שמות | EXODUS

A PARSHA COMPANION

Rabbi David Fohrman

AlephBeta
PRESS

מגיד

MAGGID

Exodus: A Parsha Companion
First edition, 2020

Aleph Beta Press
EMAIL info@alephbeta.org
WEBSITE www.alephbeta.org

Maggid Books
An imprint of Koren Publishers Jerusalem Ltd.

PO Box 8531, New Milford, CT 06776-8531, USA
& PO Box 4044, Jerusalem 9104001, Israel
www.maggidbooks.com

Series design by Cory Rockliff
Volume design by Estie Dishon

ISBN 978-1-59264-567-1 (hardcover)

A CIP catalog record for this title is
available from the British Library

Printed and bound in the United States

About Our Parents

Our parents surmounted great tragedy and hardship to live exemplary lives. They loved us, nourished us, and sacrificed much to help us flourish and become committed Jews. In their example, we saw sacred values of the Torah brought to life. We live in the shadow of their deeds.

ABRAHAM AND ESTHER HERSH hailed originally from the Carpathian mountains. They were both survivors of Auschwitz, and they met after the war in a displaced persons camp in Germany. Shortly thereafter, they made their way from the ashes of Europe to the Land of Israel, where Abraham fought in Israel's War of Independence. He was a fierce lover of both the land and the Torah of Israel. Together, Abraham and Esther lived difficult lives but, through it all, somehow always maintained a deep faith in Hashem. Their strong values — commitment to family and to Judaism, and an abiding love of the State of Israel and the Jewish people — made powerful impressions upon their children.

RABBI MOSHE AND RIVKA ZYTELNY made their way from Europe to America. Toby's father was, in his younger years, a yeshiva bachur in Kletzk. Before Lakewood was a gleam in the eye of history, he became a close student of Rabbi Aharon Kotler, and a *chevrusa* of his son, Rabbi Shneur. He escaped the ravages of war by heading, with his yeshiva, first to Siberia and then to Kazakhstan, where he met his wife, Rivka. The couple moved from Kazakhstan to France — and all this time, despite war and constant upheaval, Rabbi Aharon remained like a father to him. To this day, Ronny and Toby cherish letters in their possession that Rabbi Aharon sent to Rabbi Moshe in France, advising him on major life decisions. Eventually, Rabbi Moshe and Rivka came to America, where he rejoined his rebbe and yeshiva in Lakewood. There, he became part of an unlikely success story, as he helped reestablish a vibrant center of Torah on new and distant shores. All in all, Moshe was the only one in his entire immediate family to survive the war. Together, he and Rivka raised seven children.

Our parents lived through harrowing times and emerged with a steely, strengthened faith; they sacrificed much to pass on their vibrant heritage. We remember them with love, and are honored to carry their legacy forward.

Ronny & Toby Hersh

The Shemot volume of the *Parsha Companion* is lovingly dedicated by

Daniel & Jamie Schwartz

In honor of their children

רחל נתניה ורפאל שמחה

Jennifer Schwartz &
Raffi Holzer

חנה ליאת ויצחק משה גד

Hannah & Isaac Landa

and beloved grandchildren

May all of you, our progeny, serve as faithful and
secure links in the sacred chain of our heritage,
passing on to your own children the deep love and
appreciation for the beauty and wisdom of our Torah,
and a firm commitment to live by its precepts and
practices — as we have tried to model for you.

– Love, Ima and Abba, Savti and Sabi

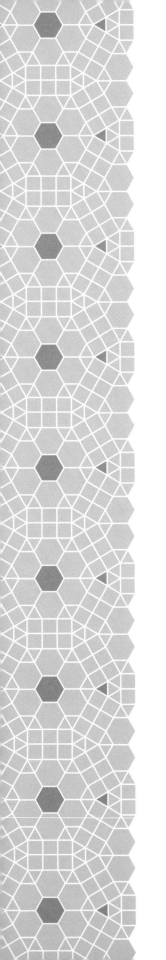

We gratefully acknowledge the following patrons who, with generosity and vision, have dedicated individual volumes of this *Parsha Companion* series:

BEREISHIT

Tuvia & Barbara Levkovich

SHEMOT

Daniel & Jamie Schwartz

VAYIKRA

Mark & Erica Gerson

Chaim & Livia Jacobs

Yaron & Lisa Reich

Alan & Fran Broder

Yanky & Aliza Safier

Dr. Hillel & Chayi Cohen

Avram M. Cooperman MD & family

BAMIDBAR

Dr. Bruce Wayne Greenstein
& Ms. Monica Patricia Martinez

DEVARIM

Andrew & Terri Herenstein

We also wish to acknowledge

Legacy Heritage Fund

for its generous support to help
make this series of books possible.

LEGACY HERITAGE FUND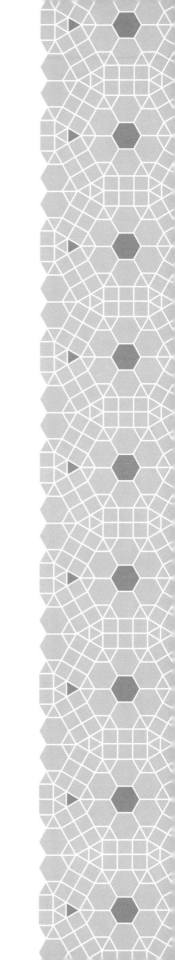

Contents

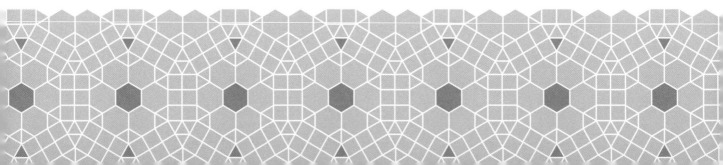

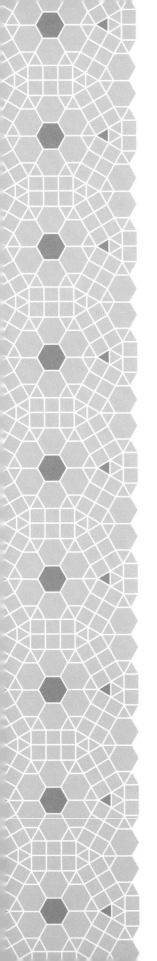

Some Words of Appreciation

WHILE THE IDEAS IN these pages are my own, I have benefited from the partnership of many in creating this volume. Their care, attention, generosity, and wisdom helped transform mere ruminations into the volume you hold in your hands.

Chief among those partners are Ronny and Toby Hersh, the patrons of this five-volume series of books. Ronny and Toby have dedicated the series to the memory of their parents, Abraham and Esther Hersh, *z"l* and Moshe and Rivka Zytelny, *z"l,* whose own personal stories were great journeys in their own right. The first volume of the series contains an appreciation of their lives; I am honored that this series of volumes bears their name.

This particular volume of the series (essays on Shemot) has been generously sponsored by Dan and Jamie Schwartz, in honor of their children and grandchildren. I originally got to know Dan and Jamie over a Pesach we spent together a few years back. One of the first things that impressed me about them was how eager they were not just to learn Torah themselves, but to share the depth of that learning widely. Ultimately, their vision was to open up the treasures of the Torah's wisdom even to those who never benefited from a traditional yeshiva background. Early on, Dan and Jamie found a trusted partner in these endeavors: They befriended Rabbi Yaakov Horowitz, and helped him spearhead a groundbreaking series of books that made basic parsha study (and ultimately, basic Gemara learning, as well) accessible to novices of all ages. In sponsoring this volume of the *Parsha Companion*, they are taking this vision another step forward, and I am grateful to partner with them in these efforts.

I would also like to acknowledge Legacy Heritage Fund for its generous support to help make this series of books possible. The foundation focuses much of its effort on supporting Jewish education in innovative and trendsetting ways. I am honored that Legacy Heritage Fund has chosen to include this series of books among the many worthy projects they've chosen to support.

Many have helped take mere words and craft out of those words the book that you hold in your hands. I am greatly indebted to these good folks, so let me introduce you to them:

First, Matthew Miller, Rabbi Reuven Ziegler, and the rest of the team at Koren/Maggid have been spectacular to work with. They are proudly bringing a new generation of original Jewish thought to the public, one beautiful book at a time, and we are all enriched by their efforts.

Shoshana Brody (from Aleph Beta) capably and carefully managed the production of this volume, and helped edit and sharpen just about each and every essay. Immanuel Shalev and Beth Lesch (from Aleph Beta), as well as Debbie Ismailoff and Ita Olesker (from Koren), lent their editing talents to this work as well. Rabbis Eli Raful and Elinatan Kupferberg contributed valuable research. The beautiful cover design was created by Cory Rockliff, who also designed the series' overall aesthetic, while the pages of this volume were crafted by Estie Dishon.

Many of the ideas in this book on Shemot had their *own* genesis, as it were, in parsha videos I created with the help and support of the amazing team at Aleph Beta (you can find those videos at **www.alephbeta.org**). I want to take this opportunity to acknowledge, with gratitude, those behind the scenes who have, over the years, helped to transform Aleph Beta from mere idea, to fledgling startup, to a viable, going concern: its founders, board of directors, and officers. They are Etta Brandman, Alan Broder, David Hamburger, Jeff Haskell, Josh Malin, David Pollack, Donny Rosenberg, Robbie Rothenberg, Dan Schwartz (who, with his wife, is also the sponsor for this volume), Kuty Shalev, Steve Wagner, and Moishe Wolfson. I want to thank, as well, the manifold subscribers of Aleph Beta, who each support our work in ways great and small, and provide us with meaningful feedback, appreciation, as well as a dose of constructive criticism. It is a privilege to take this journey through Torah along with you; having you by our side gives us the drive and motivation to continue.

I want to also take this opportunity to recognize three men, each of whom is no longer with us; all three played an outsized role in nurturing my development over the years. My father, Moshe Fohrman, *z"l*, passed away when I was quite young, but he taught me so much about life, people, and relationships in the short years we had together; his love and influence continues to pervade my work. My stepfather, Zev Wolfson, *z"l*, a man of towering accomplishments, took me under his wing, believed in me, and helped me thrive. LeRoy Hoffberger, *z"l*, a bulwark of the Baltimore Jewish community, became a dear friend and mentor. Roy and I first met when he attended a class that I taught at the Johns Hopkins University; he took a keen interest in my work and ultimately helped give it life by creating the Hoffberger Foundation for Torah Studies. The love of all three I shall carry with me as long as the One Above deigns that I walk the earth.

Finally, I want to acknowledge my family. My wife, Reena, and my kids—Moshe, Shalva, Avigail, Shana, Yael, Ariella, and Avichai—what can I say? They are not only wonderful in and of themselves; they have built a network of love and support for one another that makes me proud. In times of quarantine, when it is all too natural to feel jittery and on edge, their good cheer and love have been a welcome and refreshing constant in my life. Beyond that, they have helped shape this book in ways great and small, for they really are *my* "parsha companions." Many of the ideas contained in these pages were born, shaped, or refined in animated discussions with them around the Shabbos table. I treasure those moments: Learning Torah with my family is a constant opportunity to talk about things that matter deeply with people I care about the most—and what could be better than that?

Rabbi David Fohrman

Inwood, NY
September 2020

Introduction
Exodus: A Book of Names?

SHEMOT. IN ENGLISH, NAMES. What a strange title for a book of the Torah. Why call it that?

The simple answer, of course, is that *shemot,* "names," show up in the very beginning of the book. It begins with these words:

וְאֵלֶּה שְׁמוֹת בְּנֵי יִשְׂרָאֵל
הַבָּאִים מִצְרָיְמָה

These are the names of the Children of Israel who came to Egypt.

Exodus 1:1

And then, in just two verses, the Torah goes ahead and recounts the names of the children of Jacob who had come down to Egypt back in the days of Joseph. But allow me to pose this question to you: Do you really think this is a good reason to name the book *Shemot*?

The English and Latin translators of the Torah evidently didn't seem to think so. They routinely speak of the book of *Shemot* as "the book of Exodus."

Exodus. Now *that* would seem like a very good name for this book. After all, the Exodus from Egypt really is *the* great event that dominates the book. Indeed, once we are done with the first two verses of *Shemot,* the Torah seems to drop the idea of names like a hot potato and moves on to the story of the Israelites' enslavement and subsequent redemption from Egypt, a saga that dominates the next twenty or so chapters of text. So, if you're looking for a theme to name a book of the Torah after, "Exodus" seems perfect: The Exodus redemption narrative is riveting — it's got suffering, drama, miracles, redemption, you name it. So "Exodus" seems like a terrific name for this book. But in Hebrew, that's not what we call it. We call it *Shemot,* the Book of Names.

Why?

I want to suggest that an answer to this question may lie buried in the very first comment made by Rashi in this book. I want to read it together with you and see if we can make sense of what he's trying to get at.

Rashi's Starting Point

Rashi looks at the copious list of names the Torah gives in the first verses of Exodus and wonders why it was necessary. For, as it happens, the Torah has already listed the names of those who came down to Egypt, all the way back in the book of Genesis. Yes, that's correct; back in Genesis, right at the moment when Joseph's family comes down to Egypt, we have this verse:

Genesis 46:8

וְאֵלֶּה שְׁמוֹת בְּנֵי־יִשְׂרָאֵל הַבָּאִים מִצְרַיְמָה יַעֲקֹב וּבָנָיו בְּכֹר יַעֲקֹב רְאוּבֵן:

These are the names of the Children of Israel who came to Egypt: Jacob and his descendants; Jacob's firstborn, Reuven.

From there, the text in Genesis goes on to list not only the names of the twelve children of Jacob who came down to Egypt, but the names of *their* children, too. Moreover, take a glance at the syntax of that verse back in Genesis, and you'll notice that it is identical to the opening verse in Exodus. Both begin with the exact same words:

Genesis 46:8	Exodus 1:1
וְאֵלֶּה שְׁמוֹת בְּנֵי־יִשְׂרָאֵל הַבָּאִים מִצְרַיְמָה יַעֲקֹב וּבָנָיו בְּכֹר יַעֲקֹב רְאוּבֵן:	וְאֵלֶּה שְׁמוֹת בְּנֵי יִשְׂרָאֵל הַבָּאִים מִצְרַיְמָה אֵת יַעֲקֹב אִישׁ וּבֵיתוֹ בָּאוּ:
These are the names of the Children of Israel who came to Egypt: Jacob and his descendants; Jacob's firstborn, Reuven.	These are the names of the Children of Israel who came to Egypt with Jacob, each coming with his household.

So Rashi's question, to open *Sefer Shemot*, is: *We've heard all this already.* We don't need another recitation of the names of those who came down to Egypt. Not only is such a recitation tangential to the theme of the book, it is also just repetitious, plain and simple.

Rashi's Answer

To resolve his question, Rashi cites a midrash. Let's read his language together and try to understand clearly what he is telling us:

אַע"פּ שֶׁמְּנָאָן
בְּחַיֵּיהֶם בִּשְׁמוֹתָם,
חָזַר וּמְנָאָם בְּמִיתָתָם,
לְהוֹדִיעַ חִבָּתָם,
שֶׁנִּמְשְׁלוּ לְכוֹכָבִים,
שֶׁמוֹצִיאָם וּמַכְנִיסָם
בְּמִסְפָּר וּבִשְׁמוֹתָם שֶׁנֶּ'
"הַמּוֹצִיא בְמִסְפָּר
צְבָאָם לְכֻלָּם בְּשֵׁם
יִקְרָא".

Although the Torah counted the Children of Israel in their lifetimes [back in the book of Genesis], still [the Torah] went back and counted them [at the beginning of Exodus] when they died, to let you know how dear they were [to the Almighty], inasmuch as they were compared to the stars. [For when it comes to the stars, we know that] God brings them out and returns them by number and by name, as it says [in Isaiah 40:26]: "He takes out the stars according to their number, and all of them He calls by name."

Rashi, from Exodus Rabbah 1:3; Tanchuma Yashan 1:1:2

Now, at face value, what Rashi tells us here is puzzling, for it is not immediately clear exactly how he has answered his question. Rashi seems to think that his question disappears, as it were, once we realize that the people of Israel are compared by the Almighty to stars. Stars get named, so we get named. Stars apparently get named twice: once at night, when God "takes them out," so to speak, and once in the morning, when He snuggles them back in their resting places, so that they can come back out again the next night. So…just like the stars, it seems to follow that we, too, should get named twice: once when the Children of Israel are alive, when they first come down to Egypt, and once when they are dying out, at the beginning of Exodus.

The comparison of Israel to stars, though, sounds fanciful, even whimsical. What, if anything, is the midrash that Rashi cites really trying to get at here? I think the midrash is alluding to something very deep. Here's how we might puzzle out its meaning.

Like the Stars

The midrash says that the key to understanding the naming of Israel in the beginning of Exodus is to remember that Israel is compared to stars. To begin to understand the significance of this, we need to ask: Exactly *when* did it happen that Israel was compared to stars? The midrash just states that it happened, putting it out there as a blind fact, assuming the reader immediately understands what event in the Torah it is referencing. But *when*, as a matter of fact, was that comparison to stars actually made?

The answer, of course, is that it happened in the times of Abraham.

Back in Genesis, chapter 15, Abraham had worried that he was an old man but he did not yet have an heir. Who would carry on his legacy? And in response to his fear, God had told him to go outside:

Genesis 15:5

הַבֶּט־נָא הַשָּׁמַיְמָה וּסְפֹר הַכּוֹכָבִים אִם־תּוּכַל לִסְפֹּר אֹתָם וַיֹּאמֶר לוֹ כֹּה יִהְיֶה זַרְעֶךָ:

"Look toward the heavens and count the stars, if you are able to count them." And [God] said to him, "So shall your offspring be."

In telling Abraham that his children would be like the stars, God was issuing an almost playful challenge: *Can you count the stars? Just try counting them.* The implication, of course, is: *Abraham, you can't count them. They're not countable. They are innumerable! And that's how your children will be, too.*

So isn't that interesting: The moment the Almighty first associated the Children of Israel with stars was the moment God also brought up the idea of counting them. And *that* brings us face-to-face with a fascinating paradox. For when, in Genesis, God told Abraham that the nation of Israel will be like the stars, God's real point to him was that his descendants would be…*impossible* to count. They would be innumerable. But now, here comes this midrash, and it references this very moment in Genesis, this promise that God made to Abraham that his descendants will be like the stars — and what does the midrash make of that? That God, as a token of love, treats us just like the stars and *counts* each one of us. So the midrash seems to be directly at odds with the plain sense of the text! Are we countable, like the midrash suggests, or uncountable, like God once told Abraham?

Countable or Uncountable? It Depends

The answer, I would suggest, is: It depends on when.

To explain, what God was really telling Abraham back in Genesis was that, *at a certain point in time,* your children are going to become virtually innumerable. I think we can agree that, in its plain meaning, that is really the point of the verse. So let me ask you: *When,* historically, did that actually happen? When did God's promise actually come true?

The answer, interestingly enough, would have to be: *Right at the beginning of the book of Exodus.*

Yes, right there at the beginning of Exodus. Look at what happens right after the Torah goes and counts the people by name:

וַיָּמָת יוֹסֵף וְכָל־אֶחָיו וְכֹל הַדּוֹר הַהוּא: וּבְנֵי יִשְׂרָאֵל פָּרוּ וַיִּשְׁרְצוּ וַיִּרְבּוּ וַיַּעַצְמוּ בִּמְאֹד מְאֹד וַתִּמָּלֵא הָאָרֶץ אֹתָם:	Joseph died, and all his brothers, and all that generation. And the Israelites were fertile and they swarmed; they multiplied, and increased very greatly, so that the land was filled with them.	Exodus 1:6–7

An incredible population explosion takes place, and it happens, according to the text, right after the death of Joseph and his brothers. It was *then,* with the advent of that population explosion, that the Children of Israel started to become "innumerable." It was then that they began to make the transition from family to nation, from a small family clan whose cousins you more or less knew by name, to a nation whose population seemed virtually innumerable, to a people so big that nobody really knows everybody anymore.

It turns out, then, that what God told Abraham was, on the one hand, a great blessing. But the blessing also had a potential downside to it as well. It contained, inherently, a bit of a darker side…

The Dark Side of "Uncountable"

"Your progeny will go from being a mere family to a teeming nation." "They'll be like the stars." "You'll be unable to count them." When you put it like that, it all seems wonderful; to father a whole nation is an amazing blessing. But on the other hand, what happens when a group makes the transition from family to nation? Knowing the numbers starts to become hard. Knowing the *names* becomes hard.

Names and numbers. You're a kid in middle school. What does it say to you when, in your rather large class, the teacher doesn't even know how many of you there are in the room? Or when the teacher loses track of your names and mixes up Deloris and Doris? What does it say when you have seventy-eight grandchildren — *or was it seventy-nine?* — and you mix up Shloime with Shimmy, and the prospect of attending yet another bar mitzvah party two and a half hours down the New Jersey Turnpike starts to seem less and less appealing? There's a kind of intimacy that can get lost as a family goes from a family to a clan, from a clan to a nation. What can get lost is the sense that each and every individual…really matters.

It is this issue, I would argue, that the midrash intends to address. Yes, God had told Abraham that his children will eventually be like the stars. *Can he count the stars? Can anyone?* It might seem like a loss of intimacy, a loss of individual purpose, is inevitable when this blessing comes to fruition. But that is where the midrash comes in…

The Stars: Man's Perspective and God's Perspective

The midrash notes that just at the point in history when Israel made the transition from an easily countable family group to a virtually innumerable mass of people that would form a nation, the Torah insisted on something. It insisted upon naming the people and counting them. And it does so twice:

Exodus 1:1   וְאֵלֶּה שְׁמוֹת בְּנֵי יִשְׂרָאֵל
הַבָּאִים מִצְרָיְמָה

These are the names of the Children of Israel who came to Egypt.

Why? The midrash suggests that, at this juncture in history, it is as if God is completing the promise He once made to Abraham. It is as if God is saying to Abraham: You, an ordinary human being, may be unable to count your progeny, once they become like the stars. But that's you. *Not Me.* For precisely at the moment the people of Israel are poised to become innumerable, it is then that God stops to tell us, and all future generations, their names; and it is then that He stops to tell us how many there were. Why? *Because God treats them just like the stars.*

A human being looks at the stars and, face it, they all look the same. The innumerable points of light are impressive, but they seem virtually interchangeable. *Who even knows how many of them there are up there?* But that is a human being's way of looking at the stars; it is not *God's* way of looking at the stars. That's the point of the verse the midrash quotes in Isaiah: "God counts the stars, and deals with each one by name." The Almighty does so, the midrash suggests, every night when the stars first come out, and then one more time, in the morning, when the stars seem to melt away and die in the growing, brightening dawn.

Even as we become innumerable, God can and does count us — because in His eyes, each of us counts. Even as we become innumerable, God knows our names — because in His eyes, each of us matters. Only a human gets dizzy staring at the multitudes that comprise a nation. Not God. In our Maker's eyes, we are all stars.

Slavery and Stars

Let's return to our question about the name of this book. It is the Book of Names, not the book of Exodus. Why? Or, to put that question more sharply, the dominant theme in this book is clearly slavery and our miraculous deliverance from it. Does the designation of this book as *Shemot, Names,* completely deviate from that theme… or does it somehow relate to it?

I think that perhaps the latter is the case. I want to suggest that the name of the book indeed relates to the themes of slavery, oppression, and deliverance that make up the book's central theme. Given what we've seen above, the word "names" may actually have something powerful to say about that.

Go back for a moment to the title of the first book of the Torah, Genesis. Why name it that? The most obvious answer is that the book begins with the story of creation, and hence, the name *Bereishit,* or Genesis, which means "the beginning." But creation is only the first story in the book.

Why name the *whole* book after that? Is it just a matter of convenience and happenstance — the word *bereishit* appears in the first verse of the book — or might the name also somehow relate to the themes of the book as a whole?

The answer may well be that the first book of the Torah deals with more than one kind of creation. It is not just a universe that first comes into being in that book, but a people: The genesis of the people of Israel takes place in the first book of the Torah. Indeed, when does Genesis come to an end? It ends, fittingly enough, at the last moment of this "beginning." The people, still one large, extended family, have made their way down to Egypt. Their future has been secured with the lifesaving grain Joseph provides to his brothers and their families. And yet, slavery looms on the horizon…

That is where Genesis ends. And the very first event in the Torah's next book, the book of *Shemot*, marks a new stage in the life of the people. Just after giving us the names of those who came down to Egypt, *Shemot* tells of a population explosion that occurred in Egypt. With that sudden ballooning of numbers, the people are becoming not just a family, but an incipient nation. And so…the book is called "Names." Why? Not only because in the very first verses, the people get named. That's only half the story. Just as there was more than one reason to call Genesis "Genesis," there is also more than one reason to call *Shemot… Names*. Which is to say: Just as in Genesis, there was an overt moment of creation at the beginning of the book, but a larger, more subtle process of creation would unfold that would span the whole book (the creation of the family of Israel), more deeply justifying the name "Genesis"…so it is with the Book of Names, too. The people are overtly named by God, in just a verse or two, at the beginning of the book, but the book is called *Names* for a reason that pervades the book as a whole. It is as if the name of the book were saying: *God continues to know our names, to keep track of each and every one, throughout all the events that happen in the book.*

For, after all, what *does* happen in the book?

In this book, not only do we attain the numbers to become a nation. That's the nice part of the book. The not-so-nice part is what happens to us, just as we reach this stage of maturation: We are brutally enslaved. Our babies are thrown into the Nile. We become victims of brutality, of history's first quasi-genocidal act of anti-Semitism.

It is a dark moment in history, a moment when God seems to hide His face. And yet…it is *still* the Book of Names. It is as if the title of the book itself suggests that even in our moments of greatest suffering, God knows our names. God attends to each and every one of us, individually. For consider this: When, after all, was it that God told Abraham that his children would be like the stars? It was immediately before He told him something else:

יָדֹעַ תֵּדַע כִּי גֵר
יִהְיֶה זַרְעֲךָ בְּאֶרֶץ
לֹא לָהֶם וַעֲבָדוּם
וְעִנּוּ אֹתָם אַרְבַּע מֵאוֹת
שָׁנָה:

You shall know, yes know, that your progeny will be strangers in a land not their own. And [the inhabitants of that land] will enslave them, and oppress them, for four hundred years.

Genesis 15:13

It was as if God were saying to Abraham: *Yes, there is darkness on the horizon. But know this: You will be like stars to Me. Never forget that.* To a human, individual stars may not matter. But you and I *see stars differently*. God names the stars and counts them. Even in your darkest moments, in My eyes, you still continue to shine.

In the end, perhaps when we call the book *Names* we are not attempting to evade discussion of Egyptian enslavement. On the contrary, this, itself, is a way we talk about that enslavement. Through it all, God knows our names. He cares about each and every one of us, in all of our pain, all of our anguish. For we are like stars, indeed.

The Long Arm
of Pharaoh's Daughter

וַתֵּרֶא אֶת־הַתֵּבָה בְּתוֹךְ
הַסּוּף וַתִּשְׁלַח אֶת־
אֲמָתָהּ וַתִּקָּחֶהָ:

She spied the basket among the
reeds and sent her handmaiden,
and took it.

EXODUS 2:5

The Long Arm of Pharaoh's Daughter

A NUMBER OF YEARS ago, my oldest child, Moshe, came home from kindergarten one day with a project he had made in class: a long, white, cardboard… arm. I came home and saw it, lying on the kitchen table — this long, unnaturally stretched-out, disembodied arm, and in an instant, I knew what it was. The Torah portion that week was **Parshat Shemot**, and my son's art project apparently came straight from one of the more famous statements of Rashi on the parshah. My son had brought home a kindergartner's replica of the daughter of Pharaoh's arm.

Of Handmaidens and Arms

What Rashi has to say about the arm of the daughter of Pharaoh comes from the midrash. But to understand both what the midrash and what Rashi are saying, you first have to go back to the core biblical text it is all based upon.

First, a little context: Moses was born at a time when the Egyptian king had commanded his people to cast all male babies born to the Children of Israel into the Nile River. Moses' mother initially hid her child but eventually found herself unable to conceal him — at which point she put the baby in a small basket of sorts in the reeds by the side of the Nile. There, the infant was discovered by the daughter of the Pharaoh, who, escorted by her maidservants, had come to bathe in the river's waters:

וַתֵּרֶא אֶת־הַתֵּבָה בְּתוֹךְ הַסּוּף
וַתִּשְׁלַח אֶת־אֲמָתָהּ וַתִּקָּחֶהָ׃

She spied the basket among the reeds and sent her handmaiden, and took it.

Exodus 2:5

Now, here is where things get tricky. In the plain, straightforward sense of the text — its *peshat* — the princess sent her maidservant to go fetch the child. But the Sages of the Midrash see something else in these words. They pick up on the fact that the Hebrew word for "maidservant" in that verse, *amah,* is a homonym; it can also mean "arm" or "arm's length."[1] Given this, the rabbis expounded the verse differently. In their reading, the daughter of Pharaoh didn't send her handmaiden to that child; she sent her *arm*. That is, the princess's arm miraculously extended from wherever she was standing, grasped the little baby in that faraway little basket — and then, one would suppose, it retracted, bringing the child back to her. And that explains why my son proudly came home one day with a cardboard cutout of one very long arm belonging to a princess.

I have to confess that I found myself struggling at that moment as to how I ought to respond to my wide-eyed kindergartner. Sure, it was a great art project. And I could (and did) compliment him on his prowess with scissors, cardboard, and glue. But how do I explain to him what happened at the Nile? What if he wanted to know which story *really* happened? Did she send her maidservant, or her arm? It can't have been both. Did the Rabbis mean their interpretation to somehow replace the basic, straight-forward interpretation of the verse?

How Did the Sages Expect Us to Understand Their Words?

Midrash sometimes gets a bad reputation. Some folks look at it and find themselves suppressing the urge to roll their eyes and think: *This seems like the strangest interpretation in the world. Why can't the Rabbis just leave a perfectly fine story the way it is?* Behind that skepticism is an important question: Could the Rabbis themselves have possibly truly believed in their interpretation? Imagine, in our case, that events *really* transpired the way the Sages of the Midrash say they transpired. Put yourself in the shoes of the daughter of Pharaoh. There you are, approaching the river, looking forward to a cool, refreshing swim in the waters of the Nile, and you spy this little basket in the reeds. You see this little baby and you have compassion upon him. Sure, you're a little nervous because he's evidently a child of the Israelites, but you are about to send your maidservant to go fetch the baby, when all of a sudden … your arm just stretches, magically, like a

---

1   Indeed, the word *amah,* besides meaning "maidservant," is used throughout the Torah to denote a measurement: an "arm's length," generally interpreted as the length of an adult forearm.

fishing rod. It goes and grabs that child, and then — *whoosh!* — it miraculously retracts with said baby in hand.

Now, if you were the daughter of Pharaoh, and *that just happened to you* — what do you think you would probably do next?

I don't know about you, but if I were that princess, I would drop everything and run all the way back to the palace, probably screaming the whole time: *"My arm! My arm! What's happened to my arm?"*

And, because any normal person would probably react that way, I think we can draw some inferences about how the Rabbis meant us to understand their words here. The Sages simply *can't* have been asking us to "replace" the simple understanding of the verse with their new interpretation, for an outlandish, unexpected miracle of the sort they are describing, with this tale of an elongated arm, would have hopelessly and completely disrupted the chain of events the Torah goes on to describe. The daughter of Pharaoh never would have raised Moses in the palace. In all likelihood, the helpless infant would have been left alone in the Nile, as a horrified princess tried to figure out what to do about her arm.

But if the Sages didn't mean to replace the *peshat* of the verse, what *did* they mean to do?

How Should We Understand Midrash?

The question I'm raising, to be fair, isn't just a question about this particular midrashic comment. It is a question about many, if not most, midrashic comments. The Rabbis have a way of saying the strangest things sometimes: Jonah gets swallowed by a fish. But the Sages of the Midrash don't leave it at that. They happen to notice that the fish, when it was first mentioned, was called a *dag* (masculine); and when the fish is mentioned next in the text, it is a *dagah* (feminine).

וַיְמַן יְקֹוָה דָּג גָּדוֹל לִבְלֹעַ אֶת יוֹנָה וַיְהִי יוֹנָה בִּמְעֵי הַדָּג שְׁלֹשָׁה יָמִים וּשְׁלֹשָׁה לֵילוֹת: וַיִּתְפַּלֵּל יוֹנָה אֶל יְקֹוָה אֱלֹהָיו מִמְּעֵי הַדָּגָה:	The Lord provided a huge fish to swallow Jonah; and Jonah remained in the fish's belly three days and three nights. Jonah prayed to the Lord his God from the belly of the fish.	Jonah 2:1–2

Seizing on the discrepancy, the Sages (cited by Rashi to Jonah 2:1) tell us their conclusion: First, Jonah was swallowed by a male fish, but he never prayed to God in that fish. So God instructed the male fish to expel Jonah, at which point he was promptly swallowed by a female fish — who just happened to be pregnant. It was crowded inside that female fish, and it was there that Jonah, beset by discomfort, finally prayed to God.[2]

Why would the Rabbis say such a thing? Why didn't they just leave a perfectly good story — the "Jonah and the Great Fish" narrative we all know and love — alone?

The answer to these questions, I believe, lies in a basic misunderstanding many of us harbor about what the Sages of the Midrash were trying to do. We mistakenly assume that the midrash is trying to tell us what actually transpired — and in so doing, we confuse midrash with what we might call *peshat* — the plain meaning of the verse it is commenting on. But midrash was never meant to be *peshat*. Generally speaking, the Sages of the Midrash were not trying to tell us *what* it was that happened (the verses themselves do that); they were trying to tell us about the *meaning* of what happened.

Two Hands at the Piano

In other words, *drash* and *peshat* aren't in competition with one another; they complement one another. One can think of them almost as if they were the two hands of an expert pianist, playing music on a piano. If you've ever played piano, you know that the right hand of a pianist will generally carry what we call the melody, while the left hand will carry the harmony. We usually listen to both together. But ask yourself: What would it be like to listen to each hand in isolation?

Well, if you were listening to *just* the right-hand notes of a song — say, "Old MacDonald Had a Farm" — the tune you're hearing might sound plain and unsophisticated, but it would at least make sense. It would be plainly recognizable as "Old Macdonald Had a Farm." But now imagine you are listening to only the left-hand notes of that same song. What would *that* sound like?

It wouldn't sound like anything at all. It would just sound like nonsense.

---

2   See Rashi to Jonah 2:1.

Now, put the two hands together, and listen to the notes that emanate from both. Well, that *really* sounds like "Old Macdonald Had a Farm." Through those two hands, and the confluence of notes between them, emerge all the richness and glory one could possibly muster out of that tune.

And so it is with the Torah. The simple meaning of a piece of text is like the notes played with the right hand. It gives you the basic picture of what is going on. It has coherence. It sounds like a story, even if that story might seem basic or unadorned. The midrash, on the other hand, is like the notes played with the left hand. It is the harmony to that story. Looked at in isolation, it sounds fanciful and random, almost like nonsense. But read in consonance with the "right hand's notes," with the biblical text it is commenting upon, all of a sudden the composite story jumps out at you with a vibrance and richness you'd never have expected.

With midrash, the Sages are weaving a careful thread of commentary, often allegorical in nature, around the plain sense of the biblical text.[3] It is a kind of harmony. Just as harmony emphasizes and draws out certain notes in the melody of a song, so midrash does something similar with elements of the biblical text. The Sages, exquisitely careful readers that they were, noticed things in the *peshat* — the simple meaning of the text — that might easily be overlooked, and they sought to bring our attention to those elements, and to tease out their implications for us. The result of that exercise is midrash: easily misunderstood if read in isolation,

---

3   The notion that midrash usually has allegorical, rather than literal, meaning has deep roots in Jewish tradition. Rambam suggested this in his Commentary on the Mishnah as well as on his commentary to Chelek (the tenth chapter of tractate Sanhedrin), as did his son, R. Abraham ben HaRambam (see his *Ma'amar al HaDerashot*). Similar approaches were adopted by Maharal of Prague, throughout his works, as well as by Ramchal in his *Ma'amar al HaAggadot*, and Maharsha throughout his aggadic commentary. Given this strong trend in our tradition, it is remarkable (and regrettable) that in contemporary education, midrash is often presented to children as indistinguishable from *peshat*, and in competition with it for the plain meaning of a biblical passage. Many children are needlessly left to worry whether they are being blasphemous in some way by doubting whether a midrashic teaching "really" represents what happened in any given story.

but intensely profound if read in consonance with the underlying biblical text it comments upon.[4]

When seeking to read Midrash then, the trick is to peruse the underlying biblical text *first*. Look carefully at that, and ask yourself: Are there any difficulties or surprises here? What, if anything, is puzzling about the flow of this story? Once you have done your careful reading of the Torah's text, then, and only then, go back and read the midrash. As you do, you might well find yourself nodding along, saying to yourself: *Oh, I get it. So that's what these Sages were talking about.*

Let's try that here.

Rereading the Story

Revisiting that story of the daughter of Pharaoh at the Nile, I want to ask you, for just a moment, to put yourself into the shoes of that handmaiden — the maidservant that was dispatched by the princess to fetch the child. Ask yourself: What is your job description? When you were "hired" for this job, to accompany the princess as she went about her day — what did your employer, as it were, want from you?

The interest of the palace, it seems to me, is clear. Your number one goal, as a lady-in-waiting for the princess, is to look after her. Tend to her needs if possible, but above all, keep her safe. With that in mind, let me ask you: What would be going through your head when the daughter of Pharaoh tells you to go and fetch that little baby in the reeds for her?

A little context will quickly shed light on the difficulty you face. The princess's father is the king. He is the one who has decreed a kind of genocide against this incipient Jewish nation. A mass extermination is underway, carried out by the citizenry at large. People throughout Egypt, throughout all strata of society, are murdering little baby boys; casting them into the Nile to be drowned. It can't be easy on folks. It can't be simple for the respectable folks living in the suburbs of Raamses to drown little kids. But the citizens of Egypt are doing it, because the king has insisted that their national security depends upon it.

---

4   Not all midrash works the way I'm suggesting here — there are, indeed, different strands of midrash, with different interpretive aims, but much of it does. A good book to peruse for those interested in exploring the profundity of midrash further is *Learning to Read Midrash* by Simi Peters (Urim Publications, 2005).

And now here you are, at the shores of the Nile, accompanying the daughter of this king — and all of a sudden, she spies an Israelite baby in the distance. You see the look in your mistress's face and you immediately know what she's feeling:

וַתַּחְמֹל	[The princess] had compassion	Exodus 2:6
עָלָיו	[on the child]	

But just as immediately, she realizes something:

וַתֹּאמֶר מִיַּלְדֵי	She said, "This must be	Exodus 2:6
הָעִבְרִים זֶה:	a Hebrew child."	

The princess's first reaction is to feel compassion. Who isn't moved by the sight of an infant crying? But an instant later, the cognitive part of her brain kicks in and confronts her with a cold, hard truth: *It's a Jewish child.*

The Handmaid's Tale

Nevertheless, the princess makes a decision. She asks you, her handmaiden, to go fetch that child for her. So what would you do, in that moment?

Well, what's your job now? *Keep the princess safe!* That's your number one imperative. So, you've got to be the grown-up in the room. It's up to you to say no.

So let's say you do that. You tell the princess this is madness, that she can't just defy her father like this. *"Look who you are! You're a princess of the Egyptian Empire!"*

But what if the daughter of Pharaoh won't take no for an answer? What if she says: Go fetch the child anyway!

Well, if she really insists, you might cut your losses and try a different tack: *"Look, your Highness. Let's be reasonable. Save the child, if you must. But don't bring him home with you. Don't adopt him as yours. It is too great a risk. We can find a nice Hebrew family to pass him off to."*

And what if the daughter of Pharaoh would not accept even *that* as a solution? What if she told you in reply: "No! I saw this pitiable child in the reeds, I am responsible for his welfare. I *must* take care of him, directly and personally." If she said that, you might take one last stab at helping her see things rationally. You might tell her: "Fine! Take the child; even bring him into the palace, if you think that's what you have to do. But please, Your Highness, come what may — don't tell him who he is. Don't raise him as an Israelite. He must never know his real identity."

Even here, the princess, in our little thought experiment, doesn't give an inch. She replies firmly: "No, that wouldn't be *right*! He must know who he is. He has to know his true heritage. He must know that he is an Israelite. I will raise him to understand this."

Now let's leave our little thought experiment, for in fact, something like this last courageous stand must have been adopted by the princess (whether her maidservant ever in fact challenged her or not). That much is clear from the biblical text. For shortly after the Torah tells us that the princess sent that handmaiden to fetch the child, it tells us that after the baby was weaned, the princess raised the child as her own — until, one day:

Exodus 2:11

וַיִּגְדַּל מֹשֶׁה וַיֵּצֵא אֶל־אֶחָיו
וַיַּרְא בְּסִבְלֹתָם וַיַּרְא אִישׁ
מִצְרִי מַכֶּה אִישׁ־עִבְרִי
מֵאֶחָיו:

Moses grew up, and he went out to his brothers and saw their suffering. He saw an Egyptian beating a Hebrew, one of his brothers.

Ask yourself: How did Moses come to know those slaves were "his brothers"? Ever since he was weaned, as a baby, he had grown up in the palace, raised as a prince by the daughter of Pharaoh. There is only one possibility: *The princess must have told him.*[5] Why? There was no practical reason

---

5   One could perhaps protest my interpretation, and suggest that Moses learned his true identity from his birth mother, Yocheved, who nursed him as a very young child — but such a contention is exceedingly difficult to support. For although the Torah tells us that Miriam sought out Yocheved to be the nursemaid for the princess, it is equally clear that the daughter of Pharaoh was unaware that she was actually Moses' mother. We know this because when the princess directs her to nurse the child on her behalf, she says: הֵילִיכִי אֶת הַיֶּלֶד הַזֶּה וְהֵינִקִהוּ לִי וַאֲנִי אֶתֵּן אֶת שְׂכָרֵךְ,

for doing this. It would have been so convenient not to… But evidently, the daughter of Pharaoh thought otherwise: *It wouldn't be right to hide this.* So one day — and of course, we don't know exactly when — the daughter of Pharaoh must have had that difficult conversation with her adopted son, in which she tells him the truth. *I love you as my own, and always will, but part of that love is to let you know who you really are. Those Hebrews out there — those slaves — are your brothers.*

To Reach for That Which Is Beyond Your Reach

The exact dialogue in the above reenactment is obviously a creation of our own imagination — we don't know that the handmaiden ever opposed her mistress — but my point is to try to help you see how outlandish a thing the princess was doing by sending her to get that child. It seems entirely preposterous to imagine she would succeed at what she dares to do here (and actually succeeds in doing): raise this child as a proud son of Israel, in the palace of Pharaoh. It is the rough equivalent of Hitler's daughter raising an adopted Jewish child as her own, and proudly presenting him before the German Reichstag once a year on his birthday. What this princess managed to do with Moses, guided only by her allegiance to what is right, good, and noble — is nothing short of flabbergasting.

And *that*, I think, is the point of the midrash.

The notion of "within arm's reach," in English, has come to be a metaphor for that which is possible for us to actually try to achieve. Each and every one of us has certain things we can do in life, and certain things we really can't. Some things, for good or ill, are just…beyond our reach. You're the upstanding rabbi of a large congregation. You're not going to go disco dancing in a neighborhood bar in the wee hours of the morning. That's true no matter how much you may enjoy dancing. For all intents and purposes, the expectations foisted upon us by our particular status

---

"Take this child and suckle him for me, **and I will pay your wage** [**for this**]." Clearly, then, Miriam has kept the true identity of Moses' mother a secret from the princess. Which means, of course, that all the time Yocheved nursed Moses, there was one phrase she could never afford to say to him: *My son.* Moses, then, could not have learned his identity from his nursemaid mother. He could have learned it only from the daughter of Pharaoh herself.

in society exclude certain kinds of choices in our lives, effectively putting them beyond our reach.

And so it was with the daughter of Pharaoh. For ask yourself this question: When the daughter of Pharaoh sees Moses, say, thirty yards away, there in those reeds by the side of the river — at that moment, is the infant she sees *in* her reach, or *out* of her reach?

And the answer, of course, is: From a physical standpoint, obviously, the child is in her reach. He's just thirty yards away. All the princess has to do is dispatch her maidservant to get the child and she can have him. But in every other way but the physical, that child is completely unattainable. What she wants to achieve with that child — to raise him in the palace, with an understanding of who he really is — that is entirely beyond her reach. *You can't just go and do that in Pharaoh's Egypt, not if you are the king's daughter.* But the princess doesn't care. She sends her handmaiden anyway.

Exodus 2:5	וַתִּשְׁלַח אֶת־אֲמָתָהּ וַתִּקָּחֶהָ:	She sent her handmaiden, and took [the basket].

The princess reached for that which was beyond her grasp — and her arm extended; she actually got what she was reaching for. So yes, of course she sent her *amah*, her maidservant. But the midrash's point is that in doing this, in dispatching her maidservant, she was in effect sending her arm (the *other* meaning of *amah*). Miraculously, she was able to reach for something completely beyond her — and get it.[6]

---

6   So as not to leave you hanging with questions about that midrash I referenced with Jonah, allow me to suggest a possible interpretation of what the Sages might have been getting at there. The Sages of the Midrash appear to have noticed a pattern in the original biblical text, and it is this: *Jonah keeps on running away from God.* It is not just in the second or third verse of the book that he runs away, where he gets his prophecy and immediately flees to Tarshish, to evade doing what God has asked of him — he keeps on running away after that, too. When a divine storm comes, and he presumably knows that this, somehow, is God coming after him though he has fled — Jonah runs away…into sleep. The text tells us he takes a nap, a strange thing to do, indeed, on a fragile ship riding mighty waves. And when the captain wakes him up, telling him that all the heathen sailors are praying to their

The Sages seem to be telling us — through the exquisite harmony they interweave with the Torah's melody — that buried in the story of the daughter of Pharaoh lies an enduring truth: Sometimes a goal can be beyond your reach, but if it is good, noble, and right, and you reach for it anyway — sometimes, a miracle can happen. Sometimes, God can allow your arm to stretch, so you actually take hold of what would otherwise remain a mere dream.

---

gods and asking him why he is sleeping, Jonah does not, like them, get up and pray. Instead…he runs away again — this time, seemingly, into death: The sailors draw lots that point to him as the reason for the storm, and instead of confronting God then and speaking to Him — Jonah instead tells the sailors to cast him into the violent waves.

The Almighty then sends a fish to swallow Jonah, thwarting this last attempt at flight from the Divine. It is at this point that the Sages interject, having noticed the discrepancy between the text's first reference to the fish (in masculine) and its second reference to the fish (in feminine). What they are doing, seemingly, is extending the pattern they saw in the text one more step. Even in the fish, the Sages were saying, Jonah still wasn't ready to confront God. Even there, he avoided prayer. In order to force a confrontation with Jonah, God actually was compelled to quite literally put Jonah in a place where there was simply nowhere to move at all. Only then did Jonah begin to pray and confront the God from whom he fled.

Why was Jonah so desperate to flee? What is the particular, allegorical meaning of being confined in the womb of a female fish, who just happened to have been pregnant at the time? A full explanation of these points is beyond the scope of this essay, but I believe it has to do with Jonah's struggle to come to grips with, of all things, God's compassion. Compassion in Hebrew is *rachamim*, a word that derives from *rechem*, or "womb." At some level, compassion is a fundamentally feminine, womb-like way of viewing someone — hence, it is not coincidental that Jonah, in the Sages' telling, ends up in the womb of a fish, of all places. God is trying to teach Jonah something about *rachamim* and its value, a lesson which ultimately comes through in the book's final story of the worm and the gourd. For a fuller treatment of the story of Jonah and the meaning of the Sages' comments about the female fish, please see my talk on this, available at alephbeta.org.

The God Who Said to His Universe: "Enough!"

וָאֵרָא אֶל־אַבְרָהָם אֶל־יִצְחָק וְאֶל־יַעֲקֹב בְּאֵל שַׁדָּי וּשְׁמִי יְקֹוָה לֹא נוֹדַעְתִּי לָהֶם:

I appeared to Abraham, Isaac, and Jacob as El Shaddai, but I did not make Myself known to them by My name YKVK.

EXODUS 6:3

The God Who Said to His Universe: "Enough!"

THROUGHOUT THE BIBLE, GOD is known by many names — Elokim, Hashem or YKVK, Adonai. But **Parshat Va'era** highlights another name for God. In the cornucopia of divine names that appear in the Bible, this one is relatively little known. It is commonly pronounced "Shakkai," or in Hebrew שדי.[1]

וָאֵרָא אֶל־אַבְרָהָם אֶל־יִצְחָק וְאֶל־יַעֲקֹב בְּאֵל שַׁדָּי וּשְׁמִי יְקוָה לֹא נוֹדַעְתִּי לָהֶם:	I appeared to Abraham, Isaac, and Jacob as El Shaddai, but I did not make Myself known to them by My name YKVK.	Exodus 6:3

What are the implications of this mysterious name? What does it mean?

The Sages (Chagigah 12a) have an interesting midrashic interpretation of this name. They saw it as an acronym for the words *Ani Hu she'amarti le'olam dai*, "I am He who said to the world 'Enough!'"[2]

I want to ponder that phrase with you: What does it mean to say to your world "Enough!"?

The God of an Unruly Universe

There is something a bit paradoxical, for starters, in saying to your universe "enough!" On the one hand, it sounds like something a Creator would say. If I'm the boss of the world, certainly I can yell at it: "Enough!"

---

1   The name is spelled שדי, but is often pronounced Shakkai (as if spelled שקי), a mark of deference so as not to unnecessarily and casually pronounce the Divine Name.

2   See Chagigah 12a.

as in "Stop already, that's too much!" But upon reflection…why would God say something like that to His universe? First, a creator is in the business of making things, not stopping to make them. So why would a creator be putting the brakes on the creative process? Why might He be saying "Enough!" rather than, say, "Keep right on going"?

And second, we usually think of the Creator as being the One who creates. We think of God as being the prime, active agent in creation, and the universe being the passive object of that activity, "that which is being created." Yet, the phrase the Sages coined suggests that the reality is at least partially otherwise. If God says to His newly created universe "Enough!" it seems almost as if creation is burgeoning, pulsing and alive, as if the God of creation had to somehow rein in His unruly, newly created universe lest its dynamism get out of hand. But while that view of the universe might have some poetic appeal — is it really true? Is the universe really like that?

It turns out that it is.

It might seem strange to think of the universe as if it were a bit like an unruly child who needs reining in. But here's the fascinating thing: scientists of our day and age suggest that the early universe really *did* need quite a bit of reining in. Indeed, as I'd like to now show you, had God *not* said to the universe "Enough!" you and I probably wouldn't be here today to talk about it.[3]

A Brief History of the Universe

Let's review some of what modern cosmology has to say about the beginnings of the universe.[4]

---

3   To be sure, the Sages of the Talmud lived long before contemporary theories of cosmology. But their words do anticipate aspects of these modern theories in eerie ways. Thus, a brief disclaimer: I don't profess to know exactly what the Sages meant when they spoke of God "saying to the Universe, 'enough'"; but what I can tell you is what their language inspires in me; what it is that, at least in my mind, I hear, when I think of a God who said to His Universe "Enough!" This essay is my best attempt to get that across to you.

4   My summary comes, more or less, from a handy book entitled *Universes*, by John Leslie (New York: Routledge, 1989). In the common scientific view, the events I'm about to describe took place over billions of years. The Bible, of course, famously talks about them as having occurred over "six days." I won't address this apparent

There was a cataclysmic explosion; the very biggest of bangs. In that explosion, "some-thingness" suddenly came from nothingness. But that first "somethingness" was quite a bit different from what we see around us today. At first there were only super-heated subatomic particles — nearly countless amounts of them, racing out from the exploding center. Over time, those particles began to cool — and, when they cooled enough, in a blaze of brilliance, light suddenly came into the world:[5] *Vayehi ohr*.

These subatomic particles began to join with one another to form the simplest of atoms — hydrogen. Now, hydrogen is pretty simple. It is but a single electron orbiting around a single proton, and for a long time, that's all there was in the universe. But over time, gravity began to work its magic, and vast amounts of hydrogen atoms began to coalesce into huge clouds.

As gravity drew the hydrogen atoms closer and closer together, friction between the atoms began to increase, causing the hydrogen to heat up. Eventually, some of the hydrogen clouds became so dense, and so scaldingly hot, that they spontaneously ignited in a thermonuclear reaction, becoming burning furnaces in the heavens. The hydrogen in these celestial furnaces would burn and burn, and in so doing, would transform itself to helium. We call these burning clouds of hydrogen stars.

And for a long time, that was it. The universe was nothing but space, clouds of atoms…and stars. But over time, something altogether new came to the developing universe: planets.

How did *they* come to be?

Well, it turns out that if a star is big enough — that is, if it has enough mass — then, toward the end of its life cycle, something remarkable happens. As it begins to exhaust its hydrogen fuel, gravity causes the star to collapse upon itself. As the star implodes, the friction between the packed-together atoms in the dying star becomes immense. The remnants of the star's hydrogen fuel becomes superheated — and, at a critical

---

discrepancy here, but I'd refer interested readers to my lectures that address this topic on alephbeta.org; for other views, see also Aryeh Kaplan, *Immortality, Resurrection, and the Age of the Universe: A Kabbalistic View* (Hoboken, NJ: Ktav, 1993), as well as Dr. Gerald Schroeder, *Genesis and the Big Bang* (New York: Bantam, 1991).

5   Physicists speak of this as the "Era of Recombination," when temperatures in the early universe dropped to around 3000 degrees Kelvin. It was also the point at which protons and electrons began to fuse, to create the earliest hydrogen atoms (Dan Maoz, *Astrophysics in a Nutshell*, 2nd ed. [Princeton, NJ: Princeton University Press, 2016]).

point, when the hydrogen becomes dense enough and hot enough, the star explodes.

That mammoth explosion is one of the mightiest events to occur in the universe. It is what we call a supernova. In the white-hot kiln of a supernova all of the heavy elements are formed — carbon, gold, zinc, copper, you name it. And as the exploding star hurls its contents outward, all these newly formed elements are cast out into space, becoming the building blocks of what will eventually become … planets.

Well, there you have it: you start with a bang, you let gravity do its thing, and before you know it, there's a supernova here, a supernova there — and, voila! You've got a recognizable universe-as-we-know-it on your hands. It sounds like a fairly simple process. It doesn't seem so tough to engineer.

But it is actually a lot harder to engineer than you might suppose. Because remember, the thing that started it all was *an explosion* — and, typically, explosions are not terribly ordered things. If you toss a grenade in a room, let it explode, and survey the scene afterward, what are you going to find? A big mess, to put it mildly. There would be tangled clumps of debris over here, shattered glass over there, general mayhem everywhere. Indeed, explosions are the ultimate chaos makers. The problem is that the big bang couldn't afford to be chaotic. Had it truly been chaotic — had it been anything other than very finely tuned, indeed — the universe as we know it could not have come into being.

A Goldilocks World

To see how that's so, let me walk you through a few of the conclusions modern cosmologists have reached about the nature of the early, rapidly expanding universe. We'll start with what cosmologists call "the flatness problem." We spoke earlier about how, in the aftermath of the original "bang," there were all these hydrogen atoms speeding out into space, and eventually, these coalesced into clouds, and then stars. But now let's get a bit more granular. Let's inquire about exactly how fast these particles were actually moving as they sped outward from the bang.

You see, there is a potential problem here: If those atoms were moving a little bit too fast, gravity never would have been able to act upon them to bring these atoms together into clouds. All you would have had is a universe comprised of lonely, disparate hydrogen atoms — no stars, no planets, no nothing.

So these particles can't have been moving too fast. *Fine, got it.* But…
they can't have been moving too slowly, either. Because had they *indeed*
been moving too slowly, gravity would have further slowed — and eventually stopped — the acceleration of these particles altogether. Which means
gravity would have brought everything back together into…one Great Big
Crunch. Instead of a universe with stars and planets, then, you'd have a
universe with nothing at all in it.

The bottom line is that to get a universe with stars and planets and
all those good things, what you really need is a Goldilocks universe. You
need particles traveling at speeds that are not too fast, and not too slow.
You need them to be traveling at a speed that is "just right."

So now, you say to yourself: *Well, it sounds like we all got pretty lucky
living in this Goldilocks universe, but how "just right" did it have to be? When
you say "too fast" or "too slow," what exactly was the margin of error here?*

The Margin of Error

What does "just the right speed" really mean? You might be curious as
to what was the margin of error. If all those particles were moving a little
too fast we wouldn't be here to talk about it, and if they were moving a little too slow we wouldn't be here to talk about it. So…just how lucky are
we to actually be here having this discussion?

Well, what if I told you that the margin of error was 10 percent?

In other words, what if I told you that if the universe had expanded 10
percent faster than it actually did, stars would have never have come about,
and if it had expanded 10 percent slower than it did, stars would likewise
have never come about? If that was the margin of error, you might well
conclude that you are pretty lucky to be around. After all, nine chances
out of ten point to non-existence for you and all your friends and family,
not to mention the rest of the solar system and the galaxy.

Fine. But what if the actual margin of error *wasn't* one out of ten, but
was more like one out of a hundred? Meaning, had everything in the
early universe expanded at a rate just 1 percent faster than it actually did,
we'd have been left with no universe to speak of, and had everything expanded at a rate just 1 percent slower than it did, likewise, we'd have had
no universe?

Well, then maybe you'd say to yourself: *I guess we were extremely lucky.*

So now, let's exit our thought experiment and ask what the facts actually are. What *was* the margin of error? Was it 10 percent, 1 percent, or even less, perhaps — maybe one part in a thousand? Well, cosmologists have estimated that the actual margin of error was not one in ten, one in a hundred, or even one in a thousand. It was…

One part in 10^{55}.

Take a moment to comprehend the enormity of that number. It is one part in ten followed by fifty-four zeros.[6] We don't even make names for numbers that big.[7]

One in a million is ten with six zeros after it, or 10^6. One in a billion is 10^9. One in a trillion is 10^{12}. The number 10^{55} is unimaginably beyond all that. To give you a sense of its gargantuan size, consider some comparables. According to the National Report on Forest Resources,[8] there are about three hundred billion trees in all the forests in the continental United States. Assuming each tree has about half a million leaves, that would put the total number of leaves on all the trees in the United States somewhere between, say, 10^{16} and 10^{17}. The amount of atoms in the observable universe, on the other hand, has been estimated at about 10^{81}. So, somewhere between those two immense numbers, somewhere between the total number of leaves in the United States and atoms in the entire universe, somewhere in that middle, you've got 10^{54}. One part in that immense haystack — *that's* the chance you have of starting with a random, cataclysmic explosion, and getting a rate of expansion that would actually deliver to you a universe.

The problem is that if you really want a universe, it's not just the rate of expansion that you have to worry about. You have to worry about a whole lot more.

---

6   H. Guth, *Physical Review D*, vol. 23, no. 2 (1981): 348, as cited in Leslie, *Universes*.

7   My editor disputes me, and suggests that we do have a name for the number: a septendecillion. Lo and behold, a glance at Merriam-Webster's dictionary betrays the fact that she is indeed correct — that *is* the name for one, followed by 54 zeros. So we could call this ten septendecillions. But I stand by the larger point here. No one ever talks about septendecillions. We don't traffic in numbers that size, and have little comprehension of their enormity.

8   See data for the U.S. Forest Service, at www.fia.fs.fed.us.

The Grenade's Wreckage, Redux

It turns out that there are other, similar problems that would bedevil a creator seeking to get a universe out of a bang. For example, consider the analogy I gave earlier about tossing a hand grenade into a room and surveying the wreckage afterward. One might imagine the density of debris in that room would vary pretty widely. Denser clumps of wreckage would be strewn over here, with less shrapnel over there; a giant hole in the wall would yawn over on the other side.

But now consider the "debris" speeding out of an initial, big bang–style explosion. If the subatomic particles ejected from the big bang emerged in a pattern that was too clumpy, with dense regions placed quite close to one another, then the hydrogen in the early universe would never have managed to develop into stars. Instead, the hydrogen clouds would have been too massive, and their gravity would have forced them to collapse into titanic but lifeless black holes. On the other hand, if the universe emerging from a big bang wasn't clumpy *enough*, if it were too uniformly diffuse, then gravity would never have been able to bring together the hydrogen atoms to form clouds at all. Again, the result would be: no stars — just a bunch of electrons, protons, and hydrogen, scattered haphazardly throughout a cold, dark universe.

All told, we have a second Goldilocks problem on our hands. The regions emerging from the big bang needed to be *just* clumpy enough for hydrogen clouds to form, leading to stars; but not *too* clumpy, lest innumerable black holes form instead.

Once again, then, we might wonder about the margin of error. How clumpy is *too* clumpy? How diffuse is *too* diffuse? How lucky did we get to be here?

Turns out, the margin of error this time is virtually infinitesimal. It is not one in a million or even one in a billion; it is, according to cosmologists, nothing less than one part in $10^{10,123}$. This mind-boggling number, if you wrote it out, would be the numeral 1 followed by more than ten thousand zeros. And that estimate doesn't come from some fly-by-night, amateur astronomer; it comes from the British mathematician Roger Penrose, one of the scientists who first demonstrated the existence of black holes.[9]

---

9   See Leslie, *Universes*, p. 27. Moreover, Penrose isn't alone. For a sense of the scientific consensus here, see such works as Martin Rees, *Just Six Numbers* (New York:

Goldilocks and the Four Fundamental Forces

The flatness problem and what I've described above as the "clumpiness problem" are just two arenas in which, at the earliest moments of our universe's existence, fine-tuning had to occur in order for life to emerge. But there are others.[10] To give you a sense of just one more of them, let's talk briefly about the fundamental forces that underlie our universe. Scientists currently recognize four such forces. We call them gravity, electromagnetism, the nuclear weak force, and the nuclear strong force.

As it happens, these four forces have radically different strengths relative to one another. And all these force strengths — *they* had to be fine-tuned, too.

John Leslie, in his book *Universes*, explains how. Let's imagine a universe in which things were ever so slightly different from what they are, a universe in which the nuclear strong force was, say, just 1 percent stronger or weaker than it actually is. In a universe like that, stars would be incapable of manufacturing carbon in any quantities. That would in turn deprive the universe of one of the core building blocks of life, making it very hard for carbon-based life forms like you or me to exist. If, on the other hand, the nuclear strong force was, say, 2 percent *stronger* than it is, then protons could not exist, which would mean that atoms as we know them would cease to exist, too.

So, life depends on a finely tuned nuclear strong force. But it also depends on a finely tuned nuclear weak force. If, for example, the latter were just a bit stronger than it actually is, all the hydrogen in the early universe would have become helium instead, meaning there could never be any water, nor stable, long-burning stars. Make the nuclear weak force just a bit *weaker* than it is, and presto, you'd likewise destroy all the hydrogen.

Turning to electromagnetism, if that force were just a little bit stronger, the brightness of stars would fall dramatically, transforming all ordinary (main-sequence) stars into red stars, probably too cold to support

---

Basic Books, 2001); Stephen Hawking, *A Brief History of Time* (New York: Bantam, 1998), or Paul Davies, *The Mind of God* (New York: Simon & Schuster, 1992).

10 John Leslie, in his book *Universes*, delineates about a dozen other matrices in the universe, or in physics as we know it, which needed similar kinds of precise adjusting.

life.[11] On the other hand, if electromagnetism were to have been ever so slightly *weaker*, all main sequence stars would be blue stars: Very hot, and too short-lived to support life.

Finally, let's talk about gravity. Gravity, as it turns out, is dramatically, almost unimaginably, weaker than electromagnetism — roughly 10^{39} times weaker. But guess what? That ratio needed to be fine-tuned as well — because had it been, say, only 10^{33} weaker, stars would be a billion times less massive, would burn a million times faster, and would consequently leave the universe barren of life as we know it.[12]

All told, the four fundamental forces needed to be within a hair's breadth of what they actually are for us to exist.

The Dangers of Unbridled Creativity

When you add it all up, this exploding universe, in its infancy, needed quite a dose of organization and order, indeed. A mere random bang, no matter how big and how grand, would not have brought us a universe we could eventually live in. Someone needed to rein in that explosion. As the Sages said so long ago, the Almighty truly is שדי, "the One who said to His world, "Enough!" God set and enforced limits for an otherwise unruly universe.

When we think of the God of creation, we often think of "creation" as an all-consuming, overriding imperative. Indeed, what else would the God of creation be doing during the primal six days in which everything began — other than creating? But it turns out the Almighty was up to something more than creating, after all. Creation is an expansive activity; it is a breathless, burning act of bringing things into being. But it turns out that creative energy alone — no matter how powerful or overwhelming — is not, on its own, enough to create an environment stable enough to support this exquisitely delicate thing we call life. Life indeed exists only when two precarious energies are balanced — the energy that pushes existence forward, and the energy that simultaneously sets limits to it, the energy that holds creation back.

---

11 They would be unable to explode into supernovae — the explosions that would be needed to create most of the elements, besides hydrogen and helium, in the periodic table.

12 Leslie, *Universes*, pp. 3–4.

As we have seen, this is so with life on the grandest of scales — the universe. And it is so, as well, on the smallest of scales — for example, in the human cell. Our cells contain the wondrous and vital capacity to reproduce themselves: to copy their DNA, divide their organelles, and suddenly become two. But as vital as the capacity to recreate itself is, a cell that knows *only* how to do this is a malevolent actor. We have a name for cells like that. We call them cancer. A cancer cell is a cell that doesn't know when to stop, that doesn't heed limits, that doesn't know when to die. Cancer is nothing but creativity careening out of control.

Yes, God is our Creator. But, ironically, were creativity the *only* force the Almighty knew how to wield, His creation would have collapsed in on itself. It is only the Creator who is *also* שדי — the Creator who can impose limits upon expansion — who can bring into being and nurture a lush and rich world.

Of Motherhood and Death

We human beings have a hard time with limits sometimes. The dizzying rush of creativity is far more seductive to us than the need to call a halt to the creative process. Bringing an idea to life, an invention to fruition, a person into being — that is intoxicating. Knowing when to call it quits, by comparison, isn't terribly fun. Painting with life feels good; with death, not so much. But being a responsible creator requires that kind of discipline.

The Sages tell us something intriguing about God. It is a pithy little saying that encapsulates the delicate balancing act we've been talking about:

Shabbat 55a	אמר רבי חנינא: חותמו של הקדוש ברוך הוא אמת. Rabbi Chanina said: The seal of God is truth.

Think about that Hebrew word for "truth," the word that the Sages identify as God's hallmark: אמת. Look at how it is spelled. Its structure conveys an exquisite sense of balance. Its first letter is the first letter of the Hebrew alphabet, א, and its last letter is the last letter of the alphabet, ת. And its middle letter? Yes, you might have guessed — it is the letter that appears right in the middle of the alphabet, מ.

But it isn't just in the layout of its letters that אמת conveys balance. It conveys balance in another way, too. For אמת can be seen as the marriage of two words, formed by its component letters.

Take the first two letters of אמת: What do they spell? Put *alef* and *mem* together and you get אם, the Hebrew word for "mother." And now, consider the *last* two letters of אמת — the *mem* and the *tav*. What do *they* spell? The answer is: מת, the Hebrew word for "death."

Mother and death.

The first is the one we humans associate most with the idea of nurturing. She, in her tenderness, encapsulates the drive to bring life into the world, to guard it from harm, and to foster its growth, come what may. The second is that which we humans associate with the ultimate limit. Death is the ultimate "no," the ultimate cry "Enough!"

To be God is to paint with both energies. It is to be the Creator when possible, but שדי when necessary. To have enough compassion to nurture life insistently, but to possess enough wisdom to know that without limits, life cannot last. To be God is to be true; to know that sometimes, compassion means having to say "enough."

We Could Have Been Back Twice Already

וּמוֹשַׁב בְּנֵי יִשְׂרָאֵל אֲשֶׁר יָשְׁבוּ בְּמִצְרָיִם שְׁלֹשִׁים שָׁנָה וְאַרְבַּע מֵאוֹת שָׁנָה:

The stay that Israel stayed in Egypt was four hundred and thirty years.

EXODUS 12:40

We Could Have Been Back Twice Already

THE CLIMACTIC TENTH PLAGUE takes place, and the Egyptians finally decide to cast the children of Israel out of their land. At that point, we get a few verses that describe succinctly what actually happened as the Israelites left Egypt. We hear that the departing Israelites ask for gold and silver from their Egyptian neighbors, and they receive it from them. We hear that the people leave 600,000 strong, not counting children. The Israelites leave so quickly, we are told, there is no time for their bread to rise, and so they take unleavened dough on their backs. And finally, we hear how long Israel's sojourn in Egypt lasted: They had spent 430 years there before they finally left.

That's the story we all know and love. But if you look carefully at the original Hebrew language in the verses that tell us all this, you'll find a hidden pattern lurking just beneath the surface of the text. The pattern is remarkable, and it suggests there is more to this picture than immediately meets the eye.

Let's take a look at those verses, and the pattern, I think, will reveal itself.

The Pattern Begins

Let's start with that part about the unleavened bread. The people didn't have time to let their bread rise, the verse tells us, because they left Egypt so fast, and they didn't have time to tarry, to hang around. The Hebrew for that is *velo yachlu lehitmahmei'ah,* as in the following verse:

Exodus 12:39

וַיֹּאפוּ אֶת־הַבָּצֵק אֲשֶׁר
הוֹצִיאוּ מִמִּצְרַיִם עֻגֹת
מַצּוֹת כִּי לֹא חָמֵץ כִּי־
גֹרְשׁוּ מִמִּצְרַיִם וְלֹא יָכְלוּ
לְהִתְמַהְמֵהַּ וְגַם־צֵדָה לֹא־
עָשׂוּ לָהֶם:

And they baked unleavened loaves out
of the dough that they had taken out of
Egypt, for it was not leavened, since they
had been driven out of Egypt and could
not **dally**; nor had they prepared any
provisions for themselves.

Now, that word *lehitmahmei'ah* is an unusual word. It doesn't appear all
that often in the Torah. As it happens, the last time the reader encountered that word was way back in the book of Genesis. Let's take a moment
to revisit how the word appears there; I'll set the scene for you…

A Debate about Benjamin

The land of Canaan had been struck by a terrible famine, and Jacob's family
was desperate for food. Egypt, breadbasket of the ancient world, had the
grain necessary to sustain the family — but when Jacob's children made a
trip there to procure it, they had been less than successful.

The problem had revolved around Benjamin. The children of Jacob,
upon arriving in Egypt to buy grain, had encountered a high-ranking
Egyptian official who was inexplicably harsh with them. He accused the
band of brothers of being spies, and imprisoned one of them, Shimon.
Moreover, he told the brothers that he would not sell them the grain they
sought unless they returned with their last remaining brother, Benjamin,
whom they had left back in Canaan.

So the brothers traveled back to Canaan and told their father, Jacob,
about all this. But unfortunately, when Jacob heard of the demand for
Benjamin, things came to an impasse. Jacob refused to let Benjamin
leave his side. Joseph, he said, had already mysteriously gone missing,
and Benjamin was now his only remaining child from his beloved wife
Rachel. He was not prepared to let him out of his sight.

Time goes by, and the family's food supplies dwindle. And finally, Judah
finds a way to break the impasse. He tells Jacob that he will take personal
responsibility for Benjamin:

Genesis 43:9

אָם־לֹא הֲבִיאֹתִיו אֵלֶיךָ
וְהִצַּגְתִּיו לְפָנֶיךָ וְחָטָאתִי לְךָ
כָּל־הַיָּמִים:

If I don't bring him back to you and stand
him up before you — I will have sinned
against you, all the days [of my life].

Finally, ending his plea to his father, Judah says this:

כִּי לוּלֵא הִתְמַהְמָהְנוּ כִּי־עַתָּה
שַׁבְנוּ זֶה פַעֲמָיִם:

Indeed, had we not been dallying around [like this], we could have been there and back [to Egypt] twice already!

Genesis 43:10

And there, of course, is that word *hitmahmahnu*, "dallying around." It just happens to be the same phrase that appears later, in the book of Exodus, in **Parshat Bo,** when the text tells us: *lo yachlu lehitmahmei'ah*, "the Israelites didn't have time to *dally around*" in Egypt long enough to let their dough rise before they left.

Could It Be Mere Coincidence?

Now this recurrence of the unusual phrase *lehitmahmei'ah* is not in and of itself particularly earth-shattering. Unusual words do have a way of appearing and recurring now and then — and therefore, the mere fact that such a word appears first here and then there is not necessarily cause to infer that the Torah means to paint any larger connections between the stories. Could well be just a coincidence.

But here's the thing: This recurrence of *lehitmahmei'ah* isn't an isolated connection between the two stories. Not by any stretch of the imagination. In fact, there are no less than six different word pairings that connect the two biblical passages we've been looking at. And not only that, but these six recurring phrases aren't scattered randomly throughout each episode. No, there's a pattern that animates their recurrence. In each of the episodes, the common phrases actually appear … *in precisely the same order.*

That kind of correlation doesn't seem coincidental at all.

To show you what I mean, let's reproduce the two episodes side by side. Look them over yourself for a moment or two and see if any of the connections between the episodes jump out at you. Then read on, and we'll compare notes.

THE PEOPLE OF ISRAEL
LEAVE EGYPT

Exodus 12:34–41

(לד) וַיִּשָּׂא הָעָם אֶת־בְּצֵקוֹ טֶרֶם יֶחְמָץ
מִשְׁאֲרֹתָם צְרֻרֹת בְּשִׂמְלֹתָם עַל־שִׁכְמָם:
(לה) וּבְנֵי־יִשְׂרָאֵל עָשׂוּ כִּדְבַר מֹשֶׁה
וַיִּשְׁאֲלוּ מִמִּצְרַיִם כְּלֵי־כֶסֶף וּכְלֵי זָהָב
וּשְׂמָלֹת: (לו) וַה' נָתַן אֶת־חֵן הָעָם בְּעֵינֵי
מִצְרַיִם וַיַּשְׁאִלוּם וַיְנַצְּלוּ אֶת־מִצְרָיִם:
(לז) וַיִּסְעוּ בְנֵי־יִשְׂרָאֵל מֵרַעְמְסֵס סֻכֹּתָה
כְּשֵׁשׁ־מֵאוֹת אֶלֶף רַגְלִי הַגְּבָרִים לְבַד
מִטָּף: (לח) וְגַם־עֵרֶב רַב עָלָה אִתָּם
וְצֹאן וּבָקָר מִקְנֶה כָּבֵד מְאֹד: (לט) וַיֹּאפוּ
אֶת־הַבָּצֵק אֲשֶׁר הוֹצִיאוּ מִמִּצְרַיִם עֻגֹת
מַצּוֹת כִּי לֹא חָמֵץ כִּי־גֹרְשׁוּ מִמִּצְרַיִם
וְלֹא יָכְלוּ לְהִתְמַהְמֵהַּ וְגַם־צֵדָה לֹא־
עָשׂוּ לָהֶם: (מ) וּמוֹשַׁב בְּנֵי יִשְׂרָאֵל אֲשֶׁר
יָשְׁבוּ בְּמִצְרָיִם שְׁלֹשִׁים שָׁנָה וְאַרְבַּע
מֵאוֹת שָׁנָה: (מא) וַיְהִי מִקֵּץ שְׁלֹשִׁים
שָׁנָה וְאַרְבַּע מֵאוֹת שָׁנָה וַיְהִי בְּעֶצֶם
הַיּוֹם הַזֶּה יָצְאוּ כָּל־צִבְאוֹת יְקֹוָה
מֵאֶרֶץ מִצְרָיִם:

JUDAH SPEAKS WITH
JACOB

Genesis 43:6–10

(ו) וַיֹּאמֶר יִשְׂרָאֵל לָמָה
הֲרֵעֹתֶם לִי לְהַגִּיד לָאִישׁ
הַעוֹד לָכֶם אָח: (ז) וַיֹּאמְרוּ
שָׁאוֹל שָׁאַל־הָאִישׁ לָנוּ
וּלְמוֹלַדְתֵּנוּ לֵאמֹר הַעוֹד
אֲבִיכֶם חַי הֲיֵשׁ לָכֶם אָח
וַנַּגֶּד־לוֹ עַל־פִּי הַדְּבָרִים
הָאֵלֶּה הֲיָדוֹעַ נֵדַע כִּי
יֹאמַר הוֹרִידוּ אֶת־אֲחִיכֶם:
(ח) וַיֹּאמֶר יְהוּדָה אֶל־
יִשְׂרָאֵל אָבִיו שִׁלְחָה הַנַּעַר
אִתִּי וְנָקוּמָה וְנֵלֵכָה וְנִחְיֶה
וְלֹא נָמוּת גַּם־אֲנַחְנוּ גַם־
אַתָּה גַּם־טַפֵּנוּ: (ט) אָנֹכִי
אֶעֶרְבֶנּוּ מִיָּדִי תְּבַקְשֶׁנּוּ אִם־
לֹא הֲבִיאֹתִיו אֵלֶיךָ וְהִצַּגְתִּיו
לְפָנֶיךָ וְחָטָאתִי לְךָ
כָּל־הַיָּמִים: (י) כִּי לוּלֵא
הִתְמַהְמָהְנוּ כִּי־עַתָּה שַׁבְנוּ
זֶה פַעֲמָיִם:

34 So the people took their dough before it was leavened, their kneading bowls wrapped in their cloaks upon their shoulders. 35 The Israelites had done Moses' bidding and asked from the Egyptians objects of silver and gold, and clothing. 36 And the Lord had disposed the Egyptians favorably toward the people, and they let them have their request; thus they stripped the Egyptians. 37 The Israelites journeyed from Raamses to Succoth, about six hundred thousand men on

6 And Israel said, "Why did you serve me so ill as to tell the man that you had another brother?" 7 They replied, "But the man kept asking about us and our family, saying, 'Is your father still living? Have you another brother?' And we answered him accordingly. How were we to know that he would say, 'Bring your brother here'?"

foot, aside from children. **38** Moreover, a mixed multitude went up with them, and very much livestock, both flocks and herds. **39** And they baked unleavened loaves out of the dough that they had taken out of Egypt, for it was not leavened, since they had been driven out of Egypt and could not dally; nor had they prepared any provisions for themselves. **40** The stay that Israel stayed in Egypt was four hundred and thirty years; **41** at the end of the four hundred and thirtieth year, to the very day, all the ranks of the Lord departed from the land of Egypt.

8 Then Judah said to his father Israel, "Send the boy in my care, and let us be on our way, that we may live and not die—you and we and our children. **9** I myself will be surety for him; you may hold me responsible: if I do not bring him back to you and stand him up before you, I will have sinned against you, all the days [of my life]. **10** For had we not been dallying around, we could have been there and back twice already!"

Double *Sha'al*

Let's start with the Genesis narrative. During the impasse we were talking about, when the family was running low on food, Jacob asks his children why they voluntarily gave that high-ranking Egyptian official the information they did, namely, that they had another brother left at home. To this, the brothers retort that it wasn't their fault; they didn't really "volunteer" that information. On the contrary, the Egyptian had been directly interrogating them about it:

שָׁאוֹל שָׁאַל־הָאִישׁ לָנוּ וּלְמוֹ־
לַדְתֵּנוּ לֵאמֹר הַעוֹד אֲבִיכֶם חַי
הֲיֵשׁ לָכֶם אָח וַנַּגֶּד־לוֹ עַל־פִּי
הַדְּבָרִים הָאֵלֶּה הֲיָדוֹעַ
נֵדַע כִּי יֹאמַר הוֹרִידוּ אֶת־
אֲחִיכֶם:

The man **kept asking** about us and our family, saying, "Is your father still living? Have you another brother?" And we answered him accordingly. How were we to know that he would say, "Bring your brother here"?

Genesis 43:7

When the brothers spoke of the Egyptian incessantly questioning them, the Hebrew phrase for that is: *Sha'ol sha'al ha'ish lanu.* The thing to notice is that the Hebrew employs a doubled form of the word *sha'al* — as if to say, "The man *questioned us and questioned us*" (and we did nothing but answer him truthfully).[1] Now glance over to the other side of your page at the Exodus narrative, and — wouldn't you know it — you'll find a version of that same phrase, a double *sha'al* appearing there as well:

<table>
<tr>
<td>Exodus
12:35–36</td>
<td>וּבְנֵי־יִשְׂרָאֵל עָשׂוּ כִּדְבַר
מֹשֶׁה וַיִּשְׁאֲלוּ מִמִּצְרַיִם
כְּלֵי־כֶסֶף וּכְלֵי זָהָב וּשְׂמָלֹת:
וַה' נָתַן אֶת־חֵן הָעָם
בְּעֵינֵי מִצְרַיִם וַיַּשְׁאִלוּם
וַיְנַצְּלוּ אֶת־מִצְרָיִם:</td>
<td>The Israelites did Moses' bidding **and asked** from the Egyptians objects of silver and gold, and clothing. And the Lord had disposed the Egyptians favorably toward the people, and they let them have their request; thus **they stripped** the Egyptians.</td>
</tr>
</table>

To be sure, in Exodus, the two occurrences of *sha'al* each have a differ-ent meaning[2] — but that's why you need to look at the Hebrew, not just the English. In Hebrew, the parallel jumps out at you: *sha'al,* once again, is appearing twice.

Children

So just to keep track of things — let's highlight what we've found thus far:

---

1   The doubled form of verbs is used on occasion by the Torah; it generally conveys a sense of intensity.

2   Or, perhaps, they might have the same meaning — for one could render the sec-ond וַיַּשְׁאִלוּם: "They let them have what they asked for" (see Rashi to Exodus 12:36, from Mechilta de-Rabbi Yishmael 12:35).

THE PEOPLE OF ISRAEL LEAVE EGYPT	JUDAH SPEAKS WITH JACOB
Exodus 12:34–41	Genesis 43:6–10

THE PEOPLE OF ISRAEL LEAVE EGYPT

Exodus 12:34–41

(לד) וַיִּשָּׂא הָעָם אֶת־בְּצֵקוֹ טֶרֶם יֶחְמָץ
מִשְׁאֲרֹתָם צְרֻרֹת בְּשִׂמְלֹתָם עַל־שִׁכְמָם:
(לה) וּבְנֵי־יִשְׂרָאֵל עָשׂוּ כִּדְבַר מֹשֶׁה
וַיִּשְׁאֲלוּ מִמִּצְרַיִם כְּלֵי־כֶסֶף וּכְלֵי זָהָב
וּשְׂמָלֹת: (לו) וַיהֹוָה נָתַן אֶת־חֵן הָעָם בְּעֵינֵי
מִצְרַיִם וַיַּשְׁאִלוּם וַיְנַצְּלוּ אֶת־מִצְרָיִם:
(לז) וַיִּסְעוּ בְנֵי־יִשְׂרָאֵל מֵרַעְמְסֵס סֻכֹּתָה
כְּשֵׁשׁ־מֵאוֹת אֶלֶף רַגְלִי הַגְּבָרִים לְבַד
מִטָּף: (לח) וְגַם־עֵרֶב רַב עָלָה אִתָּם
וְצֹאן וּבָקָר מִקְנֶה כָּבֵד מְאֹד: (לט) וַיֹּאפוּ
אֶת־הַבָּצֵק אֲשֶׁר הוֹצִיאוּ מִמִּצְרַיִם עֻגֹת
מַצּוֹת כִּי לֹא חָמֵץ כִּי־גֹרְשׁוּ מִמִּצְרַיִם
וְלֹא יָכְלוּ לְהִתְמַהְמֵהַּ וְגַם־צֵדָה לֹא־
עָשׂוּ לָהֶם: (מ) וּמוֹשַׁב בְּנֵי יִשְׂרָאֵל אֲשֶׁר
יָשְׁבוּ בְּמִצְרָיִם שְׁלֹשִׁים שָׁנָה וְאַרְבַּע
מֵאוֹת שָׁנָה: (מא) וַיְהִי מִקֵּץ שְׁלֹשִׁים שָׁנָה
וְאַרְבַּע מֵאוֹת שָׁנָה וַיְהִי בְּעֶצֶם הַיּוֹם הַזֶּה
יָצְאוּ כָּל־צִבְאוֹת יְהֹוָה מֵאֶרֶץ מִצְרָיִם:

JUDAH SPEAKS WITH JACOB

Genesis 43:6–10

(ו) וַיֹּאמֶר יִשְׂרָאֵל לָמָה
הֲרֵעֹתֶם לִי לְהַגִּיד לָאִישׁ הַעוֹד
לָכֶם אָח: (ז) וַיֹּאמְרוּ שָׁאוֹל
שָׁאַל־הָאִישׁ לָנוּ וּלְמוֹלַדְתֵּנוּ
לֵאמֹר הַעוֹד אֲבִיכֶם חַי הֲיֵשׁ
לָכֶם אָח וַנַּגֶּד־לוֹ עַל־פִּי
הַדְּבָרִים הָאֵלֶּה הֲיָדוֹעַ נֵדַע
כִּי יֹאמַר הוֹרִידוּ אֶת־אֲחִיכֶם:
(ח) וַיֹּאמֶר יְהוּדָה אֶל־יִשְׂרָאֵל
אָבִיו שִׁלְחָה הַנַּעַר אִתִּי
וְנָקוּמָה וְנֵלֵכָה וְנִחְיֶה וְלֹא
נָמוּת גַּם־אֲנַחְנוּ גַם־אַתָּה גַּם־
טַפֵּנוּ: (ט) אָנֹכִי אֶעֶרְבֶנּוּ מִיָּדִי
תְּבַקְשֶׁנּוּ אִם־לֹא הֲבִיאֹתִיו
אֵלֶיךָ וְהִצַּגְתִּיו לְפָנֶיךָ
וְחָטָאתִי לְךָ כָּל־הַיָּמִים: (י) כִּי
לוּלֵא הִתְמַהְמָהְנוּ כִּי־עַתָּה
שַׁבְנוּ זֶה פַעֲמָיִם:

Now, take another look back at this text above, and keep reading each narrative, side by side. Just below each "green highlight," you'll discover another connection lurking between the stories…

Did you see it?

Going back to Genesis, look what happens after that double *sha'al*: Judah pleads with his father, proposing that they should just get up and go back to Egypt already, so that they and their children will be able to get the food they need to survive. Now the word for children Judah uses there is *taf*. It is a relatively infrequently used term; the more common term for children might be *banim* or perhaps *yeladim*. But, lo and behold, glance over at the corresponding section of text in **Parshat Bo,** and right after that double *sha'al*…we also hear a mention of children, characterized by that same word, *taf*: The text tells us that there were about six hundred thousand men who left Egypt, except for children — which is to say, except for the *taf*:

THE PEOPLE OF ISRAEL LEAVE EGYPT	JUDAH SPEAKS WITH JACOB
Exodus 12:34–41	Genesis 43:6–10

(לד) וַיִּשָּׂא הָעָם אֶת־בְּצֵקוֹ טֶרֶם יֶחְמָץ מִשְׁאֲרֹתָם צְרֻרֹת בְּשִׂמְלֹתָם עַל־שִׁכְמָם: (לה) וּבְנֵי־יִשְׂרָאֵל עָשׂוּ כִּדְבַר מֹשֶׁה וַיִּשְׁאֲלוּ מִמִּצְרַיִם כְּלֵי־כֶסֶף וּכְלֵי זָהָב וּשְׂמָלֹת: (לו) וַיהֹוָה נָתַן אֶת־חֵן הָעָם בְּעֵינֵי מִצְרַיִם וַיַּשְׁאִלוּם וַיְנַצְּלוּ אֶת־מִצְרָיִם: (לז) וַיִּסְעוּ בְנֵי־יִשְׂרָאֵל מֵרַעְמְסֵס סֻכֹּתָה כְּשֵׁשׁ־מֵאוֹת אֶלֶף רַגְלִי הַגְּבָרִים לְבַד מִטָּף: (לח) וְגַם־עֵרֶב רַב עָלָה אִתָּם וְצֹאן וּבָקָר מִקְנֶה כָּבֵד מְאֹד: (לט) וַיֹּאפוּ אֶת־הַבָּצֵק אֲשֶׁר הוֹצִיאוּ מִמִּצְרַיִם עֻגֹת מַצּוֹת כִּי לֹא חָמֵץ כִּי־גֹרְשׁוּ מִמִּצְרַיִם וְלֹא יָכְלוּ לְהִתְמַהְמֵהַּ וְגַם־צֵדָה לֹא־ עָשׂוּ לָהֶם: (מ) וּמוֹשַׁב בְּנֵי יִשְׂרָאֵל אֲשֶׁר יָשְׁבוּ בְּמִצְרָיִם שְׁלֹשִׁים שָׁנָה וְאַרְבַּע מֵאוֹת שָׁנָה: (מא) וַיְהִי מִקֵּץ שְׁלֹשִׁים שָׁנָה וְאַרְבַּע מֵאוֹת שָׁנָה וַיְהִי בְּעֶצֶם הַיּוֹם הַזֶּה יָצְאוּ כָּל־צִבְאוֹת יְקֹוָה מֵאֶרֶץ מִצְרָיִם:

(ו) וַיֹּאמֶר יִשְׂרָאֵל לָמָה הֲרֵעֹתֶם לִי לְהַגִּיד לָאִישׁ הַעוֹד לָכֶם אָח: (ז) וַיֹּאמְרוּ שָׁאוֹל שָׁאַל־הָאִישׁ לָנוּ וּלְמוֹלַדְתֵּנוּ לֵאמֹר הַעוֹד אֲבִיכֶם חַי הֲיֵשׁ לָכֶם אָח וַנַּגֶּד־לוֹ עַל־פִּי הַדְּבָרִים הָאֵלֶּה הֲיָדוֹעַ נֵדַע כִּי יֹאמַר הוֹרִידוּ אֶת־אֲחִיכֶם: (ח) וַיֹּאמֶר יְהוּדָה אֶל־יִשְׂרָאֵל אָבִיו שִׁלְחָה הַנַּעַר אִתִּי וְנָקוּמָה וְנֵלֵכָה וְנִחְיֶה וְלֹא נָמוּת גַּם־אֲנַחְנוּ גַם־אַתָּה גַּם־ טַפֵּנוּ: (ט) אָנֹכִי אֶעֶרְבֶנּוּ מִיָּדִי תְּבַקְשֶׁנּוּ אִם־לֹא הֲבִיאֹתִיו אֵלֶיךָ וְהִצַּגְתִּיו לְפָנֶיךָ וְחָטָאתִי לְךָ כָּל־הַיָּמִים: (י) כִּי לוּלֵא הִתְמַהְמָהְנוּ כִּי־עַתָּה שַׁבְנוּ זֶה פַעֲמָיִם:

So that's a second correspondence. Let's keep reading and see if we can find a third.

Erev

Return with me to the Genesis side of the page. Exactly two words after that mention of *taf*, Judah will now make use of another unusual term. Judah said to his father, about Benjamin: אָנֹכִי אֶעֶרְבֶנּוּ, I will personally stand as an *orev*, a guarantor, for Benjamin. And now, glance at the corresponding section of text in Exodus. There you'll find that exactly *two words* after the term *taf*, a variation of the same root *ayin-reish-bet* appears as well. This time, it spells *erev*, as in **וְגַם־עֵרֶב רַב עָלָה אִתָּם**; along with those six hundred thousand men and all the other Israelites, a mixed multitude — a great *erev* — of people went up.[3]

THE PEOPLE OF ISRAEL LEAVE EGYPT	JUDAH SPEAKS WITH JACOB
Exodus 12:34–41	Genesis 43:6–10

(לד)וַיִּשָּׂא הָעָם אֶת־בְּצֵקוֹ טֶרֶם יֶחְמָץ מִשְׁאֲרֹתָם צְרֻרֹת בְּשִׂמְלֹתָם עַל־שִׁכְמָם: (לה)וּבְנֵי־יִשְׂרָאֵל עָשׂוּ כִּדְבַר מֹשֶׁה וַיִּשְׁאֲלוּ מִמִּצְרַיִם כְּלֵי־כֶסֶף וּכְלֵי זָהָב וּשְׂמָלֹת: (לו)וַהי׳ נָתַן אֶת־חֵן הָעָם בְּעֵינֵי מִצְרַיִם וַיַּשְׁאִלוּם וַיְנַצְּלוּ אֶת־מִצְרָיִם: (לז)וַיִּסְעוּ בְנֵי־יִשְׂרָאֵל מֵרַעְמְסֵס סֻכֹּתָה כְּשֵׁשׁ־מֵאוֹת אֶלֶף רַגְלִי הַגְּבָרִים לְבַד מִטָּף: (לח)וְגַם־עֵרֶב רַב עָלָה אִתָּם וְצֹאן וּבָקָר מִקְנֶה כָּבֵד מְאֹד: (לט)וַיֹּאפוּ אֶת־הַבָּצֵק אֲשֶׁר הוֹצִיאוּ מִמִּצְרַיִם עֻגֹת מַצּוֹת כִּי לֹא חָמֵץ כִּי־גֹרְשׁוּ מִמִּצְרַיִם וְלֹא יָכְלוּ לְהִתְמַהְמֵהַּ וְגַם־צֵדָה לֹא־עָשׂוּ לָהֶם: (מ)וּמוֹשַׁב בְּנֵי יִשְׂרָאֵל אֲשֶׁר יָשְׁבוּ בְּמִצְרָיִם שְׁלֹשִׁים שָׁנָה וְאַרְבַּע מֵאוֹת שָׁנָה: (מא)וַיְהִי מִקֵּץ שְׁלֹשִׁים שָׁנָה וְאַרְבַּע מֵאוֹת שָׁנָה וַיְהִי בְּעֶצֶם הַיּוֹם הַזֶּה יָצְאוּ כָּל־צִבְאוֹת יְקֹוָה מֵאֶרֶץ מִצְרָיִם:	(ו)וַיֹּאמֶר יִשְׂרָאֵל לָמָה הֲרֵעֹתֶם לִי לְהַגִּיד לָאִישׁ הַעוֹד לָכֶם אָח: (ז)וַיֹּאמְרוּ שָׁאוֹל שָׁאַל־הָאִישׁ לָנוּ וּלְמוֹלַדְתֵּנוּ לֵאמֹר הַעוֹד אֲבִיכֶם חַי הֲיֵשׁ לָכֶם אָח וַנַּגֶּד־לוֹ עַל־פִּי הַדְּבָרִים הָאֵלֶּה הֲיָדוֹעַ נֵדַע כִּי יֹאמַר הוֹרִידוּ אֶת־אֲחִיכֶם: (ח)וַיֹּאמֶר יְהוּדָה אֶל־יִשְׂרָאֵל אָבִיו שִׁלְחָה הַנַּעַר אִתִּי וְנָקוּמָה וְנֵלֵכָה וְנִחְיֶה וְלֹא נָמוּת גַּם־אֲנַחְנוּ גַם־אַתָּה גַּם־טַפֵּנוּ: (ט)אָנֹכִי אֶעֶרְבֶנּוּ מִיָּדִי תְּבַקְשֶׁנּוּ אִם־לֹא הֲבִיאֹתִיו אֵלֶיךָ וְהִצַּגְתִּיו לְפָנֶיךָ וְחָטָאתִי לְךָ כָּל־הַיָּמִים: (י)כִּי לוּלֵא הִתְמַהְמָהְנוּ כִּי־עַתָּה שַׁבְנוּ זֶה פַעֲמָיִם:

---

3   The words *erev* and *orev* seem related, not just phonetically, but conceptually. *Erev rav* means a great *mixed* multitude. An *orev* is a guarantor, but the idea of being a guarantor seems related to being "mixed in": a third party, who would otherwise be outside a transaction between a borrower and a lender, nevertheless gets involved — mixes in on the transaction — and assumes responsibility as if he himself were the borrower.

An Anagram Becomes a Mirror

All of which brings us to a fourth and fifth word pairing. For right after this, in both stories, we get to that word *lehitmahmei'ah* that we were talking about before. But don't stop there; the connection runs deeper. Take a glance at the two words in each story that immediately *precede* the term *lehitmahmei'ah*, and you'll see what I mean:

THE PEOPLE OF ISRAEL LEAVE EGYPT	JUDAH SPEAKS WITH JACOB
Exodus 12:39	Genesis 43:10
(לט) ...כִּי־גֹרְשׁוּ מִמִּצְרַיִם וְלֹא יָכְלוּ לְהִתְמַהְמֵהַּ וְגַם־צֵדָה לֹא־עָשׂוּ לָהֶם:	(י) כִּי לוּלֵא הִתְמַהְמָהְנוּ כִּי־עַתָּה שַׁבְנוּ זֶה פַעֲמָיִם:

Even if you don't know Hebrew well, just look at the phrases **כִּי לוּלֵא** and **וְלֹא יָכְלוּ** and ask yourself: Is there a resemblance between them?

Looking at the letters, you can readily see that the phrases are anagrams of one another; which is to say, their letters are precisely the same, just rearranged.

But it is not just at the lexical level that the phrases are related; their meanings are related, too. At the conceptual level, the two phrases — **כִּי לולא** and **ולא יכלו** — are actually mirror images of one another. *Ki lulei* means "had we not." In Genesis, it means: dallying is what we *did* do, but *we wish we hadn't*. In Exodus, the opposite is the case, **וְלֹא יָכְלוּ לְהִתְמַהְמֵהַּ**: dallying is what we *wished* we could do, so we could have time to bake some decent bread, but *we couldn't do it* (because we were thrust out of Egypt too quickly).

A Summary of the Connections — So Far

All in all, then, here is where we are at with our developing, composite picture of connections that link the Genesis and Exodus passages:

THE PEOPLE OF ISRAEL LEAVE EGYPT

Exodus 12:34–41

(לד) וַיִּשָּׂא הָעָם אֶת־בְּצֵקוֹ טֶרֶם יֶחְמָץ מִשְׁאֲרֹתָם צְרֻרֹת בְּשִׂמְלֹתָם עַל־שִׁכְמָם: (לה) וּבְנֵי־יִשְׂרָאֵל עָשׂוּ כִּדְבַר מֹשֶׁה וַיִּשְׁאֲלוּ מִמִּצְרַיִם כְּלֵי־כֶסֶף וּכְלֵי זָהָב וּשְׂמָלֹת: (לו) וַה' נָתַן אֶת־חֵן הָעָם בְּעֵינֵי מִצְרַיִם וַיַּשְׁאִלוּם וַיְנַצְּלוּ אֶת־מִצְרָיִם: (לז) וַיִּסְעוּ בְנֵי־יִשְׂרָאֵל מֵרַעְמְסֵס סֻכֹּתָה כְּשֵׁשׁ־מֵאוֹת אֶלֶף רַגְלִי הַגְּבָרִים לְבַד מִטָּף: (לח) וְגַם־עֵרֶב רַב עָלָה אִתָּם וְצֹאן וּבָקָר מִקְנֶה כָּבֵד מְאֹד: (לט) וַיֹּאפוּ אֶת־הַבָּצֵק אֲשֶׁר הוֹצִיאוּ מִמִּצְרַיִם עֻגֹת מַצּוֹת כִּי לֹא חָמֵץ כִּי־גֹרְשׁוּ מִמִּצְרַיִם וְלֹא יָכְלוּ לְהִתְמַהְמֵהַּ וְגַם־צֵדָה לֹא־עָשׂוּ לָהֶם: (מ) וּמוֹשַׁב בְּנֵי יִשְׂרָאֵל אֲשֶׁר יָשְׁבוּ בְּמִצְרָיִם שְׁלֹשִׁים שָׁנָה וְאַרְבַּע מֵאוֹת שָׁנָה: (מא) וַיְהִי מִקֵּץ שְׁלֹשִׁים שָׁנָה וְאַרְבַּע מֵאוֹת שָׁנָה וַיְהִי בְּעֶצֶם הַיּוֹם הַזֶּה יָצְאוּ כָּל־צִבְאוֹת ה' מֵאֶרֶץ מִצְרָיִם:

JUDAH SPEAKS WITH JACOB

Genesis 43:6–10

(ו) וַיֹּאמֶר יִשְׂרָאֵל לָמָה הֲרֵעֹתֶם לִי לְהַגִּיד לָאִישׁ הַעוֹד לָכֶם אָח: (ז) וַיֹּאמְרוּ שָׁאוֹל שָׁאַל־הָאִישׁ לָנוּ וּלְמוֹלַדְתֵּנוּ לֵאמֹר הַעוֹד אֲבִיכֶם חַי הֲיֵשׁ לָכֶם אָח וַנַּגֶּד־לוֹ עַל־פִּי הַדְּבָרִים הָאֵלֶּה הֲיָדוֹעַ נֵדַע כִּי יֹאמַר הוֹרִידוּ אֶת־אֲחִיכֶם: (ח) וַיֹּאמֶר יְהוּדָה אֶל־יִשְׂרָאֵל אָבִיו שִׁלְחָה הַנַּעַר אִתִּי וְנָקוּמָה וְנֵלֵכָה וְנִחְיֶה וְלֹא נָמוּת גַּם־אֲנַחְנוּ גַם־אַתָּה גַּם־טַפֵּנוּ: (ט) אָנֹכִי אֶעֶרְבֶנּוּ מִיָּדִי תְּבַקְשֶׁנּוּ אִם־לֹא הֲבִיאֹתִיו אֵלֶיךָ וְהִצַּגְתִּיו לְפָנֶיךָ וְחָטָאתִי לְךָ כָּל־הַיָּמִים: (י) כִּי לוּלֵא הִתְמַהְמָהְנוּ כִּי־עַתָּה שַׁבְנוּ זֶה פַעֲמָיִם:

We have a double *sha'al, taf, orev/erev, couldn't dally* versus *didn't dally*… Had it been only one or two of these correspondences, we might chalk it up to mere happenstance. But *five* correspondences — coming as they do in precisely the same order in each passage — that doesn't seem all that coincidental. It feels instead like there's some intentionality here, that the Torah wants the astute reader to perceive some kind of link between these two very different episodes. But the question is: *Why?* The events described in the two passages seem disconnected from one another. One is about a band of brothers figuring out how to get food; the other is about a nation exiting Egypt. Why do these correspondences exist? What are we meant to see in them?

A Sixth Connection

I want to suggest that the meaning of the five correspondences we've just seen might very well be revealed in … a sixth correspondence. For indeed, there is one last word pair that links the stories. It takes the form of a clever play on words, and in each story, it comes right *after* the five pairs we've seen thus far.

Back in Genesis, Judah had said to his father: If we hadn't been waiting around like this,

Genesis 43:10   כִּי־עַתָּה שַׁבְנוּ זֶה פַעֲמָיִם: We could have been there and back [to Egypt] twice already!

Or, literally, we could have been *shav* — we could have *returned* — twice already. And now, glance over at the Exodus passage we've been looking at, and right after the five pairs we've discovered thus far, can you find the sixth pair? Something that reminds you of … returning twice?

Again, because this is a play on words, this is something you'll really be able to see only in the original Hebrew. You'll find the pair if, after the first five pairs in each passage, you scan the Hebrew for … the word *shav* appearing not once, but twice:

THE PEOPLE OF ISRAEL LEAVE EGYPT	JUDAH SPEAKS WITH JACOB
Exodus 12:34–41	Genesis 43:6–10

(לד) וַיִּשָּׂא הָעָם אֶת־בְּצֵקוֹ טֶרֶם יֶחְמָץ מִשְׁאֲרֹתָם צְרֻרֹת בְּשִׂמְלֹתָם עַל־שִׁכְמָם: (לה) וּבְנֵי־יִשְׂרָאֵל עָשׂוּ כִּדְבַר מֹשֶׁה וַיִּשְׁאֲלוּ מִמִּצְרַיִם כְּלֵי־כֶסֶף וּכְלֵי זָהָב וּשְׂמָלֹת: (לו) וַה' נָתַן אֶת־חֵן הָעָם בְּעֵינֵי מִצְרַיִם וַיַּשְׁאִלוּם וַיְנַצְּלוּ אֶת־מִצְרָיִם: (לז) וַיִּסְעוּ בְנֵי־יִשְׂרָאֵל מֵרַעְמְסֵס סֻכֹּתָה כְּשֵׁשׁ־מֵאוֹת אֶלֶף רַגְלִי הַגְּבָרִים לְבַד מִטָּף: (לח) וְגַם־עֵרֶב רַב עָלָה אִתָּם וְצֹאן וּבָקָר מִקְנֶה כָּבֵד מְאֹד: (לט) וַיֹּאפוּ אֶת־הַבָּצֵק אֲשֶׁר הוֹצִיאוּ מִמִּצְרַיִם עֻגֹת מַצּוֹת כִּי לֹא חָמֵץ כִּי־גֹרְשׁוּ מִמִּצְרַיִם וְלֹא יָכְלוּ לְהִתְמַהְמֵהַּ וְגַם־צֵדָה לֹא־עָשׂוּ לָהֶם: (מ) וּמוֹשַׁב בְּנֵי יִשְׂרָאֵל אֲשֶׁר יָשְׁבוּ בְּמִצְרָיִם שְׁלֹשִׁים שָׁנָה וְאַרְבַּע מֵאוֹת שָׁנָה: (מא) וַיְהִי מִקֵּץ שְׁלֹשִׁים שָׁנָה וְאַרְבַּע מֵאוֹת שָׁנָה וַיְהִי בְּעֶצֶם הַיּוֹם הַזֶּה יָצְאוּ כָּל־צִבְאוֹת ה' מֵאֶרֶץ מִצְרָיִם:

(ו) וַיֹּאמֶר יִשְׂרָאֵל לָמָה הֲרֵעֹתֶם לִי לְהַגִּיד לָאִישׁ הַעוֹד לָכֶם אָח: (ז) וַיֹּאמְרוּ שָׁאוֹל שָׁאַל־הָאִישׁ לָנוּ וּלְמוֹלַדְתֵּנוּ לֵאמֹר הַעוֹד אֲבִיכֶם חַי הֲיֵשׁ לָכֶם אָח וַנַּגֶּד־לוֹ עַל־פִּי הַדְּבָרִים הָאֵלֶּה הֲיָדוֹעַ נֵדַע כִּי יֹאמַר הוֹרִידוּ אֶת־אֲחִיכֶם: (ח) וַיֹּאמֶר יְהוּדָה אֶל־יִשְׂרָאֵל אָבִיו שִׁלְחָה הַנַּעַר אִתִּי וְנָקוּמָה וְנֵלֵכָה וְנִחְיֶה וְלֹא נָמוּת גַּם־אֲנַחְנוּ גַם־אַתָּה גַּם־טַפֵּנוּ: (ט) אָנֹכִי אֶעֶרְבֶנּוּ מִיָּדִי תְּבַקְשֶׁנּוּ אִם־לֹא הֲבִיאֹתִיו אֵלֶיךָ וְהִצַּגְתִּיו לְפָנֶיךָ וְחָטָאתִי לְךָ כָּל־הַיָּמִים: (י) כִּי לוּלֵא הִתְמַהְמָהְנוּ כִּי־עַתָּה שַׁבְנוּ זֶה פַעֲמָיִם:

The double *shav* in the Exodus passage appears in the words: *umoshav benei Yisrael asher yashvu beMitzrayim…* In English, one might translate that as: *The **stay** that Israel **stayed** in Egypt was four hundred and thirty years.* And, of course, that sounds very different from Judah's plea to his father that we could have *returned twice* already. Except that in Hebrew, it doesn't sound all that different. The Hebrew root for "return" and "stay"…is exactly the same: *shav.* Thus, it is not just Genesis that talks about *shav*, returning, twice; Exodus also speaks of *shav* twice:

וּמוֹשַׁב בְּנֵי יִשְׂרָאֵל אֲשֶׁר יָשְׁבוּ בְּמִצְרַיִם שְׁלֹשִׁים שָׁנָה וְאַרְבַּע מֵאוֹת שָׁנָה:

The **stay** that Israel **stayed** in Egypt was four hundred and thirty years.

Exodus 12:40

There's that root *shav*. And it appears *pa'amayim*, twice.

But…What Does It Mean?

Yes, a clever play on words, but that connection, I think, isn't only meant to serve as wry entertainment for the linguistically inclined reader. There is meaning in the double entendre. For there is a deep connection to be seen in the "stay that Israel stayed" for four hundred some years, and the "we could have returned twice!" exclamation of Judah. To see it, one just has to overlay the two passages on top of one another, such that one sheds light on the other.

To put it differently, the Torah is asking us to consider the events described in the Exodus passage *in light of* the events of the Genesis passage. For in the grand sweep of history, the two passages are very connected, indeed; they are like a pair of bookends to one another. In a very real way, the Egypt experience starts in one story… and ends in the other.

There and Back Again, Indeed

Let's consider the first of the bookends, in Genesis. Listen to those words that Judah said, oh so confidently, to his father: *If we hadn't dallied around, bickering about Benjamin so much, we could have been back and forth to Egypt twice already.* Taken on its own, it seems like just an off-the-cuff comment. But the Torah, in recording it for us, allows the reader to evaluate what Judah is saying with the benefit of considerable hindsight. Because, from our own perch in history, many centuries later, we can ask: How long *did* it, in fact, take for everyone Judah was talking about to "go back and forth to Egypt twice"? That second "return trip back from Egypt" — did it happen at all, and if so, *when* did it actually happen?

Well, do the math.

After Judah says these words, Father finally consents to let Benjamin go with him. So the brothers head down to Egypt, with Benjamin, to buy grain. When they get there, the high-ranking Egyptian official finally reveals to the shocked band of brothers his true identity: *He is in fact Joseph, their long-lost brother.* At that point, Joseph sends them all back to Canaan, to go pick up their father.

That's back and forth to Egypt *once.*

What happens next? Having arrived back in Canaan, they bring word to Jacob that Joseph is yet alive — and that catalyzes a second journey. The entire family of Israel packs up, and they travel down to Egypt, to live near Joseph in the land of Goshen.

Fine, so that's the first leg of a *second* trip.

But now ask: When does the return leg happen? When did the entire family of Israel return (*shav*) to Canaan that second time (*pa'amayim*)? And the answer is… They didn't return — or, at least, not in the way they thought. Quite unexpectedly for them, it took 430 years for the family, now a nation, to make it back to Canaan again.[4] Judah had surmised the family was looking at a quick trip or two back and forth. But that's not the way history worked out. Instead, Judah's *shavnu zeh pa'amayim* transmogrified itself into:

וּמוֹשַׁב בְּנֵי יִשְׂרָאֵל אֲשֶׁר יָשְׁבוּ בְּמִצְרָיִם
שְׁלֹשִׁים שָׁנָה וְאַרְבַּע מֵאוֹת שָׁנָה:

The **stay** that Israel **stayed** in Egypt was four hundred and thirty years.[5]

Exodus 12:40

What Judah Doesn't Know

The text is calling our attention to how Judah's words to his father contained a chilling irony. Judah had thought it a simple thing to go back and forth to Egypt. *Father, let's stop arguing about that Benjamin thing. Instead of wasting time, we could have been back and forth twice already!* But… Judah is not really in a position to know how very not simple getting back from Egypt really would be.

Indeed, at that moment, there is so much Judah *doesn't* know. He *doesn't* know that the high-ranking Egyptian official he is bargaining with is really his long-lost brother, Joseph. He *doesn't* know that Joseph will reveal himself, reunite with the family, and that the family will choose to relocate to Egypt, to be near Joseph. And what Judah certainly doesn't know is that, as nice as being near Joseph might seem when everyone first

---

4   Yes, some of them made a quick trip to Canaan for Jacob's funeral, but the children had conspicuously been left behind in Egypt; the family *as a whole* didn't return until the end of Egyptian slavery, centuries later.

5   The interpretation we've advanced here receives added color from the very next verse in Exodus, as well. וַיְהִי בְּעֶצֶם הַיּוֹם הַזֶּה יָצְאוּ כָּל־צִבְאוֹת יְקוָה מֵאֶרֶץ מִצְרָיִם, "And it happened, on that very day, that all the hosts of God left the land of Egypt." In other words: When *did* the children of Israel finally come back on that return leg? When all those hundreds of years elapsed, Judah's casually forecasted return finally happened. At last, the children of Israel were starting that fateful second trip home.

makes the choice to go there, future generations would look on that act of relocation as rather ominous. To be sure, the people of Israel will enter Egypt as honored guests, but they will slowly become captives there. And once that happens, the question of *how fast they can return a second time…* will be taken entirely out of their hands.

The Many Meanings of *Shav*

This word *shav* that Judah has been using in conversation with his father is slippery indeed. It has at least three meanings.[6] One meaning is "return," and that's the meaning Judah has in mind when he confidently says: *Shavnu zeh pa'amayim,* "We could have returned twice already." Likewise, as we've seen, *shav* can also mean "to stay," which is how the verse in Exodus uses the word when it states, *The **stay** that Israel **stayed** in Egypt was four hundred years."* But in the Five Books of Moses, *shav* also possesses at least one more meaning:

<table>
<tr>
<td>Deuteronomy
21:10</td>
<td dir="rtl">כִּי־תֵצֵא לַמִּלְחָמָה עַל־
אֹיְבֶיךָ וּנְתָנוֹ יְקוָה אֱלֹהֶיךָ
בְּיָדֶךָ וְשָׁבִיתָ שִׁבְיוֹ:</td>
<td>When you take the field against your enemies, and Hashem your God delivers them into your power and **you take some of them captive.**</td>
</tr>
</table>

Alarmingly, *shav* can also mean "to take captive."

What if, when Judah speaks his fateful words, all *three* meanings of the word are in play? He intends just the **first** sense of *shav*: we could have **returned** twice already. But fate will decree that the **second** and **third** meanings of "*shav*" will have their say, too. For how, indeed, will it happen that Israel will **stay** for centuries in Egypt? By **being taken captive** there; by being enslaved there, against their will.

Indeed, consider carefully this third, hidden implication of Judah's words:

---

6   The three meanings actually come from three different but phonetically related roots: ‏שוב/שבי/ישב‎.

כִּי־עַתָּה שַׁבְנוּ זֶה
פַעֲמָיִם:

We could have been taken captive twice already!

Think about how true those words become. As Judah says them, the Israelites really *were* on the brink of being "taken captive *twice*." Because yes, the family happily and willingly comes down to Egypt to live near Joseph — but, dependent on Joseph for life-sustaining grain, they are, in effect, prisoners there already. Sure, the cage is gilded; they have food and family. But they can't just get up and go; they are "captives."

That's being taken captive once.

But then, their imprisonment deepens. It unexpectedly becomes an entirely new kind of captivity. They become slaves. And once that happens, they end up **staying** in Egypt for 430 years. Until one day, by the Hand of God, they all go free, finally bringing Judah's words to a close, finally **returning** for that second and last time to Canaan.

Sitting Down to Break Bread

Shav. What a kaleidoscope of meanings it has. Turns out it has a fourth meaning, too: *to sit down.*[7]

This apparently innocuous sense of the word adds, perhaps, one last layer of irony to our story. Because when Judah says: *Shavnu zeh pa'amayim,* with hindsight, his words can also be read to mean: *We could have "sat down" twice already.*

Consider the dual saga of Judah and his brothers, and the Israelites' 430-year sojourn in Egypt. How would *sitting down twice* resonate with those two stories?

Well, back in the Genesis story involving Judah and his brothers, "sitting down" reminds the reader of a particularly fraught moment in the family — the moment the very first Israelite was **captured** and brought

---

7   In other words, when *shav* derives from the root *yashav* (ישב), it has two connotations. More broadly, *yashav* can mean "to stay" (as we saw earlier), but more literally, it can mean to actually sit down — and it is that meaning which comes into play here.

to Egypt as a slave. It happened when the brothers were "sitting down" to eat bread:

Genesis 37:25

וַיֵּשְׁבוּ לֶאֱכָל־לֶחֶם וַיִּשְׂאוּ
עֵינֵיהֶם וַיִּרְאוּ וְהִנֵּה אֹרְחַת
יִשְׁמְעֵאלִים בָּאָה מִגִּלְעָד

And [the brothers] **sat down** to eat bread. Looking up, they saw a caravan of Ishmaelites coming from Gilead.

That was when Judah had proposed selling Joseph to the Ishmaelite traders as a slave. That event — Joseph's sale into slavery — caused a cascade of consequences which in the end brought the whole family to live in Egypt, eventually to become enslaved there. Which makes it all the more ironic that — hundreds of years later, when the family of Israel finally recovers from the sale of Joseph, when they finally get ready to leave, to return to Canaan that second and last time — they don't have enough time to sit down, with leisure, to bake and eat their bread:

Exodus
12:39–40

וַיֹּאפוּ אֶת־הַבָּצֵק אֲשֶׁר הוֹצִיאוּ
מִמִּצְרַיִם עֻגֹת מַצּוֹת כִּי לֹא
חָמֵץ כִּי־גֹרְשׁוּ מִמִּצְרַיִם וְלֹא
יָכְלוּ לְהִתְמַהְמֵהַּ וְגַם־צֵדָה לֹא־
עָשׂוּ לָהֶם: וּמוֹשַׁב בְּנֵי יִשְׂרָאֵל
אֲשֶׁר יָשְׁבוּ בְּמִצְרָיִם שְׁלֹשִׁים
שָׁנָה וְאַרְבַּע מֵאוֹת שָׁנָה:

And they baked unleavened loaves out of the dough that they had taken out of Egypt, for it was not leavened, since they had been driven out of Egypt and could not dally; nor had they prepared any provisions for themselves. The stay that Israel stayed in Egypt was four hundred and thirty years.

The family of Jacob sat (*shav*) and ate their bread *once*, when Joseph had just been cast into a pit. They then journeyed to Egypt, breadbasket of the ancient world, where they sat (*shav*), with plenty of bread to eat, for centuries. That's when they sat and ate bread *twice*. And then, at the moment they leave Egypt and slavery behind forever, it is then that they must suddenly hurry, and they find themselves with no time to sit and eat bread, one last time.[8]

Judah's Secret

Looking back on Judah's declaration to his father that "we could have been there and back twice already," the reader of the Torah discerns a certain heroism in Judah's words. He was pledging to his father that he would personally ensure Benjamin's welfare. A child of Leah was taking responsibility for a child of Rachel, a brother from "the other side" of the family, and was committing to shield him from peril. That meant enough to Jacob that he agreed to allow Benjamin to travel, despite his fears. And yet, at the same time, even as Judah tells his father this, there is also something he is *not* telling his father. There is something he is hiding.

Judah's secret is that, years before this, there was another child of Rachel's that he did *not* take responsibility for: the brother that was crying from a pit while everyone else sat down to eat bread just over the next hill. That secret — *What became of Joseph that day?* — will become a kind of wild card in the family's fortunes. It will ultimately upend Judah's confident talk of an easy, second return from Egypt.

With the benefit of hindsight, we can see how that was so. The sale of Joseph would start a series of events that would eventually drag the entire family down to Egypt, where they would stay — first as guests, then as slaves — for centuries. The Torah's sobering message: Judah might speak confidently of a quick return, back and forth. But his secret would, in the long run, delay a second return from Egypt, far longer than he or his brothers ever could have imagined.

---

8   One wonders whether, upon our exit from Egypt, the injunction not to eat *chametz* — not to sit around leisurely while bread has time to rise — has its roots in the moment that catalyzed our entrance into Egypt: the leisurely consumption of bread, by the brothers, while Joseph was imprisoned in a pit and was sold as a slave to Egypt.

What Does It Mean to Have Faith?

אַל־תִּירָאוּ הִתְיַצְּבוּ וּרְאוּ
אֶת־יְשׁוּעַת יְקֹוָה אֲשֶׁר־
יַעֲשֶׂה לָכֶם הַיּוֹם

Do not fear. Stand and watch the salvation that God performs for you today.

EXODUS 14:13

What Does It Mean to Have Faith?

PARSHAT BESHALACH BEARS WITNESS to what is the Torah's most dramatic miracle: a sea splits in a moment of triumph. The people of Israel walk through as the pursuing Egyptian army is engulfed by waves behind them. As soon as their deliverance is complete, Moses leads the people in a rapturous song praising God for the miraculous salvation of the Jewish people.

That seems like it would be the natural end of the story — and yet, surprisingly, it is not. For no sooner does Moses complete singing that song with the entire Jewish people than Miriam takes aside the women, and leads them in singing, too:

וַתִּקַּח מִרְיָם הַנְּבִיאָה אֲחוֹת אַהֲרֹן אֶת־הַתֹּף בְּיָדָהּ וַתֵּצֶאןָ כָל־הַנָּשִׁים אַחֲרֶיהָ בְּתֻפִּים וּבִמְחֹלֹת: וַתַּעַן לָהֶם מִרְיָם שִׁירוּ לַיקֹוָק כִּי־גָאֹה גָּאָה סוּס וְרֹכְבוֹ רָמָה בַיָּם:

Then Miriam the prophetess, Aaron's sister, took a timbrel in her hand, and all the women went out after her in dance with timbrels. And Miriam chanted for them: Sing to the Lord, for He has triumphed gloriously; horse and driver He has hurled into the sea.

Exodus 15:20–21

Why does Miriam do this? A song for everyone had already been sung, led by Moses himself. Why wasn't that good enough? Indeed, the Torah records other songs of thanksgiving. In the book of Numbers, the people sing a song of praise when they discover water — but there is no record of men and women singing separate songs. In the book of Judges, Deborah sings a song of thanksgiving after winning a decisive battle against the forces of Sisera. But again, there is no separate song for Deborah and the women — one song suffices for everyone. Why is *this* song different? Why did Miriam feel that she needed to sing her very own song?

A Curious Introduction

The Sages of the Talmud[1] give an answer to this question. They find a clue as to why Miriam needed to sing in the words the Torah chooses to introduce Miriam just before we hear her sing her song. Take a look at those words of introduction, and perhaps you'll perceive the same oddities that the Sages noticed:

<table>
<tr>
<td>Exodus 15:20</td>
<td dir="rtl">וַתִּקַּח מִרְיָם הַנְּבִיאָה אֲחוֹת
אַהֲרֹן אֶת־הַתֹּף בְּיָדָהּ</td>
<td>Then, Miriam the prophetess, Aaron's sister, took a timbrel in her hand.</td>
</tr>
</table>

Why, the Sages ask, does the text insist on introducing Miriam in this particular way? Why do we have to know, for instance, that she was a prophetess? What if she *hadn't* been prophetically inclined? It isn't clear why that would make her unable to sing a song of thanksgiving. Moreover, why introduce Miriam as the sister of only **Aaron**? She was also certainly the sister of the even-more-famous Moses, so why leave her relationship with Moses out of the picture?

Starting from these two little mysteries, the Sages weave a fascinating story. They suggest that if you want to understand why Miriam sang her song, you have to understand something about Miriam the prophetess *before* she was the sister of Moses, when she was *only* the sister of Aaron. Because when Miriam was very young, before Moses was even born, Miriam had a vision. And that prophecy concerned the birth of Moses itself.

Here is a summary of the story the Sages tell:[2]

---

1   Sotah 12b–13a.

2   Ibid.

A Leap of Faith

When Pharaoh decreed that all newborn Israelite boys must be cast into the Nile, Amram and Yocheved decided to separate. They reasoned, *Why have more children, only for them to be brutally murdered?* But their young daughter, Miriam, protested to them, the Sages said. She pointed out that, viewed from a certain perspective, their actions were harsher even than those of Pharaoh: Pharaoh had decreed death on the male children only, while if everyone followed the lead of her parents, no children would be born at all![3]

Moreover, Miriam spoke to her parents of a mysterious prophecy she received: Her mother, she was given to understand, is destined to give birth to the savior of the Jewish people.

Upon hearing Miriam's argument, the Sages say, her parents reunited — and Moses was born.[4]

When he was born, though, the Rabbis contend that something miraculous happened — something that set expectations, as it were, for what might happen next:

וַתַּהַר הָאִשָּׁה וַתֵּלֶד בֵּן וַתֵּרֶא
אֹתוֹ כִּי־טוֹב

The woman conceived and bore a son; and she saw that he was good.

Exodus 2:2

That phrase, "And she saw that he was good," is puzzling. Of course, every mother naturally loves her child, but she doesn't *evaluate* the child, trying to determine whether he is good or not. What, then, does "she saw that he was good" mean? *That if he was "bad," she'd get rid of him?* Odd. The Sages picked up on the oddity of the phrase, and heard in it echoes of the

---

3 See Sotah 12a.

4 This talmudic reading is based, in part, on the introduction of Moses' birth with the apparently superfluous phrase וַיֵּלֶךְ אִישׁ מִבֵּית לֵוִי וַיִּקַּח אֶת־בַּת־לֵוִי, "A certain man of the House of Levi went and married a Levite woman." The Sages read this to mean that his parents remarried, in effect, just before his conception (see Rashi to Exodus 2:1). Moreover, the text notes the marriage of Moses' parents immediately after it records Pharaoh's cruel, genocidal decree, the mandated drowning of all Israelite baby boys. The Sages concluded from this that the marriage of Moses' parents needed to be understood in light of Pharaoh's decree.

first time someone looked upon something and decided *ki tov*. That, of course, was when God first created light; hence, the Sages continue their story by telling us that when Moses' mother gave birth to her new baby, an astounding miracle occurred: *The house suddenly filled with light.*[5]

Now stop reading for a moment, and put yourself in Yocheved's situation. Consider what it might have been like to have seen that light when Moses was born. Yes, months before, your daughter had told you of her mysterious vision: *You are destined to give birth to the savior of Israel.* But you didn't *really* know what to make of that. Was it really a prophecy? Or was it perhaps just the fervent hope of a desperate child caught up in a terrible, genocidal moment in history? But you and Amram took a chance and reunited anyway, and you had this child. Imagine, then, your shock when, upon his birth, the house suddenly... fills with the shining of a miraculous light?

You'd be overjoyed: *A miracle has taken place!* And that miracle seems to confirm your daughter's vision. *She was right after all!*

The Talmud suggests that this is exactly how Yocheved, and for that matter, Amram, *did* react. In the words of the talmudic Sages:

Sotah 13a

וְכֵיוָן שֶׁנּוֹלַד מֹשֶׁה נִתְמַלֵּא כָּל הַבַּיִת כּוּלָהּ אוֹר, עָמַד אָבִיהָ וּנְשָׁקָהּ עַל רֹאשָׁהּ, אָמַר לָהּ: בִּתִּי נִתְקַיְּימָה נְבוּאָתֵיךְ.

Once Moses was born, [and] the entire house was filled with light, her father rose, kissed Miriam on her head, and said to her: My daughter, your prophecy has been fulfilled!

And now, take the next logical step: If you were Miriam's mother or father, and the house had suddenly just filled with this miraculous light, convincing you that, yes, your daughter had been right all along — *what might you imagine would happen next?*

Well, if this child is really destined to save the people from Egyptian slavery — that means, at a minimum, that he is destined to *survive*. God can't therefore allow him to be drowned in the Nile like almost all other baby boys born to other mothers. Somehow, that means, a miracle is in

_____

5   See Sotah 13a; Shemot Rabbah 1; cf. Rashi to Sotah 12a.

the offing. The Almighty would somehow intervene and save this child, so he could go on to fulfill his destiny.

Yes, the miraculous light seemed to assure them that the hard part was over. God was smiling upon them now.

But with this in mind, let's return to the very next phrase in the biblical verse, which tells us what happened after that miraculous light showed up:

וַתִּצְפְּנֵהוּ שְׁלֹשָׁה יְרָחִים: וְלֹא־ יָכְלָה עוֹד הַצְּפִינוֹ	She hid him for three months; but [then], she could not hide him any longer.	Exodus 2:2–3

What terrible disappointment attends those words! After giving birth, long months passed … and nothing further, of a supernatural sort, happened. Had God abandoned them?

During those months, Yocheved did her best to hide the baby. But as time passed, his cries were getting louder and louder, and it became more and more difficult to hide him from the omnipresent Egyptian storm troopers. There had been no special, miraculous Fedex delivery of sound-proofing material, no divine force field, no intervention from the Almighty to save the child. Seemingly history had returned to its ordinary, mundane march forward. It seemed that the heavens were silent in the face of this child's plight. And so, in desperation, when it became simply impossible to hide him any longer…

וַתִּקַּח־לוֹ תֵּבַת גֹּמֶא וַתַּחְמְרָה בַחֵמָר וּבַזָּפֶת וַתָּשֶׂם בָּהּ אֶת־ הַיֶּלֶד וַתָּשֶׂם בַּסּוּף עַל־שְׂפַת הַיְאֹר:	She got a wicker basket for him and caulked it with pitch. She put the child into it, and placed it among the reeds by the bank of the Nile.	Exodus 2:3

Commenting on the devastation the child's parents must have felt, the Sages of the Talmud suggest that, at this terrible moment, Miriam's father came to his daughter and slapped her on the forehead — telling her in bitterness:

Sotah 13a

בְּתִּי, הֵיכָן נְבוּאָתֵיךְ.

My daughter! Where is your prophecy [now]?

To Stand and Watch

One of the problems we often encounter in studying the Torah's stories is that we know them too well. We've read them over and over, so we know their endings. But if we really want to learn Torah meaningfully, we have to find a way to forget what we already know. Which means: We need to read the stories without their end already in our minds. We have to do that if we are to truly perceive the plight of the stories' protagonists, who likewise didn't know how their stories would end.

Let's try that with the story of Moses' improbable birth and survival. Abandon your knowledge of how this story ends. Just live in the moment for a bit, and taste what that would be like: *You're Moses' mother. As you place that child in the reeds at the side of the Nile… as you walk back to your home with a heavy heart, what do you think the odds are that the child will actually survive?* Egyptian troops are everywhere. The nights are full of the screams of infants torn from the arms of their mothers. What chance is there, really, that this little baby of yours, alone in the reeds, will actually survive? Seemingly, those odds are vanishingly close to zero.

So now, let me ask you a question: If you were in Yocheved's position, and you had put your child in that little basket; when you returned home… *would you be able to watch from the window to see what happens next?*

Most of us wouldn't be able to watch.

But someone *did* watch.

Being Miriam

That someone was Miriam:

Exodus 2:4

וַתֵּתַצַּב אֲחֹתוֹ מֵרָחֹק לְדֵעָה
מַה־יֵּעָשֶׂה לוֹ:

And his sister stood from afar, to learn what would be with him.

If Miriam was able to bear to watch, what does that tell you about her? It tells you that Miriam hadn't lost hope. She wasn't convinced it was over. *I had a prophecy!* Miriam must have said to herself — as the Sages of the Talmud put it:

> לֵידַע מַה יְּהֵא בְּסוֹף נְבוּאָתָהּ
> She wanted to see what, in the end, would be with her prophecy.
>
> Sotah 13a

If you had interviewed Miriam at that moment, and asked her why she was still watching, *why* did she still have hope — what would she tell you? What does she know that others around her don't?

The answer is: Nothing. Miriam doesn't really have any privileged information at this point. She doesn't know the end of the story, she doesn't have the benefit of reading the book of Exodus as you and I do and flipping forward a few verses to see what happens. All she could have told you at that moment is: *Yes, it is true; things look bleak. And no, I can't explain to you how my brother can possibly be saved. But… just because I can't explain that to you, doesn't mean he is doomed. I stand by my vision.*

I'm waiting to see what will be with that prophecy of mine.

Part of faith entails realizing that human imagination is limited. Miriam faced a cruel, dead-end situation. But she still held to the belief that what seemed inevitable *wasn't* inevitable; that once you put God in the mix, the situation in which she found herself was actually rife with hidden possibility.

An Unlikely Savior

Stay with Miriam for just a bit longer; try to keep imagining yourself in her situation, as the next event in the story unfolds. There you are, standing from afar, watching your brother in that little box in the reeds, waiting against all odds for God's salvation to assert itself — when, all of a sudden, you perceive someone coming. *Who is it?*

Turns out, it is the worst possible person imaginable.

Of all the people to decide to take a dip in the river just at this propitious moment, who happens to show up, but the daughter of Pharaoh. Again, if you're reading this without the end in mind, if you're viewing things as a sympathetic bystander to these events would have viewed them, you would have traded anything for someone else — for *anyone* else — but her to appear. Her father is literally the originator of the horrifying decree to throw all baby boys into the Nile. She is princess in his palace. How could she possibly defy him? Surely, if there was ever a time for Miriam to turn away and go home, it is now. Who could bear to watch what happens next?

But Miriam doesn't turn away. She continues to stand there and watch, as the Egyptian princess discovers the tiny basket.

Here's how the biblical text describes what happens next:

Exodus 2:6

וַתִּפְתַּח וַתִּרְאֵהוּ אֶת־
הַיֶּלֶד וְהִנֵּה־נַעַר בֹּכֶה
וַתַּחְמֹל עָלָיו וַתֹּאמֶר
מִיַּלְדֵי הָעִבְרִים זֶה:

[The daughter of Pharaoh] opened it, and saw that it was a child, a boy crying. She took pity on it. And [then] she said, "This is a Hebrew child!"

Read those words slowly, and you will see a bitter conflict begin to unfold.

A Miracle in the Reeds

Pharaoh's daughter was immediately drawn to the whimpering child, and her first reaction was one of compassion. As the text puts it, **וַתַּחְמֹל עָלָיו**, *She took pity on [the child]*. But immediately after this, the text tells us of something else: Not a broad, human reaction, but a narrow, Egyptian one:

Exodus 2:6

מִיַּלְדֵי הָעִבְרִים זֶה:

"This is a Hebrew child!"

This second reaction comes not from her heart but from her head. The daughter of Pharaoh cognizes just who she is, and who, by contrast, this baby is. *As a good Egyptian princess, this is the child she's supposed to kill.* And just like that, she is caught in a bind. What will she do?

It is here, right at this moment, that Miriam enters the picture. It is here that Miriam ceases to be a bystander, someone who watches from afar, and instead becomes an actor in the unfolding drama. Seeing the uncertainty in the princess's eyes, Miriam offers an unexpected but welcome solution:

וַתֹּאמֶר אֲחֹתוֹ אֶל־בַּת־פַּרְעֹה הַאֵלֵךְ וְקָרָאתִי לָךְ אִשָּׁה מֵינֶקֶת מִן הָעִבְרִיֹּת וְתֵינִק לָךְ אֶת־הַיָּלֶד:

Then his sister said to Pharaoh's daughter, "Shall I go and get you a Hebrew nurse to suckle the child for you?"

Exodus 2:7

Miriam's suggestion offers Pharaoh's daughter a way. Previously, it had seemed like an impossible dilemma had faced the princess: Throw the child in the river to die, or immediately bring back the child to the palace as her own. There were only two choices, and neither seemed remotely palatable. Her humanity could not abide the former, and her station as an Egyptian princess rebelled against the latter. But now, as Miriam arrives on the scene, comes a solution: *Shall I go and get you a Hebrew nurse to suckle the child for you?*

The suggestion offers the princess a chance to buy time. She could pay someone to nurse him for a year or two. She could visit the child, and slowly figure out a plan for his future, a way to become his mother. *I don't need to decide this all right now. I can take the time necessary to make this work.*

In a flash, she tells Miriam to go do it:

וַתֹּאמֶר־לָהּ בַּת־פַּרְעֹה לֵכִי וַתֵּלֶךְ הָעַלְמָה וַתִּקְרָא אֶת־אֵם הַיָּלֶד:

And Pharaoh's daughter answered, "Yes; go!" And the girl went and called the child's mother.

Exodus 2:8

The rest is history. Moses is saved. A good while later, the child is weaned and brought to the daughter of Pharaoh. By this time, she has crafted a plan that will allow her to nurture the child on the sidelines of Pharaoh's court, and raise him to adulthood.

In a deliciously ironic twist, Miriam, the girl of faith; the girl who merely stood and watched, waiting to see how God would intervene — *that girl* actually became the architect of Moses' salvation. Her faith created an opening for her to act. And when she *did* act, she herself became the un-likely instrument through which her own prophecy was realized.

The Rest of Miriam's Story

Let us return now to the questions we started with: Why *did* Miriam need to sing that song at the sea? Why was the one song, led by Moses, not enough?

Now we are perhaps in a position to understand. As we noted earlier, the Sages of the Talmud had found allusions to Miriam's earlier deeds in the Torah's introduction to Miriam's song (she is the sister of Aaron; she is a prophetess). In effect, the Sages were connecting the story of Miriam at the Nile and the story of Miriam at the sea.

In connecting these events, I would suggest they were drawing not just upon what they pointed to overtly — the introduction of Miriam as a prophetess, and as the sister of Aaron — they were also drawing upon something else: a network of thematic and linguistic connections between these stories that lies just under the surface of the text.

To see what I mean, consider carefully these two narratives, Miriam at the Nile and Miriam at the sea. *Do you, perchance, see any similarities between them?*

The Nile and the Sea

Water. A body of water figures prominently in each story: a river in the first episode, a sea in the second.

Threatened Israelites. In the first episode, a single Hebrew child is threatened by the water. In the second, an entire nation of Israelites is threatened by the water.

Egyptians. In the first episode, a single Egyptian approaches. In the second episode, an entire Egyptian army approaches.

Reeds. In the first episode, the setting for the story is marked by a dom-inant natural feature: reeds (וַתָּשֶׂם בַּסּוּף עַל־שְׂפַת הַיְאֹר, "She placed [the child] in the reeds by the shore of the river"). In the second ep-isode, reeds are also the dominant natural feature. Except instead of there being just a few reeds by the side of a river, now there is a whole sea of them.

Miracle. In the first episode, a hidden miracle saves the endangered child. In the second, a dramatic, open miracle saves the endangered nation.

Standing and Watching. And perhaps most crucially, note the words that trigger the miracle in each instance. They are eerie echoes of one another. In the first episode, Miriam had stood and watched (וַתֵּתַצַּב אֲחֹתוֹ מֵרָחֹק, "And his sister stood from afar") as Pharaoh's daughter approached. Now listen to what Moses tells the people to do as Pharaoh's armies approach:

אַל־תִּירָאוּ הִתְיַצְּבוּ וּרְאוּ אֶת־ יְשׁוּעַת יְקֹוָה אֲשֶׁר־יַעֲשֶׂה לָכֶם הַיּוֹם כִּי אֲשֶׁר רְאִיתֶם אֶת־מִצְרַיִם הַיּוֹם לֹא תֹסִפוּ לִרְאֹתָם עוֹד עַד־עוֹלָם׃	Do not fear. **Stand and watch** the salvation that God performs for you today. For as you've seen Egypt today, you shall never again see them, forever.	Exodus 14:13

Microcosm, Macrocosm

Everything that happened at the Nile happens again at the sea — only on a grander scale. It is as if the first story is a microcosm of the second.

Miriam's prophecy, when she was but a child, had been that her mother would give birth to the one who was destined to save the people of Israel. When, indeed, did that prophecy become irrefutably confirmed? The answer is: When the pursuing Egyptian armies were destroyed, with utter finality, at the Sea of Reeds. Is it any wonder, then, that at that moment, Miriam felt an overwhelming need to sing a song of thanksgiving? It was then that her story became complete. Not only because it was then that her prophecy was confirmed, but also because of *how* it became confirmed. The people, who were saved at the Sea of Reeds, *needed to do what she once did*. They had needed to stand there, fearfully, watching a malevolent force approach them — and place their fate in the lap, as it were, of the Almighty. Indeed, Moses tells the people to "stand and watch" the salvation that will come — but he does not tell them *how* that salvation will come. Never in a million years would anyone have thought the sea would split. At that moment, they people had work to do — the work of faith: They had to *not* surrender to the odds; not give up hope, but ... *stand and watch*, as the most improbable of outcomes somehow materialized before their eyes.

It was only when the people as a whole could evince, for just a few moments, the faith that Miriam had shown as a child — it was only *then* that the people were saved. It was as though Miriam had somehow, through her belief and through her actions, paved the way for Moses and the people to act on the faith she taught them. When they did, they relived a collective, grander version of her own miraculous experience.

And when it finally happened — she sang. How could she not?

The Ten Commandments, by the Light of the Burning Bush

וַיִּקַּח יִתְרוֹ חֹתֵן מֹשֶׁה
עֹלָה וּזְבָחִים לֵאלֹהִים
וַיָּבֹא אַהֲרֹן וְכֹל זִקְנֵי
יִשְׂרָאֵל לֶאֱכָל־לֶחֶם
עִם־חֹתֵן מֹשֶׁה לִפְנֵי
הָאֱלֹהִים:

And Yitro, Moses' father-in-law, brought a burnt-offering and sacrifices for God, and Aaron came with all the elders of Israel to break bread before God with Moses' father-in-law.

EXODUS 18:12

The Ten Commandments, by the Light of the Burning Bush

1 MARRIAGE AT THE MOUNTAIN: METAPHOR OR REALITY?

PARSHAT YITRO TELLS THE story of Revelation at Mt. Sinai. That encounter, and the giving of the Torah that is its centerpiece, has been famously analogized in the Mishnah and Midrash to a kind of marriage — almost as if God were the groom, the Children of Israel were the bride, and the Torah were the ring.[1] It is certainly a romantic notion. The question I want to pose is, how seriously did the Sages want us to take this marriage analogy? Is it merely a fanciful, poetic metaphor? Or did they want us to regard the comparison as actually true in a basic kind of way?

I want to propose that the Sages were being quite serious when they suggested this, and that they perhaps got the idea in the first place from a close reading of the Torah itself. Indeed, if you look carefully at the story of the giving of the Ten Commandments, you'll find a pattern lurking there that leads straight to the Sages' startling conclusion: the Sinai experience really *was* a kind of marriage. Moreover, the text doesn't just establish this as a blind fact; it explains it, too. It helps us understand what we mean when we say God "loves" Israel, and more broadly, what love is about, in any shape or form.

The pattern I'm referring to is embedded in a section of text that covers a good portion of **Parshat Yitro**. We will find elements of it starting all the way back at Yitro's meeting with Moses, before Israel even arrives at Mt. Sinai, and the pattern will continue to interweave itself in the text, all the way through at least the first five of the Ten Commandments. The

---

1 Mishnah Ta'anit 4:8; Mechilta Exodus 19:17; *Pirkei de-Rabbi Eliezer* 41; cf. Rosh to Exodus 20:13 and *Kli Yakar* to Numbers 1:1.

essence of this pattern is found in a series of echoes. And the easiest way to begin to see them is to read the text at the beginning of the parshah with a question hovering in the back of your mind: *Where have I heard all this before?*

Let's try it.

Yitro Rejoices

Here are the main themes **Parshat Yitro** opens with. A visitor comes to the people of Israel as they make their way toward Mt. Sinai. That visitor is Yitro, father-in-law of Moses:

Exodus 18:1	וַיִּשְׁמַע יִתְרוֹ כֹהֵן מִדְיָן חֹתֵן מֹשֶׁה אֵת כָּל־אֲשֶׁר עָשָׂה אֱלֹהִים לְמֹשֶׁה וּלְיִשְׂרָאֵל עַמּוֹ כִּי־הוֹצִיא יְקֹוָה אֶת־יִשְׂרָאֵל מִמִּצְרָיִם:	Yitro, priest of Midian, Moses' father-in-law, heard of all that God had done for Moses and for Israel His people, how God had brought Israel out of Egypt.

Hearing this news of Israel's miraculous victory over their Egyptian over-lords, Yitro leaves his home in Midian and comes to see his son-in-law, Moses. Moses greets him, and tells him, firsthand, about all the miracles God performed for Israel. In response, Yitro rejoices:

Exodus 18:9–10	וַיִּחַדְּ יִתְרוֹ עַל כָּל־הַטּוֹבָה אֲשֶׁר־עָשָׂה יְקֹוָה לְיִשְׂרָאֵל אֲשֶׁר הִצִּילוֹ מִיַּד מִצְרָיִם: וַיֹּאמֶר יִתְרוֹ בָּרוּךְ יְקֹוָה אֲשֶׁר הִצִּיל אֶתְכֶם מִיַּד מִצְרַיִם וּמִיַּד פַּרְעֹה אֲשֶׁר הִצִּיל אֶת־הָעָם מִתַּחַת יַד־מִצְרָיִם:	And Yitro rejoiced for all the goodness that God did for the Jews: that God had saved the Jewish people from Egypt. "Blessed be the Lord," Yitro said, "who saved you from the Egyptians and from Pharaoh; who saved the people from under the hand of the Egyptians."

After that, Yitro goes and convenes a feast. While the Torah does not provide the meaning of the feast explicitly, it seems to constitute a further expression of Yitro's joy. The feast is an act of thanksgiving:

וַיִּקַּח יִתְרוֹ חֹתֵן מֹשֶׁה עֹלָה
וּזְבָחִים לֵאלֹהִים וַיָּבֹא אַהֲרֹן
וְכֹל זִקְנֵי יִשְׂרָאֵל לֶאֱכָל־לֶחֶם
עִם־חֹתֵן מֹשֶׁה לִפְנֵי הָאֱלֹהִים:

And Yitro, Moses' father-in-law, brought a burnt-offering and sacrifices for God; and Aaron came with all the elders of Israel to break bread before God with Moses' father-in-law.

Exodus 18:12

Intriguingly, someone is missing at that feast. Yitro is there, the elders of Israel are there, Aaron is there, even God is there (they eat, according to the text, "before God"). One important person who is missing is…*Moses.* The text doesn't tell us *why* Moses isn't there, but seemingly he wasn't. Perhaps his other duties were so pressing that they didn't allow him time to join in the festivities. For indeed, the very next verses of the Torah detail that the next day, Moses was judging the people from morning until night, a practice Yitro sharply criticizes:

וַיֹּאמֶר חֹתֵן מֹשֶׁה אֵלָיו לֹא־
טוֹב הַדָּבָר אֲשֶׁר אַתָּה עֹשֶׂה:
נָבֹל תִּבֹּל גַּם־אַתָּה גַּם־הָעָם
הַזֶּה אֲשֶׁר עִמָּךְ כִּי־כָבֵד מִמְּךָ
הַדָּבָר לֹא־תוּכַל עֲשֹׂהוּ לְבַדֶּךָ:

Moses' father-in-law said to him, "It is not good, this thing you are doing. You will surely wear yourself out, and these people as well. For the task is too heavy for you; you cannot do it alone."

Exodus 18:17–18

Perhaps part of Yitro's critique comes from the fact that Moses absented himself from the festivities: *If you don't have enough time to join a feast of thanksgiving to the Almighty for this salvation, it is clear that this job is getting to you.* Perhaps — that is clearly speculation — but we do know that Moses doesn't come to Yitro's feast, and we do know that Yitro immediately afterward sees him trying to do something all by himself that in Yitro's eyes is simply beyond the capabilities of any one person.

We've seen enough to get started. Now let's play our little game. *Where else, earlier in the Torah, have we come across a set of events that seems eerily similar to these?*

Déjà Vu All Over Again

A hint comes from the fact that this is not the first time we have encountered Yitro. The reader met him earlier, in the opening chapters of the book of Exodus. And if we look carefully at the events that occurred back then, we will find that they are an uncanny harbinger of the events that are occurring now. The narratives are remarkable in their confluence.

Consider the circumstances in which Yitro first met Moses. Then, as now, Yitro had heard news about a great act of salvation. And back then, Yitro had *also* invited people to join him in a feast to celebrate it. Then, as now, bread was served at that feast. And then, as now, someone important — namely, Moses — was missing, provoking Yitro's concern.

Let's review the story and you'll see how that's all true: The Torah tells us that Moses as a young man flees Pharaoh's wrath after killing an Egyptian. He runs to Midian, where he rests at a well. There, he encounters a group of young shepherdesses who he sees are being menaced by a group of shepherds. Moses drives away the harassing shepherds and provides water from the well for the shepherdesses' sheep. The young women then go home and tell their father, Yitro, about the man they met at the well, and about how he saved them. Yitro asks them where this man is and admonishes them for leaving him behind all by himself. "Call him!" he says. "Let him come and break bread with us!" And so they do.

Strikingly, if you add all this up, you'll find that point by point, the events of Moses' first encounter with Yitro presage what happens the next time he encounters Yitro:[2]

---

2   The parallels, illustrated in the table on the next page, between Moses giving water to the shepherdesses' sheep (Ex. 2:17) and Moses giving water to the Children of Israel (Ex. 15:25) are especially sharp. In the first case, initially the thirsting flock of sheep is at a well, but can't access it (the menacing shepherds were preventing the flock from getting to the water). Then, Moses intervenes, allowing the flock access to the water. The second time around, something similar happens: First the thirsting flock (in this case, the Children of Israel) come to a body of water, but they can't access it, because it is too bitter to drink. Then, Moses intervenes. God instructs him to cast a stick into the water, which sweetens it, allowing the flock access to the lifesaving water.

THE FIRST TIME YITRO MEETS MOSES	THE SECOND TIME YITRO MEETS MOSES

Salvation

Moses saves shepherdesses who are being threatened at a body of water (a well). (Ex. 2:17)	Moses, acting as an agent of God, saves an entire people who were threatened at a body of water (the Sea of Reeds). (Ex. 14:30)
Moses then gives their thirsting sheep water to drink. (Ex. 2:17)	Moses then gives the thirsting Children of Israel water to drink. (Ex. 15:25)

The One Who Is Saved Tells Yitro about the Deeds of the Savior

The young women tell their father how Moses delivered them from the shepherds. (Ex. 2:19)	Moses tells his father-in-law how God delivered them from the Egyptians. (Ex. 18:8)

Yitro Convenes a Celebratory Feast, Inviting Both Savior and Beneficiary to the Gathering

Yitro convenes a feast in which his daughters, who were saved, dine in the presence of Moses, the one who saved them. (Ex. 2:20)	Yitro convenes a feast, in which representatives of those who were saved (Aaron and the elders of Israel) dine "in the presence of God," the One who saved them. (Ex. 18:12)

Yitro Expresses Consternation That Moses Finds Himself All Alone

Moses doesn't initially join the gathering. Yitro scolds his daughters: "So where is he? Why did you leave the man behind, all by himself?" (Ex. 2:20)	Moses doesn't attend the gathering. The next day, Yitro scolds Moses for judging the people all by himself. (Ex. 18:12–14)

The convergence between the stories seems undeniable. For it is not just the general themes of the narratives that are similar. The actual *words* of the stories are markedly parallel, too.

For example, note how, in both narratives (let's just call them Yitro I and Yitro II), the Torah uses nearly identical words to describe the act of saving that Yitro celebrates:

YITRO I	YITRO II
Salvation	
וַיָּקָם מֹשֶׁה וַיּוֹשִׁעָן	וַיּוֹשַׁע יְקֹוָה בַּיּוֹם הַהוּא אֶת־יִשְׂרָאֵל מִיַּד מִצְרָיִם
And Moses rose to and delivered them. (Ex. 2:17)	Thus the Lord delivered Israel that day from the Egyptians. (Ex. 14:30)

Now look at the next theme in our series — the moment when the "saved person" tells the father (or father-in-law) about what just happened:[3]

---

3   The parallel illustrated in the table on the next page is suggested by the connection between the confluence of the words לְהַצִּיל ("to rescue") and מִיַּד ("from the hand of") in both cases. The skeptical reader might wonder, though: What does Moses' act of salvation of the women from the shepherds have to do with God's salvation of Israel from the Egyptians? The parallel structure seems to suggest that the shepherds in one story parallel the Egyptians in the other. But why?

The simple answer to that question is that both the shepherds in the Moses story, and the Egyptians in the story of Israel represent aggressors who harass a weaker, vulnerable target. Especially intriguing is the fact that when the Torah itself retells the story of the Exodus later in the book of Deuteronomy (26:6), it characterizes God's salvation of Israel from the aggressor in a striking way. The text there tells us וַיָּרֵעוּ אֹתָנוּ הַמִּצְרִים — "and the Egyptians acted perversely against us." But the Hebrew verb for the perverse aggression of Egypt just happens to be וַיָּרֵעוּ, a word whose root form is *resh, ayin, heh* — the very same root as the רֹעִים, the shepherds who harassed Yitro's daughters.

YITRO I	YITRO II

The One Who Is Saved Tells Yitro about the Deeds of the Savior

וַתֹּאמַרְןָ אִישׁ מִצְרִי הִצִּילָנוּ מִיַּד הָרֹעִים

וַיְסַפֵּר מֹשֶׁה לְחֹתְנוֹ אֵת כָּל־אֲשֶׁר עָשָׂה יְהוָה לְפַרְעֹה וּלְמִצְרַיִם עַל אוֹדֹת יִשְׂרָאֵל אֵת כָּל־הַתְּלָאָה אֲשֶׁר מְצָאָתַם בַּדֶּרֶךְ וַיַּצִּלֵם יְהוָה: וַיִּחַדְּ יִתְרוֹ עַל כָּל־הַטּוֹבָה אֲשֶׁר־ עָשָׂה יְהוָה לְיִשְׂרָאֵל אֲשֶׁר הִצִּילוֹ מִיַּד מִצְרָיִם: וַיֹּאמֶר יִתְרוֹ בָּרוּךְ יְהוָה אֲשֶׁר הִצִּיל אֶתְכֶם מִיַּד מִצְרַיִם וּמִיַּד פַּרְעֹה אֲשֶׁר הִצִּיל אֶת־הָעָם מִתַּחַת יַד־מִצְרָיִם:

They answered, "An Egyptian rescued us from the hand of the shepherds." (Ex. 2:19)

Moses then recounted to his father-in-law everything that the Lord had done to Pharaoh and to the Egyptians for Israel's sake, all the hardships that had befallen them on the way, and how the Lord had rescued them. And Yitro rejoiced over all the kindness that the Lord had shown Israel when He rescued them from the hand of the Egyptians. "Blessed be the Lord," Yitro said, "who rescued you from the hand of the Egyptians and from the hand of Pharaoh, and who rescued the people from under the hand of the Egyptians." (Ex. 18:8–10)

And finally, glance at the next parallel element, the celebratory feast. There too, a strikingly similar expression is used in each case:

YITRO I	YITRO II
Yitro Convenes a Celebratory Feast, Inviting Both Savior and Beneficiary to the Gathering	
וַיֹּאמֶר אֶל־בְּנֹתָיו וְאַיּוֹ לָמָּה זֶּה עֲזַבְתֶּן אֶת־הָאִישׁ קִרְאֶן לוֹ וְיֹאכַל לָחֶם:	וַיִּקַּח יִתְרוֹ חֹתֵן מֹשֶׁה עֹלָה וּזְבָחִים לֵאלֹהִים וַיָּבֹא אַהֲרֹן וְכֹל זִקְנֵי יִשְׂרָאֵל לֶאֱכָל־לֶחֶם עִם־חֹתֵן מֹשֶׁה לִפְנֵי הָאֱלֹהִים:
He said to his daughters, "Where is he then? Why did you leave the man? Ask him in to break bread." (Ex. 2:20)	And Yitro, Moses' father-in-law, brought a burnt-offering and sacrifices for God; and Aaron came with all the elders of Israel to break bread before God with Moses' father-in-law. (Ex. 18:12)

Connect the Dots

The pattern of correspondence we've uncovered doesn't seem like the product of mere coincidence. It seems like these two narratives are somehow meant to be read in concert with one another, or to shed light on one another. To my mind, then, this puts two questions before us: What is the meaning of this pattern, which is to say, what, if anything, are we meant to learn from it? And how far do these correlations between the stories extend? If we keep reading the Yitro I narrative past the point where Moses breaks bread with Yitro, will it continue to echo events in the Yitro II narrative?

I think the answer to the latter question is yes, the echoes do continue further. And if we follow their trail, it may help us develop some answers to the first question, too: What meaning are we, the reader, meant to find in the parallels?

Let's continue reading the Yitro I narrative, and explore what happens next. After Yitro hears the news from his daughters about how a man came and saved them, and after he makes a feast to celebrate that salvation, we read this:

וַיּוֹאֶל מֹשֶׁה לָשֶׁבֶת אֶת־הָאִישׁ וַיִּתֵּן אֶת־צִפֹּרָה בִתּוֹ לְמֹשֶׁה׃	Moses consented to stay with the man, and he gave to Moses his daughter Tziporah as wife.	Exodus 2:21

In Yitro I, the savior went on to marry the one he saved. So we might wonder: Does something analogous happen in Yitro II? Does the savior marry the one he saved?

In order to answer that, let's remember who is the savior this time, and who is the one he saved.

This time, the savior is none other than the Almighty Himself. And the one he saved is the entire nation of Israel. As Yitro himself said:

בָּרוּךְ יְקֹוָה אֲשֶׁר הִצִּיל אֶתְכֶם מִיַּד מִצְרַיִם וּמִיַּד פַּרְעֹה	Blessed be God, who rescued you from the hand of the Egyptians and from the hand of Pharaoh.	Exodus 18:10

So it feels like we can make a prediction here. The pattern leads us to expect that shortly after Yitro comes to the recently saved people of Israel and makes that thanksgiving feast…God should somehow take the hand of Israel in marriage. And *that*, I believe, is exactly where the Sages were coming from when they insisted that we should view the giving of the Torah at Sinai as a kind of marriage. For, indeed, the Revelation at Sinai is the great, earthshaking event lurking just around the corner in the Yitro II sequence: The people leave Rephidim, where Yitro came to greet Moses, and they travel into the Sinai Desert and encamp at the foot of Mt. Sinai (Exodus 19:2). There, God speaks to Moses and instructs him to deliver the following message to Israel:

כֹּה תֹאמַר לְבֵית יַעֲקֹב וְתַגֵּיד
לִבְנֵי יִשְׂרָאֵל אַתֶּם רְאִיתֶם
אֲשֶׁר עָשִׂיתִי לְמִצְרָיִם וָאֶשָּׂא
אֶתְכֶם עַל־כַּנְפֵי נְשָׁרִים וָאָבִא
אֶתְכֶם אֵלָי: וְעַתָּה אִם־
שָׁמוֹעַ תִּשְׁמְעוּ בְּקֹלִי וּשְׁמַרְתֶּם
אֶת־בְּרִיתִי וִהְיִיתֶם לִי סְגֻלָּה
מִכָּל־הָעַמִּים כִּי־לִי כָּל־
הָאָרֶץ: וְאַתֶּם תִּהְיוּ־לִי מַמְלֶכֶת
כֹּהֲנִים וְגוֹי קָדוֹשׁ.

This is what you shall you say to the
House of Jacob and declare to the
Children of Israel: "You have seen what
I did to the Egyptians, how I bore you
on eagles' wings and brought you to Me.
Now then, if you will listen to My voice
and keep My covenant, you shall be My
treasured possession among all nations,
for indeed, all the earth is Mine. You
shall be for Me a kingdom of priests and
a holy nation."

Consider the import and tone of those words. They are strikingly tender.
God, in essence, has made … a proposal of marriage to Israel here. She has
the chance to accept or decline. *I have saved you; I have brought you to Me.
Keep My covenant and you will be Mine; I will treasure you.* God is asking
Israel to allow herself to be claimed by God, to engage in a committed re-
lationship with the Master of the Universe that will change her forever.[4]

---

4   Indeed, the language the Torah uses in the run-up to the Revelation at Sinai is striking in its similarity to the words the Torah employs before the very first marriage
in the Torah: that of Adam and Eve. Yitro declares to Moses, for example, לֹא־טוֹב
הַדָּבָר אֲשֶׁר אַתָּה עֹשֶׂה…לֹא־תוּכַל עֲשֹׂהוּ לְבַדֶּךָ, "It is not good this thing you are
doing … you can't do it all by yourself" (Ex. 18:17–18). Similarly, before Adam takes
Eve as his wife, God declares: לֹא־טוֹב הֱיוֹת הָאָדָם לְבַדּוֹ, "It is not good for man
to be all by himself" (Gen. 2:18). Moreover, when God proposes His covenant to
Israel, He states: אַתֶּם רְאִיתֶם אֲשֶׁר עָשִׂיתִי לְמִצְרָיִם וָאֶשָּׂא אֶתְכֶם עַל־כַּנְפֵי נְשָׁרִים
וָאָבִא אֶתְכֶם אֵלָי, "You have seen what I did to the Egyptians, how I bore you on
eagles' wings and brought you to Me" (Ex. 19:4). Likewise, right before the marriage of Adam and Eve, the text tells us: וַיְבִאֶהָ אֶל־הָאָדָם, "And [God] brought
her to the man" (Gen. 2:22). All told, the echoes of history's very first marriage
seem to resonate throughout the Revelation narrative at Sinai.

    Note as well that the woman Moses took as a wife was named Tziporah, mean-
ing "bird." Interestingly, bird metaphors also pervade God's "proposal of marriage"
to Israel: אַתֶּם רְאִיתֶם אֲשֶׁר עָשִׂיתִי לְמִצְרָיִם וָאֶשָּׂא אֶתְכֶם עַל־כַּנְפֵי נְשָׁרִים וָאָבִא
אֶתְכֶם אֵלָי, "You have seen what I did to the Egyptians, how I bore you on eagles'
wings and brought you to Me" (Ex. 19:4). God compares Himself to the most powerful bird in the sky, who brought Israel on His wings to Sinai. Who would ride on
a bird's wings if not another bird, another *tzipor*?

How Far Do These Parallels Extend?

Having seen the possibility that the experience of Revelation at Sinai forged a marriage-like bond between a nation and God, the question now becomes: Does the pattern that yielded this insight — the string of parallels between Yitro I and Yitro II — continue still further? And if it does, what else is it trying to teach us?

To see if the parallels extend further, we can begin by asking: After Moses saves the daughters of Yitro, after he gets left behind and Yitro calls him to join them in breaking bread, after he is given the hand of Tziporah in marriage … what happens *next* in the Yitro I story?

A Journey through the Wilderness to Chorev

Next, we have this:

וּמֹשֶׁה הָיָה רֹעֶה אֶת־צֹאן יִתְרוֹ חֹתְנוֹ כֹּהֵן מִדְיָן וַיִּנְהַג אֶת־הַצֹּאן אַחַר הַמִּדְבָּר וַיָּבֹא אֶל־הַר הָאֱלֹהִים חֹרֵבָה:	Now Moses was tending the flock of his father-in-law, Yitro, the priest of Midian, and he led the flock into the wilderness, and came to Chorev, the mountain of God.	Exodus 3:1

So ask yourself: Where else in the Torah do you hear something like that? Where *else* does Moses lead his father's sheep through a desert, until he gets to "Chorev, the mountain of God"? Well, keeping in mind that Mt. Chorev is another name for Mt. Sinai … [5] it all happens again in Yitro II. Consider the following verse in the Yitro II sequence, which tells of what takes place after Yitro came to greet Moses and celebrate with him:

וַיִּסְעוּ מֵרְפִידִים וַיָּבֹאוּ מִדְבַּר סִינַי וַיַּחֲנוּ בַּמִּדְבָּר וַיִּחַן־שָׁם יִשְׂרָאֵל נֶגֶד הָהָר:	They journeyed from Rephidim, and they entered the wilderness of Sinai — and they encamped in the wilderness. Israel encamped there in front of the mountain.	Exodus 19:2

---

5 See Deuteronomy 4:10; see also Exodus 33:6.

Once again, Moses is leading a flock to Mt. Chorev, but this time, the flock is comprised of people, not sheep.[6] Once again, the flock belongs to his "father" — but not his father-in-law; instead, they belong to Moses' Heavenly Father.[7]

Clearly, then, the parallels between Yitro I and Yitro II are continuing apace: Moses' first journey through a wilderness to Mt. Sinai prefigures his second journey to that very same place. The first time, he was leading sheep; the second time, he was shepherding an incipient nation. And where will each journey culminate? At the same desert mountain, known as Chorev, or Sinai.

The Burning Bush and the Burning Mountain

Waiting for Moses at each destination is a great sight: *Something burns but is not being consumed.* The first time, it is a humble bush:

Exodus 3:2

הַסְּנֶה בֹּעֵר בָּאֵשׁ וְהַסְּנֶה
אֵינֶנּוּ אֻכָּל׃

There was a bush all aflame, yet the bush was not consumed.

The second time around, it is a whole mountain that is ablaze, but not destroyed:[8]

---

6   Later, Moses analogizes Israel specifically to a flock of sheep; see, for example, Numbers 27:17.

7   The parallel is remarkably precise. In both stories, not only is Moses leading a flock of his "father" to Chorev, but in each case, the verses emphasize that he is leading them through a *midbar* — a wilderness — to get there. Moreover, notice the strange phraseology in Exodus 3:1, which describes Moses leading Yitro's sheep "to the Mountain of God at Chorev." At this point in the text, the reader would have no idea why Chorev is known as "the Mountain of God," for this, indeed, is the first time the reader has been introduced to that mountain. It seems almost as if the text, in characterizing Chorev as "the mountain of God," is relying on the reader to notice the parallel-journey Moses undertakes, leading Israel to this mountain later — for it is there that the mountain is quite obviously "the mountain of God," being the site at which divine revelation occurs.

8   Indeed, one might go as far as to say that the parallels between the stories help explain *why* the bush at Chorev wasn't being consumed. In the Revelation narrative,

וְהַר סִינַי עָשַׁן כֻּלּוֹ מִפְּנֵי אֲשֶׁר
יָרַד עָלָיו יְקוָה בָּאֵשׁ

The mountain of Sinai was full of smoke because God had descended upon it in fire.

Exodus 19:18

And the parallels continue still further. In each episode, the Almighty then calls out to Moses. First, at the Burning Bush, when Moses has arrived alone at Chorev:

וַיִּקְרָא אֵלָיו אֱלֹהִים   And God called to him.

Exodus 3:4

And later, in Yitro II, when Moses arrives at the same mountain along with hundreds of thousands of his countrymen:

וַיִּקְרָא יְקוָה לְמֹשֶׁה   And God called to Moses.

Exodus 19:20

Moreover, consider what God had said after calling out to Moses, back at the Burning Bush:

---

the Torah explains that the mountain itself was covered in smoke, "because God had descended upon it in fire." Perhaps that, then, is the reason the bush is burning, too: God had descended upon it, through the medium of fire. In other words, normally, a burning object becomes consumed by the flames engulfing it because the object serves as a source of fuel for the flames. So, of course, as the fuel is used up, the item that's burning becomes consumed. But in the case of the Burning Bush, the source of the fire, its fuel, was not the bush. The flames came from elsewhere: from "God descending" on the bush, much as God later descends upon Sinai (in the verse in Yitro II that runs parallel to this). Hence, given the general parallels in the stories, the Yitro II explanation — *because God descended upon it in fire* — helps explain the rationale for the mysterious ability of the bush in Yitro I to withstand the flames that engulf it.

Exodus 3:5   אַל־תִּקְרַב הֲלֹם   Don't get too close.

Later, before the Revelation at Sinai, God pronounces to Moses a similar warning:

Exodus 19:12   וְהִגְבַּלְתָּ אֶת־הָעָם סָבִיב לֵאמֹר   You shall set bounds to the people
                   הִשָּׁמְרוּ לָכֶם עֲלוֹת בָּהָר וּנְגֹעַ   around, saying, Take care for yourselves,
                   בְּקָצֵהוּ כָּל־הַנֹּגֵעַ בָּהָר מוֹת   that you go not up onto the mount, or
                   יוּמָת: touch its border; whoever touches the
                                  mountain shall surely die.

The Almighty tells Moses to establish a perimeter around the mountain, to guard against the danger inherent in Revelation. Once again, people can't come "too close." If they invade the perimeter, they'll die.

Do These Parallels Extend Still Further?

We have an impressive series of parallels that run between the Yitro I and Yitro II stories. But here's the really intriguing thing: As these parallels extend still further in each story, we have seen that they begin to infiltrate the prologues to the Burning Bush episode and to the Sinai-Revelation episode, respectively. Which means that the parallels are coming perilously close to…the Ten Commandments themselves:

YITRO I	YITRO II
Moses saves shepherdesses threatened at a body of water; he then gives their thirsting sheep water to drink.	God saves an entire people threatened at a body of water; God then gives them water to drink.
Yitro's daughters tell their father how Moses delivered them from the shepherds.	Moses tells Yitro how God delivered them from the Egyptians.
Yitro convenes a feast. Moses doesn't initially join the gathering.	Yitro convenes a feast, but Moses doesn't attend the gathering.
Moses takes Tziporah as his wife.	God takes Israel as His people.
YITRO I CONTINUES: Prologue to Burning Bush	**YITRO II CONTINUES: Prologue to Revelation at Sinai**
Leading Sheep through the Desert to Chorev (Sinai)	Leading God's Sheep through the Desert to Sinai
A bush is burning and is not consumed.	A mountain is burning and is not consumed.
God called out to Moses.	God called out to Moses.
Don't get too close.	Set up a perimeter; the people can't touch the mountain.
Do the parallels extend into the next events of the Burning Bush story?	*Do the parallels extend into the next events of the Revelation at Sinai story?*

We might surmise: If the prologue to the Revelation at Sinai *really* mirrors the prologue to the Burning Bush…what about the stories that lie *beyond* those respective prologues? What about what God *says* at the Burning Bush? What about what God *says* at Sinai? Could those things be related, too?

In both stories, the next thing that happens is that God has a conversation, of sorts, with Moses. At the Burning Bush, God speaks to Moses and tells him He wants him to lead the people out of Egypt. Moses tries to avoid taking the job, and God and Moses have a somewhat testy back-and-forth about that. Moses gives five reasons, one after another, why he can't go; and God parries each of the five excuses. And at Sinai, God also speaks to Moses — in the form of the Ten Commandments. Eventually, these will appear in written form, with five commands placed on each of two stone tablets.

Do you get where this is going? *Five* exchanges...*five* pairs of commands on two tablets? Could the five and five be parallel to one another?

If they are, a fascinating possibility emerges: We might be able to gain incomparable insight into the meaning of the Decalogue...by looking at the five exchanges between God and Moses in the Burning Bush story. Indeed, in some mysterious way, those first exchanges at Sinai might well be the precursors of the Ten Commandments themselves.

Moreover, to the extent that the Yitro I and Yitro II parallels have revealed the Sinai Revelation to constitute a kind of wedding between God and Israel, this, too, augurs a kind of paradigm shift for how we might understand the Ten Commandments. For indeed, the Decalogue is God's next major declaration after the proposal of marriage He makes to the people. It would seem, then, that the Ten Commandments aren't merely a set of dictates we are expected to observe, but instead they are very possibly principles that give shape and texture to the marriage-like bond that Israel shares with the Almighty. They are, perhaps, the laws that make it possible for Israel to live in close quarters with the Divine, the code of conduct which seals the covenant between her and God.

It seems challenging, though, to interpret the Ten Commandments this way. For at face value, the document is simply a straightforward list of "thou shalts" and "thou shalt nots." What is so endearing about keeping this list of laws? How could such laws breathe life into a veritable marriage between God and Israel?

The answer to that question, I think, will become clear as we continue to explore the pattern we've begun to uncover. For as we read God's words in the Decalogue in light of God's words at the Burning Bush, we shall find, I think, that not only are the Ten Commandments part of this larger pattern of Yitro I and Yitro II parallels, but they are themselves powerfully illuminated by it.

2   A NEW WAY TO READ THE TEN COMMANDMENTS

In God's five exchanges with Moses at the Burning Bush, He tells Moses something about what He expects of Moses, what their relationship going forward will be like. Likewise, I want to suggest that in the first five commandments of the Decalogue, God tells the people something about what He expects of them, and what their relationship going forward will be like (the other five focus principally on man's relationship with his peers).[9] In this way, the private revelation of God to Moses at the Burning Bush becomes the basis for the public revelation of God at Sinai. What was said in one story in some way prefigures, or prompts, what was said in the next.

To explore this possibility, let's go through each of these stories — the Burning Bush episode on the one hand, and the Sinai Revelation on the other — and examine how the five declarations in one instance might connect or shed light on the five in the other.

What Does It Take for God to Be "Your" God?

At the Burning Bush, the first thing God says to Moses (after a prefatory warning not to come too close) is an introduction of sorts. As you read it, pay attention to its very first word:

וַיֹּאמֶר אָנֹכִי אֱלֹהֵי אָבִיךָ	And He said, "**I am** the God of your father."	Exodus 3:6

Anochi. I am… When else does God introduce Himself that way?

The answer, of course, is in Yitro II. It is the very word that introduces the Ten Commandments:

אָנֹכִי יְקֹוָה אֱלֹהֶיךָ	**I am** YHVH Your God.	Exodus 20:2

9   Those interested in exploring the possible relationship the five commands on each tablet might have with one another are encouraged to consult a lecture of mine; see "The Hidden Structure of the Ten Commandments," available as an animated lecture at alphabeta.org. There I elaborate on what I believe to be some of the deeper meaning of the symmetry in the tablets.

Interesting. But for all the similarity between these introductions, there is a key difference as well. The first time around, when God says *Anochi* at the Burning Bush, He goes on to speak of Himself as "the God of your *fathers*." The second time around, after saying *Anochi* in the Ten Commandments, God introduces Himself differently. This time, He is "*your* God," אָנֹכִי יְקֹוָה אֱלֹהֶיךָ.

One might wonder: Why, at the Burning Bush, was God perfectly happy to be the God of our fathers… and now He wants to be known as "our God"? What changed?

Almost as soon as one articulates that question, one becomes aware of the answer. For much, indeed, has changed since the days of the Burning Bush. As a matter of fact, the first commandment tells you *exactly* what's changed:

Exodus 20:2   אָנֹכִי יְקֹוָה אֱלֹהֶיךָ אֲשֶׁר
                הוֹצֵאתִיךָ מֵאֶרֶץ מִצְרַיִם מִבֵּית
                עֲבָדִים:

I am YHVH your God, **who brought you out of the land of Egypt, the house of bondage.**

God does something monumental for us. He lifts us up out of Egypt, the house of bondage. He sets us free. It is on this basis that He rightfully claims that He is no longer just the God of our fathers, but our God. He is present in our life, right here, right now.[10]

---

10 Indeed, the first of the Ten Commandments seems to be picking up on the language of the "marriage proposal" we identified above, the language God uses when addressing Israel right before the moment of Revelation:

אַתֶּם רְאִיתֶם אֲשֶׁר עָשִׂיתִי לְמִצְרָיִם וָאֶשָּׂא אֶתְכֶם עַל כַּנְפֵי נְשָׁרִים וָאָבִא
אֶתְכֶם אֵלָי. וְעַתָּה אִם שָׁמוֹעַ תִּשְׁמְעוּ בְּקֹלִי וּשְׁמַרְתֶּם אֶת בְּרִיתִי וִהְיִיתֶם
לִי סְגֻלָּה מִכָּל הָעַמִּים כִּי לִי כָּל הָאָרֶץ. וְאַתֶּם תִּהְיוּ לִי מַמְלֶכֶת כֹּהֲנִים
וְגוֹי קָדוֹשׁ.

You have seen what I did to the Egyptians, how I bore you on eagles' wings and brought you to Me. Now then, if you will listen to My Voice and keep My covenant, you shall be My treasured possession among all nations. (Ex. 19:4–6)

God is laying claim to us as His people, because He took us out of Egypt. On that basis, He is asking us to listen to His voice and to abide by His commands — not just because He had a relationship with our fathers, but because He has a relationship with *us*.

Indeed, back at the Burning Bush, God had not done this yet. Then, the people were still mired in a state of slavery that stretched back in time for centuries. So the most God could say to them on that occasion, when introducing Himself to Moses, was: *I am the God of your fathers.* When God introduces Himself to the people at Sinai, on the other hand, by that point, circumstances have changed greatly. The people have just seen the Egyptian army destroyed at the Sea of Reeds. The Exodus from Egypt is a reality now, not merely a dream. Now, God has become *"their* God."

From Intention to Action

The truth is, if one looks more closely at God's two *Anochi* introductions (the first at the Burning Bush, the next at the giving of the Ten Commandments) one sees just how dramatically this contrast springs to life. For here, below, is the totality of God's opening introduction at the Burning Bush. Note, in particular, its beginning and ending words:

"I am the God of your father, the God of Abraham, the God of Isaac, and the God of Jacob." And Moses hid his face, for he was afraid to look at God. And the Lord continued, "I have marked well the plight of My people in Egypt and have heeded their outcry because of their taskmasters; yes, I am mindful of their sufferings. I have come down to rescue them from the Egyptians and to bring them out of that land to a good and spacious land, a land flowing with milk and honey, the region of the Canaanites, the Hittites, the Amorites, the Perizzites, the Hivites, and the Jebusites. Now the cry of the Israelites has reached Me; moreover, I have seen how the Egyptians oppress them. Come, therefore, I will send you to Pharaoh, **and you shall bring My people, the Israelites, out of Egypt.**

Exodus 3:6–10

אָנֹכִי אֱלֹהֵי אָבִיךָ אֱלֹהֵי
אַבְרָהָם אֱלֹהֵי יִצְחָק וֵאלֹהֵי
יַעֲקֹב וַיַּסְתֵּר מֹשֶׁה פָּנָיו כִּי יָרֵא
מֵהַבִּיט אֶל־הָאֱלֹהִים. וַיֹּאמֶר
יְקוָה רָאֹה רָאִיתִי אֶת־עֳנִי עַמִּי
אֲשֶׁר בְּמִצְרָיִם וְאֶת־צַעֲקָתָם
שָׁמַעְתִּי מִפְּנֵי נֹגְשָׂיו כִּי יָדַעְתִּי
אֶת־מַכְאֹבָיו. וָאֵרֵד לְהַצִּילוֹ
מִיַּד מִצְרַיִם וּלְהַעֲלֹתוֹ מִן־
הָאָרֶץ הַהִוא אֶל־אֶרֶץ טוֹבָה
וּרְחָבָה אֶל־אֶרֶץ זָבַת חָלָב
וּדְבָשׁ אֶל־מְקוֹם הַכְּנַעֲנִי
וְהַחִתִּי וְהָאֱמֹרִי וְהַפְּרִזִּי וְהַחִוִּי
וְהַיְבוּסִי. וְעַתָּה הִנֵּה צַעֲקַת
בְּנֵי יִשְׂרָאֵל בָּאָה אֵלָי וְגַם
רָאִיתִי אֶת הַלַּחַץ אֲשֶׁר
מִצְרַיִם לֹחֲצִים אֹתָם.
וְעַתָּה לְכָה וְאֶשְׁלָחֲךָ אֶל־פַּרְעֹה
וְהוֹצֵא אֶת־עַמִּי בְנֵי־יִשְׂרָאֵל
מִמִּצְרָיִם.

Where else do we hear words that sound suspiciously like that beginning and ending? *In the first of the Ten Commandments, that's where.* Just take the *beginning* of God's introduction at the Burning Bush, and put it together with the *end* of that same introduction, and it magically transforms into… the first declaration in the Ten Commandments:

Exodus 20:2

אָנֹכִי יְקוָה אֱלֹהֶיךָ אֲשֶׁר הו
צֵאתִיךָ מֵאֶרֶץ מִצְרָיִם

I am YHVH your God, who brought you out of the land of Egypt.

At the Burning Bush, God declared His *intention* to take the Children of Israel out of Egypt. But when the Ten Commandments were given, God had already *fulfilled* that intention — so He updated His introduction. Now, God could rightfully say He was "their God."

The God of Radical Empathy

While we are looking at how God introduces Himself at the Burning Bush and in the Ten Commandments, we should also point out another way these introductions differ: The first commandment is a whole lot shorter and pithier than God's introduction was at the Burning Bush. Indeed, there is a very large section of text right in the middle of the Burning Bush introduction that doesn't seem to be reflected at all in the first commandment. We might wonder: If the earlier text is really a template of sorts for the later one, what about this whole missing middle? Where, if anywhere, does *it* show up in the Decalogue's first command?

The answer, I think, is that it's there; you just need to look for it carefully. Indeed, both introductions have a middle — it is just that one middle is quite long and the other is quite short. One is a few verses in length, and the other is just a single word. Look at them both, side by side:

GOD INTRODUCES HIMSELF

IN YITRO I	IN YITRO II
The Burning Bush	**The Ten Commandments**

אָנֹכִי אֱלֹהֵי אָבִיךָ אֱלֹהֵי אַבְרָהָם אֱלֹהֵי יִצְחָק
וֵאלֹהֵי יַעֲקֹב וַיַּסְתֵּר מֹשֶׁה פָּנָיו כִּי יָרֵא מֵהַבִּיט
אֶל־הָאֱלֹהִים. וַיֹּאמֶר יְקוָה רָאֹה רָאִיתִי אֶת־
עֳנִי עַמִּי אֲשֶׁר בְּמִצְרָיִם וְאֶת־צַעֲקָתָם שָׁמַעְתִּי
מִפְּנֵי נֹגְשָׂיו כִּי יָדַעְתִּי אֶת־מַכְאֹבָיו. וָאֵרֵד
לְהַצִּילוֹ מִיַּד מִצְרַיִם וּלְהַעֲלֹתוֹ מִן־הָאָרֶץ
הַהוּא אֶל־אֶרֶץ טוֹבָה וּרְחָבָה אֶל־אֶרֶץ זָבַת
חָלָב וּדְבָשׁ אֶל־מְקוֹם הַכְּנַעֲנִי וְהַחִתִּי וְהָאֱמֹרִי
וְהַפְּרִזִּי וְהַחִוִּי וְהַיְבוּסִי. וְעַתָּה הִנֵּה צַעֲקַת בְּנֵי
יִשְׂרָאֵל בָּאָה אֵלָי וְגַם רָאִיתִי אֶת הַלַּחַץ אֲשֶׁר
מִצְרַיִם לֹחֲצִים אֹתָם. וְעַתָּה לְכָה וְאֶשְׁלָחֲךָ
אֶל־פַּרְעֹה וְהוֹצֵא אֶת־עַמִּי בְנֵי־יִשְׂרָאֵל
מִמִּצְרָיִם

אָנֹכִי יְקוָה אֱלֹהֶיךָ אֲשֶׁר
הוֹצֵאתִיךָ מֵאֶרֶץ מִצְרָיִם

"I am the God of your father, the God of Abraham, the God of Isaac, and the God of Jacob." And Moses hid his face, for he was afraid to look at God. And God continued, "I have seen the suffering of My people in Egypt and have heard their cries, because of their taskmasters; yes, I know their suffering. I have come down to rescue them from the Egyptians and to bring them out of that land to a good and spacious land, a land flowing with milk and honey, the region of the Canaanites, the Hittites, the Amorites, the Perizzites, the Hivites, and the Jebusites. Now the cry of the Israelites has reached Me; moreover, I have seen how the Egyptians oppress them. And now, come, I will send you to Pharaoh, and you shall bring My people, the Israelites, out of Egypt." (Ex. 3:6–10)

I am YHVH your God, who brought you out of the land of Egypt. (Ex. 20:2)

Glance over at the left side of the table above, and look at the middle section of that introduction (in blue). What would you say its main theme is?

- *I have seen the suffering of My people in Egypt*
- *I have heard their cries*
- *I know their suffering*
- *Now, the cry of the Israelites has reached Me*
- *I have seen how the Egyptians oppress them*

We have a word for this in English, and it is "empathy."[11] To experience what someone else is experiencing as deeply as possible, even if that experience is uncomfortable or painful, is the soul of empathy. And empathy has consequences. It naturally spurs the one who experiences it to reach out and help the victim. Which, in fact, is the very next point God

---

11   Actually, if one looks carefully at this middle section of the introduction, one can discern a chiasm within it:

> *I have seen the suffering of My people in Egypt* **and have heard their cries, because of their taskmasters;** *yes, I know their suffering. I have come down to rescue them from the Egyptians and to bring them out of that land to a good and spacious land, a land flowing with milk and honey, the region of the Canaanites, the Hittites, the Amorites, the Perizzites, the Hivites, and the Jebusites.* **Now the cry of the Israelites has reached Me;** *moreover, I have seen how the Egyptians oppress them.*

The text begins and ends with God stating that He has "seen" the suffering of Israel; the second element and the second to last element of the text has God stating that He has "heard" their cries; and the middle element is God's statement that He "knows" their suffering, and will therefore act to save them.

Reflecting on this, one might say that the structure indicates God internalizing the pain of His people, so to speak. The first stage of the process involves sight. The way we humans perceive the sense of sight is that with our eyes we become aware of what is taking place outside us. But after sight, the second stage involves the hearing of sound. We humans perceive hearing as involving greater internalization than seeing; when we hear, sound "goes into" our ears and actually enters us. But the deepest level of internalization lies at our center, and this is "knowing." Knowing, or cognition, is a completely internal process: When we humans "know" something, we take the data from the outside that our senses report to us, and we come to "know it" on the inside. Thus, the structure of God's introduction points to the essence of empathy: bringing someone else's pain and suffering inside ourselves.

makes in introducing Himself at the Burning Bush. Right after saying that He "knows the people's suffering," the Almighty says:

וָאֵרֵד לְהַצִּילוֹ מִיַּד מִצְרַיִם וּלְהַעֲלֹתוֹ מִן־הָאָרֶץ הַהִוא אֶל־אֶרֶץ טוֹבָה וּרְחָבָה אֶל־אֶרֶץ זָבַת חָלָב וּדְבָשׁ	And I shall go down to save them from the hand of Egypt and to bring them from that land to a good and spacious land; to a land that flows with milk and honey.	Exodus 3:8

In short, God "feels" what the people feel, and then acts to save them. But why, then, you may ask, doesn't all this get reflected in the Ten Commandments, in that first command, where God introduces Himself? In other words, if, as we've seen, the two *ends* of the Burning Bush introduction get reflected in the first command, why does the middle part suddenly go missing?

The answer is: It doesn't go missing at all. It just gets condensed into a single word. That word is God's name, YHVH.

Indeed, back at the Burning Bush, after His opening *Anochi*, God didn't really use a name for Himself at all. He just spoke of being the nameless deity our forefathers knew:

אָנֹכִי אֱלֹהֵי אָבִיךָ	I am the God of your fathers.	Exodus 3:6

But now, in the Ten Commandments, God advances a name:

אָנֹכִי יְקֹוָה אֱלֹהֶיךָ	I am **YHVH** your God.	Exodus 20:2

I am *Yod, Heh, Vav, Heh*, your God, who took you out of Egypt.

That special, mysterious name of God, YHVH. What, if anything, does it even mean? I want to suggest a theory to you. That single word, that name by which God introduces Himself in the Ten Commandments, is shorthand for everything that was in the middle of the Burning Bush introduction. It is shorthand for "the God of empathy and, therefore, the God of action." For as we shall see later, the name YHVH is associated with states of being — being in the past, being in the present, and being in the future.[12] It is as if God, with that name, denotes Himself as the God of Being; the God who is radically present with you, so much so that He can't help but act.

Thinking about God this way has implications. And those implications express themselves in what comes next — which is to say, in the next commands of the Decalogue.

The Second Principle of the Ten Commandments

Let's move on and continue our examination of the Yitro I and Yitro II narratives, in relation to one another. That brings us to the second exchange between God and Moses at the Burning Bush on the one hand, and the second of the Ten Commandments, on the other. Here they are, side by side:

THE SECOND ELEMENT

YITRO I: THE BURNING BUSH God's Second Exchange with Moses	YITRO II: REVELATION AT SINAI The Second of the Ten Commandments
וַיֹּאמֶר מֹשֶׁה אֶל־הָאֱלֹהִים מִי אָנֹכִי כִּי אֵלֵךְ אֶל־פַּרְעֹה וְכִי אוֹצִיא אֶת־בְּנֵי יִשְׂרָאֵל מִמִּצְרָיִם: וַיֹּאמֶר כִּי־אֶהְיֶה עִמָּךְ וְזֶה־לְּךָ הָאוֹת כִּי אָנֹכִי שְׁלַחְתִּיךָ בְּהוֹצִיאֲךָ אֶת־הָעָם מִמִּצְרַיִם תַּעַבְדוּן אֶת־הָאֱלֹהִים עַל הָהָר הַזֶּה:	לֹא־יִהְיֶה לְךָ אֱלֹהִים אֲחֵרִים עַל־פָּנָי...וְלֹא תָעָבְדֵם
But Moses said to God, "Who am I that I should go to Pharaoh and bring the Israelites out of Egypt?" And [God] said, "Because **I will be with you**; that shall be your sign that it was I who sent you. When you have freed the people from Egypt, **you shall serve** God at this mountain." (Ex. 3:11–12)	There shall not **be for you** other gods... You shall not **serve them**. (Ex. 20:3, 5)

---

12 YHVH seems to be an amalgam of the Hebrew words for "being" in the past, present, and future: *hayah, hoveh,* and *yihiyeh.* For further elaboration of these points, see later in this essay.

Once again, the private conversation between God and Moses appears to presage the national conversation between God and the people of Israel. The earlier text offers a kind of rationale for the latter one, helping us understand *why* idolatry is prohibited: Why does God ask for our loyalty in worship? Why serve only Him, and not any other power, real or imagined? The answer lies in Moses' second exchange with God at the Burning Bush. Back then, a skeptical Moses had asked God how he could possibly have the temerity to go to Pharaoh, and how he could possibly liberate his enslaved people. To this, God had replied that he won't be doing it alone. "I will be with you," God had said.

And God *was* with Moses, just as He had promised. *Because* God was with him, Moses was successful when he went to Pharaoh. The people were now free. Hence, if God dedicated Himself to "be with" Moses so that the people could win their freedom, it would be a travesty for the people to "be with" other gods and enslave themselves once more.[13] Not just a travesty but a betrayal. The לֹא יִהְיֶה לְךָ of the second commandment doesn't just mean "don't worship other powers"; it means don't "be with" them. That is, don't desecrate the כִּי אֶהְיֶה עִמָּךְ (Ex. 3:12) quality of God—God's "with-you-ness"—by being with other, foreign deities. At the end of the day, our relationship with God is not transactional; you don't just go and exchange Him for some other newfangled power you decide you'd like to serve.

The Third Commandment

Let's go on and explore the third exchange between Moses and God at the Burning Bush. If our theory is right, this should correspond to the third principle of the Ten Commandments: Don't take God's name in vain. And it does. For what do you suppose that third exchange between

---

13 Another point should be made about the second exchange between Moses and God at the Burning Bush. In it, Moses repeats the word *anochi*, which the Almighty had just used to introduce Himself to Moses. Moses now takes the word and uses it himself, when he expresses his fear of confronting Pharaoh: מִי אָנֹכִי כִּי אֵלֵךְ אֶל־פַּרְעֹה, "Who am I that I should go to Pharaoh?" (Ex. 3:11). The Torah thus seems to be asking the reader to remember the previous use of the word, even as Moses uses it again. Thus, Moses is in effect saying to God: Yes, you may be *Anochi*, the great and powerful "I" of the divinity, but מִי אָנֹכִי—by contrast, who am I? (Ex. 3:11). I'm no god; I'm weak and frail. How can I possibly go to Pharaoh? To this, God essentially replies: You know why you, too, are a somebody? כִּי־אֶהְיֶה עִמָּךְ, "Because I'm going to be with you."

God and Moses at the Burning Bush was all about? As if on cue, it was about … *God's name,* of all things:

THE THIRD ELEMENT

YITRO I: THE BURNING BUSH	YITRO II: REVELATION AT SINAI
God's Third Exchange with Moses	**The Third of the Ten Commandments**

וַיֹּאמֶר מֹשֶׁה אֶל־הָאֱלֹהִים הִנֵּה אָנֹכִי בָא אֶל־בְּנֵי יִשְׂרָאֵל וְאָמַרְתִּי לָהֶם אֱלֹהֵי אֲבוֹתֵיכֶם שְׁלָחַנִי אֲלֵיכֶם וְאָמְרוּ־לִי מַה־שְּׁמוֹ מָה אֹמַר אֲלֵהֶם: וַיֹּאמֶר אֱלֹהִים אֶל־מֹשֶׁה אֶהְיֶה אֲשֶׁר אֶהְיֶה וַיֹּאמֶר כֹּה תֹאמַר לִבְנֵי יִשְׂרָאֵל אֶהְיֶה שְׁלָחַנִי אֲלֵיכֶם: וַיֹּאמֶר עוֹד אֱלֹהִים אֶל־מֹשֶׁה כֹּה תֹאמַר אֶל־בְּנֵי יִשְׂרָאֵל יְקֹוָה אֱלֹהֵי אֲבֹתֵיכֶם אֱלֹהֵי אַבְרָהָם אֱלֹהֵי יִצְחָק וֵאלֹהֵי יַעֲקֹב שְׁלָחַנִי אֲלֵיכֶם זֶה־שְּׁמִי לְעֹלָם וְזֶה זִכְרִי לְדֹר דֹּר:

לֹא תִשָּׂא אֶת־שֵׁם־יְקֹוָה אֱלֹהֶיךָ לַשָּׁוְא כִּי לֹא יְנַקֶּה יְקֹוָה אֵת אֲשֶׁר־יִשָּׂא אֶת־שְׁמוֹ לַשָּׁוְא:

Moses said to God, "When I come to the Israelites and say to them, 'The God of your fathers has sent me to you,' and they ask me, **'What is His name?'** what shall I say to them?" And God said to Moses, "Ehyeh-Asher-Ehyeh." He continued, "Thus shall you say to the Israelites, 'Ehyeh sent me to you.'" And God said further to Moses, "Thus shall you speak to the Israelites: **YHVH**, the God of your fathers, the God of Abraham, the God of Isaac, and the God of Jacob, has sent me to you: **This shall be My name** forever, this My appellation for all eternity." (Ex. 3:13–15)

You shall not take the **name of YHVH**, your God, in vain; for YHVH will not clear one who takes His name in vain. (Ex. 20:7)

In Moses' third exchange with God at the Burning Bush, he asks the Almighty what he should tell the people God's name is. The Almighty's initial answer to him seems almost to avoid the question:

אֶהְיֶה אֲשֶׁר אֶהְיֶה   I will be that which I will be   Exodus 3:14

When God uses the word *eheyeh* (I will be) here, He seems to be referencing something He said just moments before to Moses. Remember: Moses had felt incapable of going to Pharaoh to demand freedom for his people, and when He asked God how he could possibly go, God had answered him: You can do it because "I will be with you." Now God chooses to answer Moses' next question — *What name of Yours shall I give to the people?* — with nomenclature that echoes what he last told Moses: "I will be."

Why would God do that? He seems to be telling Moses: *Remember what I told you when you were in distress? Well, the same way I told you I will be with you personally in a time you felt troubled, so too, I will be with them, the entire people, in their time of trouble.* Indeed, this is how the Sages of the Midrash understood the meaning of God's words here. They asserted that God wasn't just saying here "I will be"; He was saying: "I will be *with*," as in, *"Tell the people I will be with them in their current sorrow, and in all future sorrows."*[14] He was declaring Himself the timeless God of empathy.[15]

---

14 Rashi to Exodus ad loc., from Berachot 9a.

15 *Being there now and always…* The role of time here strikes me as fascinating and instructive. To really "be with someone," in a truly empathetic way, requires a certain concentration of one's sense of being. For example, one needs to avoid distraction. If I'm your friend and you're talking to me but I'm glancing around, half-listening to other conversations in the room, that doesn't feel great. My attention is fragmented; I'm not really being with you.

But here's something to consider: Even if I really focus on what you're saying, still, there's always something *inherently* fragmented about human consciousness, despite our best intentions — because a human being can be here only right now, in this little fragment of time called the present. The present me is talking to you, but the past me is gone and the future me is not yet here. Right now, it is just the little fragment of me that happens to be here right now, in the moment, who is here with you. With God, though, that's not the case. God somehow blends past,

How did the Sages arrive at this peculiar notion? Why did they insist that "I will be what I will be" amounted to God saying, "I will *always* be with the people, no matter how beaten down they become"? I would suggest that they deduced it from what God says *next* to Moses, which is this:

Exodus 3:14–15

וַיֹּאמֶר כֹּה תֹאמַר לִבְנֵי יִשְׂרָאֵל אֶהְיֶה שְׁלָחַנִי אֲלֵיכֶם: וַיֹּאמֶר עוֹד אֱלֹהִים אֶל־מֹשֶׁה כֹּה־ תֹאמַר אֶל־בְּנֵי יִשְׂרָאֵל יְקוָה... שְׁלָחַנִי אֲלֵיכֶם

He continued, "Thus shall you say to the Israelites, 'Ehyeh sent me to you.'" And God said further to Moses, "Thus shall you speak to the Israelites: **YHVH**...has sent me to you."

God gives Himself an actual name here, YHVH. But what, after all, does YHVH mean? It has no obvious meaning in Hebrew. But YHVH is connected to the idea of "being there," and it is also connected to the idea of timelessness; indeed, it seems almost like an acronym for the Sages' idea "I will be with you *always*." For in Hebrew, there's a word for existence in the past. It is *hayah*. There's a word for existence in the future; it is *yihiyeh*. And existence in the present? That is *hoveh*. Take all those words for existence and overlay them, one on top of the other, and you get *yod, heh, vav, heh*. Thus, YHVH seems to express the notion of concentrated being — "being there" in past, present, and future — all collapsed into a single, potent present.

Later, after the Exodus from Egypt is complete, God comes to the nation of Israel and, in the Decalogue, formulates a third command that resonates with all this. It references that name YHVH, which had seemed to distill the idea of timeless "being with." If this is the name that signifies God being with Israel always — no matter how beaten down we may feel — how could you possibly think of marginalizing that name, or treating it lightly? Hence, the third command tells us:

Exodus 20:7

לֹא תִשָּׂא אֶת־שֵׁם־יְקוָה אֱלֹהֶיךָ לַשָּׁוְא

You shall not take the name of YHVH, your God, in vain.

---

present, and future existence together into one concentrated sense of being, such that everything God ever was and will be is with you right now, in a limitless kind of empathy.

The Fourth Element: Testimony through Acts

The theme of empathy that we've seen develop in the first three exchanges at the Burning Bush, as well as the first three commands in the Decalogue, takes a stark turn in the fourth element of each narrative. Let's look at that in the Burning Bush story first.

In the fourth exchange at the Burning Bush, Moses protests to God that the people are going to doubt that YHVH has appeared to him. God, in response, offers Moses proof of their encounter, which takes the form of three mysterious acts of transformation that Moses will be able to carry out: water turns to blood when it hits the ground; a hand turns white, and a staff transforms itself into a snake. God labels these acts of transformation "signs" (Exodus 4:8).

Now, the conventional way to understand all this is that Moses was protesting to God that skeptics will doubt the truth of his claim that God revealed Himself to him. That is, he fears people will think he is a charlatan or delusional. But if that's really the case, it is hard to understand how the three signs — seemingly just three glorified magic tricks — would disabuse skeptics of their suspicions. Magic wasn't unheard of in Egypt. Couldn't skeptics potentially dismiss them as sleight of hand? Why would these signs assure Moses that the people would believe that he had *for sure* experienced a divine revelation?

Allow me to propose an answer. Moses never meant to ask God how he might convince the kind of skeptic I described above. He wasn't worried that people would doubt he had spoken to God. He was worried about people doubting that this God who spoke to him could fairly be characterized as YHVH. Listen carefully to the language of the text:

וְהֵן לֹא־יַאֲמִינוּ לִי וְלֹא יִשְׁמְעוּ בְּקֹלִי כִּי יֹאמְרוּ לֹא־נִרְאָה אֵלֶיךָ יְקוָה:	But they won't believe me. They won't listen to my voice. They will say: **It is not true that YHVH appeared to you.**	Exodus 4:1

Recall what YHVH signifies: the God of radical empathy, the God who is there with us, potently, in our life, always, even in times of our greatest sorrow. The people had experienced unimaginable horrors in Egypt for many long years. They would not easily believe that God was who Moses said He was: a compassionate divine force, full of love, who is there with us, now and always. It is hard for those experiencing immense suffering to believe that the God who had been silent all this time is present with them in their sorrow. That can seem like a bridge too far.

So God says, show them these three signs. The signs weren't supposed to be magic tricks. They were designed as tangible expressions of empathy, whose self-evident meaning would resonate viscerally with the people. They would demonstrate that God knows the raw truth of their pain.

A full exploration of the three signs and their symbolic import is beyond the scope of this essay,[16] but let's at least consider the last of the three signs, and I think the flavor of the signs will begin to emerge.

Water into Blood

God tells Moses to take some water from the Nile, spill it on the ground and, as if by magic, it will turn to blood. Ponder that for a moment. Does it remind you of any phenomenon that takes place later on in the Exodus saga? *Water turning into blood, perchance?* Of course: It's the first plague, the moment when the entire Nile River turns, harrowingly, into blood. Looking at it with hindsight, it appears that the sign of the water turning into blood somehow foreshadowed that first plague. But still, what meaning was this water-turning-into-blood phenomenon supposed to have?

What meaning, indeed? Why do you think, of all things, God would choose to begin His cascade of ten plagues with … a river turning into blood?

It is because He wanted to show that He understood the truth about what happened to the people, the darkest, most terrible truth.

Consider this: What would you say was the greatest crime the Egyptians perpetrated upon the Israelite population, in all of those hundreds of years of slavery, beyond all the brickmaking, beyond all the excruciating labor? Beyond all that, there was one horrific act that was paramount. It was an act so terrible it could hardly even be held in memory without driving the bearer of that memory mad with pain. It was the casting of the little baby boys into the Nile, the drowning of generations of helpless children.

The truth is, the horror was even worse than just the killing of all those children. It extended beyond that, too. For ask yourself: Why did Pharaoh decree that the babies should be killed in precisely this fashion? Why

---

16 I treated the meaning of the three signs extensively in *The Three Great Lies of the Exodus*, a video series available at alephbeta.org.

pollute the Nile, so precious and crucial to Egypt's economy, with what must have been countless corpses?

Plausible Deniability

The answer is that the Nile offered plausible deniability. It offered the aggressor a way to avoid confronting the truth of his crime. For now ask yourself this: When all those babies perished in the Nile, did the river ever turn red with blood? The answer, of course, is no. There was just too much water.[17] The blood was diluted into virtual nothingness by the vastness of the water.

Yes, at night there would have been screams and terror as babies were ripped away from parents and cast in the water but in the morning…everything would seem to revert to normal. So what happens when the parents come before the police or the courts and ask: *Where's my child?* The magistrate files a missing persons report, shakes his head sadly, and asks if the parents can perhaps provide any evidence of the ridiculous atrocities they are alleging. But of course, there is no evidence. The screams are gone. The birds are chirping. The water of the Nile is placid and clear. Egyptians are jogging on the paths near the shore and playing Brahms on stolen pianos, while the ladies read Goethe in the parlor room. It is as if the Nile itself has conspired with the rest of nature to mask the crime. And it leaves the victim, the bereaved parents, staring at one another and wondering: *Are we the ones who are crazy?*

The God Who Gets It

So God validated what was done to the people. Indeed, the first step in redeeming a traumatized people isn't really taking them out of Egypt. Before that, there's work to do; in effect, you have to say: *I know what was done to you; I get it.* And so the first plague, foreshadowed in this sign at the Burning Bush, has one clear message: The Nile will turn to blood. It will do that, not because of magic. It will do that because…that's the reality.[18]

---

17 It is estimated that more than seventy billion gallons of water flow through the Nile every day.

18 Intriguingly, the first two signs at the Burning Bush involved a transformation of one thing into another, where the transformation was undone afterward: A staff

The aggressor will be forced to confront his crime. Egyptians will have to stare with horror and shame at the blood. And the victims will begin to find a measure of solace: We *weren't* the crazy ones. Everyone and everything around us lied. But God knows the truth. *Yes, this is what happened to you.*

God's first act of care, even before taking us out of Egypt, is that He stood up and told the truth about us. He did so without saying a word. He did it with actions: first, a symbolic act, the sign at the Burning Bush; then, a real-world act that brings the sign to fruition — the first plague, which turned the Nile into blood. At the Burning Bush, through that sign, God was saying to Israel: *I know the truth about what happened to you. I understand the horror.* God really *was* YHVH, the God of Being-There-With-You, after all.

It is a message that apparently left its intended mark:

Exodus
4:30–31

וַיַּעַשׂ הָאֹתֹת לְעֵינֵי הָעָם:
וַיַּאֲמֵן הָעָם וַיִּשְׁמְעוּ כִּי־פָקַד
יְקוָה אֶת־בְּנֵי יִשְׂרָאֵל וְכִי רָאָה
אֶת־עָנְיָם וַיִּקְּדוּ וַיִּשְׁתַּחֲווּ:

He performed the signs in front of the people, and the people began to trust. They heard that YHVH had taken note of the Children of Israel, and that He had seen their suffering. So they bowed low in homage.

---

transformed into a snake, then back into a staff. A hand turned white as snow, then reverted to its healthy, regular appearance. The fact that the object goes back to its original structure seems to signify that the transformation was an illusion; the original form of the item is its true form. But the last sign, the water turning to blood, involves a transformation that is permanent (once the water turns to blood, it doesn't revert to water again). If we are correct in assuming that this last sign recalls the crime of drowning children in the Nile, then perhaps it is fitting that the blood does *not* revert to water. The fact that the water turns to blood but doesn't go back to water again suggests that it is the *original water* that is the illusory thing, and that the blood is its more real form. Indeed, the Egyptians, in using the Nile to cover up their crime, created a situation where the pristine appearance of their river's water was the illusion. From a moral standpoint, the red of the blood of the children spilled into the water reflects the true color of the river. Hence, the plague of blood merely reveals the hidden truth of things — on some level, the water, by rights, *ought* to be blood! — and destroys the Egyptian attempt at a cover-up.

The Fourth Command: Israel Reciprocates the Signs

And so, in the fourth of the Ten Commandments — the section of Yitro II that corresponds to the signs God showed Moses in Yitro I — we try to do for God what He did for us: We tell the truth about Him. We testify that He created the world. We do it the same way He told the truth about us — not through words, but through actions. We do it by keeping the Sabbath every seventh day.

Moreover, when God first told the truth about us, He did it with something God called a *sign*: the symbolic act of water that turns to blood.[19] So, when we tell the truth about God, we also do it with a sign:

וְשָׁמְרוּ בְנֵי־יִשְׂרָאֵל אֶת־הַשַּׁבָּת
לַעֲשׂוֹת אֶת־הַשַּׁבָּת לְדֹרֹתָם
בְּרִית עוֹלָם: בֵּינִי וּבֵין בְּנֵי
יִשְׂרָאֵל אוֹת הִוא לְעֹלָם

The Children of Israel people shall keep the Sabbath, observing the Sabbath throughout the ages as a covenant for all time: **it shall be a sign** for all time between Me and the people of Israel.

Exodus 31:16–17

God told the truth about what others did to us, how they oppressed us and brought us low. We reciprocate that by observing the Sabbath, in which we tell the truth about what God did for others to provide for them and elevate them. In six primal days, He bequeathed to us, His creatures, the glorious gift of a world in which to live.

The Fifth Element

Our exploration of the Yitro I and Yitro II narratives is now nearly at an end. To bring it to a close, we are going to examine the fifth and final exchange between God and Moses at the Burning Bush (in Yitro I), which, I want to argue, corresponds to the fifth and final command on the first tablet of the Decalogue (in Yitro II).

---

19 The Torah explicitly calls this a sign. See, for example, Exodus 4:8, where the text gives this label to the transformative acts Moses was able to carry out: וְהָיָה אִם־ לֹא יַאֲמִינוּ לָךְ וְלֹא יִשְׁמְעוּ לְקֹל הָאֹת הָרִאשׁוֹן וְהֶאֱמִינוּ לְקֹל הָאֹת הָאַחֲרוֹן, "And it shall be, if they don't believe you, and don't listen to the voice of the first sign, they will listen to the voice of the last sign."

At the Burning Bush, Moses had tenaciously offered one excuse after another as to why he simply couldn't go to Pharaoh to free the Israelites. Finally, he says this to the Almighty:

Exodus 4:10

וַיֹּאמֶר מֹשֶׁה אֶל־יְקֹוָה בִּי אֲדֹנָי לֹא אִישׁ דְּבָרִים אָנֹכִי גַּם מִתְּמוֹל גַּם מִשִּׁלְשֹׁם גַּם מֵאָז דַּבֶּרְךָ אֶל־עַבְדֶּךָ כִּי כְבַד־פֶּה וּכְבַד לָשׁוֹן אָנֹכִי:

Moses said to YHVH, "Please, My Master, I have never been a man of words, neither yesterday nor the day before, nor even now that You have spoken to Your servant; I have a kind of heaviness of the mouth, a heaviness of the tongue.

Moses' last protestation to God is that he just doesn't speak well. We don't know exactly what he means by this; he might be referring to a lisp or speech impediment of some sort; he might simply think he is ineloquent. But one way or another, he makes the case that a "heaviness" of the tongue and mouth makes him unfit to do the job God has asked him to do.

To this, God responds:

Exodus 4:11–12

מִי שָׂם פֶּה לָאָדָם אוֹ מִי־יָשׂוּם אִלֵּם אוֹ חֵרֵשׁ אוֹ פִקֵּחַ אוֹ עִוֵּר הֲלֹא אָנֹכִי יְקֹוָה: וְעַתָּה לֵךְ וְאָנֹכִי אֶהְיֶה עִם־פִּיךָ וְהוֹרֵיתִיךָ אֲשֶׁר תְּדַבֵּר:

"Who is it that gives man speech? Or who makes him dumb or deaf, seeing or blind? Is it not I, YHVH? Now go, and I will be with you as you speak; I will guide you as to what to say."

God's answer to Moses has two elements to it. The first: I am the supreme Maker of humankind, the One who is responsible for all the varied deficits and gifts that any particular person has. So, by implication: *If I say you have what you need to accomplish a task I've set for you, then you probably can trust Me on that.* But God says something else, too. His second message is, in effect: *Don't worry. You're not going to have to do this alone. I'm going to be with you; I'm going to be with your mouth. I'll help you.*

With that second assurance, God returns to a theme He has reprised over and over again in speaking with Moses at the Burning Bush: *I will be with you.* Indeed, if we recall that the name YHVH, which God has given

Himself at the Burning Bush, seems to denote God in His quality of Being, the Almighty is once again using that very same idea to reassure Moses: *Yes, your heaviness of speech comes from Me; I'm the God who made you. But if I'm the One who gave you that difficulty to struggle with, I'm also the One who can give you the strength to surmount it. I'm with you, and My Presence at your side can give you strength when you feel inadequate. I am YHVH, the "being with you" God.*

The Fifth Command: Honoring Parents

Let's leave that discussion at the Burning Bush, for a moment, and turn to the corresponding text in the Decalogue. As we do, let's see if we can pick up anything in it that resonates with these words or ideas.

The fifth command — the last on the first tablet — is, of course, the imperative to honor one's parents:

כַּבֵּד אֶת־אָבִיךָ וְאֶת־אִמֶּךָ	Honor your father and honor your mother.	Exodus 20:12

At first glance, it might seem hard to perceive a connection between the idea of honoring one's parents and Moses' complaint at the Burning Bush about a heaviness of the tongue. But in fact, Moses' complaint actually has quite a bit to do with the idea of honoring parents. Indeed, his complaint could well be regarded as the quintessential argument for *not* honoring one's parents. For if I feel basically inadequate, if I feel I don't really have the fundamental tools I need to succeed in life — what relationship might I end up developing with my parents?

Consider this: Why should anyone honor his or her parents? The answer seems obvious: They give you the greatest gift of all, life, and for that we should be eternally grateful. But the truth of the matter is a bit more nuanced than that. For your parents didn't just give you a generic gift called life; they gave you a very specific gift — your *particular* life. Parents give you your singular genes, your unique upbringing, the basic hand of cards you are dealt in this world. That hand of cards comes with certain gifts, but it also comes with what may seem like overwhelming deficits or challenges. Facing the reality of one's deficits, one might well throw up their hands and say: *I don't like the hand I've been dealt. I feel like it's all wrong. I want to exchange my cards.*

If one feels that way intensely enough, they might well resent their parents rather than honor them. But the Torah insists that no matter the hand we are dealt in life, we *should* honor our parents. Why? What is the rationale for that?

The answer would seem to lie in…what God told Moses back at the Burning Bush. For what, after all, did God say when Moses complained to Him about his clumsiness of speech? *I am Your Creator. I gave you the hand of cards with which you face the world. And I gave you exactly what you need to accomplish the tasks that lie before you in this world.*

God, of course, adds to this another idea as well: I didn't just give you deficits and gifts and abandon you. I stand with you, and that, too, gives you the strength you need to surmount the challenges that you will face. This, too, is what parents do for us. They don't just create us and leave. They raise us in their homes. They stand by us. They give us attention and care. And that, too, helps us succeed in difficult moments. Together, these two factors — what our parents give us to begin with, and how they stand with us later in life — really *can* engineer success in the most improbable of ways. It is ironic, indeed, that Moses, the man who complained that he couldn't talk well, that his speech was clumsy and unpersuasive, is the one whose words are remembered for their eloquence and power by people the world over thousands of years later.[20]

---

20 To sharpen the point a bit more, the Torah seems to be saying that what our parents gave us, with our unique gifts and challenges, really *is* enough, in the sense that we all have the raw capacity to meet the challenges in life that are uniquely ours. For that alone we owe our parents a debt of gratitude. In addition, the ideal parents help their children further in life, and beyond money or violin lessons or anything else tangible or material, the most overlooked but most powerful gift they can give is really the gift of "being": Just standing with a child and being there for him or her when he feels most vulnerable. All parents do the former; all strive, with varying success, to do the latter. And we, as children, honor them for these gifts and for these efforts, however human and imperfect those efforts may be.

Of Honor and Heaviness

Thus, Moses' fifth exchange with God at the Burning Bush informs the fifth command of the Decalogue; indeed, it seems to provide a rationale of sorts for that command. But if this strikes you as fanciful, or speculative, if you find yourself doubting whether Moses' exchange with God at the Burning Bush really has anything to do with the Decalogue's injunction "honor your father and mother," I invite you to consider the words Moses used back at the Burning Bush to express his concern about the way he spoke. He doesn't just say that he doesn't speak well; he says his mouth and tongue are … *heavy*; in Hebrew, כְּבַד־פֶּה וּכְבַד לָשׁוֹן אָנֹכִי, "I am *kevad peh, kevad lashon*." So let me ask you now: Does that expression remind you of anything later in the Torah? A double use of the word t, of the root *kaf-bet-dalet*, anyone? Yes, you guessed it: That same three-letter root becomes the word the Torah uses, in the fifth of the Ten Commandments, to insist that we honor … both our parents.

Here are the two texts, side by side:

THE FIFTH ELEMENT

YITRO I: THE BURNING BUSH God's Fifth Exchange with Moses	YITRO II: REVELATION AT SINAI The Fifth of the Ten Commandments
וַיֹּאמֶר מֹשֶׁה אֶל־יְקוָה בִּי אֲדֹנָי לֹא אִישׁ דְּבָרִים אָנֹכִי גַּם מִתְּמוֹל גַּם מִשִּׁלְשֹׁם גַּם מֵאָז דַּבֶּרְךָ אֶל־עַבְדֶּךָ כִּי כְבַד־פֶּה וּכְבַד לָשׁוֹן אָנֹכִי׃	כַּבֵּד אֶת־אָבִיךָ וְאֶת־אִמֶּךָ
But Moses said to the Lord, "Please, O Lord, I have never been a man of words, neither yesterday nor the day before, nor even now that You have spoken to Your servant; I have a kind of heaviness of the mouth, a heaviness of the tongue. (Ex. 4:10)	Honor your father and honor your mother. (Ex. 20:12)

In a deliciously ironic twist, the very words Moses used at the Burning Bush to characterize his unique way of speaking — his "heaviness" (כְּבַד) of mouth and tongue — later become transformed, in the fifth commandment, into the Hebrew word for "honor" — כַּבֵּד.[21] It is as if the Torah were saying: What you think is problematic about yourself is not a reason to denigrate your parents; if anything it is cause to honor them. Why? Because your singular mix of gifts and challenges are exactly what you need to fulfill your particular destiny in this world. Your perceived deficits along with your perceived gifts make you who you are. And who you are isn't something that can simply be disassembled into components, with you taking just the elements you want and discarding others. You aren't an old car a mechanic keeps around his shop to harvest for its parts. No, the mysterious and wonderful gift your parents gave you — *your* life — is unitary and unique and in its totality is a great gift indeed. That unitary gift is reason to honor your parents, not resent them.[22]

21　There is also a second linguistic element that seems to connect the fifth exchange between Moses and God at the Burning Bush to the fifth of the Ten Commandments. This is the word God uses to suggest to Moses that He will be with his mouth and tongue and guide him as to what to say. The word for "guide" in Hebrew is הוֹרֵיתִיךְ, which seems to phonetically play off of הרה, the Hebrew word for conceiving a child. Inasmuch as the fifth commandment beckons us to honor those who conceived us, God's response to Moses assuring him that He will stand by him and offer guidance when he felt unable to speak well, can be seen as a kind of seed from which the notion of honoring parents emerges.

22　Sometimes the most profound truths are the ones we know most intuitively. The uniqueness of our own existence — the fact that we can't simply be taken apart and put back together again — resonates as true, even with young children, and sometimes our role as parents is to help our kids get in touch with those intuitions. Good children's books can occasionally help us in that quest, and here the wry but poignant words of Dr. Seuss come to mind: "Today you are You, that is truer than true. There is no one alive who is Youer than You" (*Happy Birthday to You!* [Random House Books for Young Readers, 1959]).

The Corollaries of Empathy

We have now completed our look at Yitro I and Yitro II. I freely admit there may be more to these parallels than we've seen thus far.[23] But in our (limited) look at them, we've discerned, I think, how God's private discussion with Moses at the Burning Bush (Yitro I) informs, and perhaps provides the basis for, God's public and eternal words to the nation in the Ten Commandments.[24]

At the Burning Bush, a common thread animated each of the five exchanges between God and Moses. It was the idea of "being with you." In one way or another, in His discussion with Moses, God consistently comes back to this idea: God allows Himself, as it were, to "be with us" and to "be with Moses" in times of trial, to experience something we humans call empathy, and to act on its basis. Given that, we might arrive at a generalized conclusion about the Ten Commandments — which, as we've seen,

---

23 In particular, the parallels between Yitro I and II may well extend back *earlier* than we've seen in this essay. I suspect, in fact, that the parallels we saw in **Parshat Beshalach**, between Moses' salvation as an infant, by the reeds at the Nile, and Israel's later salvation at an entire Sea of Reeds, are actually part of this larger "Yitro I and Yitro II pattern" — and may well be the point at which the parallels between the two narratives begin. If so, as I suggest later in this essay, it may be that we should update the terms "Yitro I and Yitro II" as ways of speaking about the two sets of parallel narratives. The Yitro I narrative — the one that begins with Moses being saved at the Nile and ends with the Burning Bush — can probably best be thought of as the story of Moses' personal life: how he goes from being an infant saved in Egypt to a man who encounters God at the Burning Bush. The Yitro II story shows how these events become a template, of sorts, for how similar themes play at the *national* level: It is the story of how an infant nation, newly saved from Egypt, comes to encounter God at Sinai.

24 As a coda to our discussion, I'll point out that the two icons of each "conversation" — the Burning Bush on the one hand, and the mountain called Sinai, on the other — share a commonality of name. In Hebrew, the former is a סנה (*sneh*) and the latter is סני (*sinai*). The only difference between the two comes in the final letter: A *heh* in the first case and a *yod* in the second. Bearing in mind that the letter *heh* has a numerical value of five and *yod* has a numerical value of ten, I wonder if the similarity and discrepancy between סנה and סני is shorthand for the relationship between the two: The two are the same, except one is five and the other is ten. Or: The *five* exchanges at the Burning Bush, later in the Torah, transform themselves into *Ten* Commandments at Sinai.

reflects the Burning Bush discussion. What *are* these commands, really? They are the principles that are the corollaries of this basic truth: *God is with us.* They are the ways that we, the recipients of God's love and care, are meant to respond to it.

Indeed, love is not *just* a matter of receiving someone else's care. It is a two-way street. Which is to say, it involves not just taking but giving — even when one partner is a mere human and the other is the Master of the Universe Himself. Thus, when we accepted the Ten Commandments at Sinai, part of what we were committing ourselves to was to be not merely passive recipients of God's empathy, but active agents who reciprocate that empathy. *If our Creator is there for us, we want to somehow be there for our Creator, too.* This understanding transforms the way we look at the Decalogue: Yes, the Ten Commandments are mitzvot; they are surely commands — but they are also more than mere commands. They express a means through which we human beings can become full partners in a relationship with our God. They are about how we can be a giver and not just a taker in that relationship. In accepting the Ten Commandments, we commit to respond to a loving God — with love, care, and honor of our own.

The Ten Commandments as a Window onto the Nature of Love

Looking back on the parallels we've uncovered between the Yitro I and Yitro II narratives, what shall we say about them? I think we can propose that they are copious and elegant, but they are also mysterious. At the very least, they form a remarkable, hidden thread that helps weave seemingly unrelated sections of the book of Exodus into an integrated whole. But one senses that the parallels have a larger meaning, too. The first narrative, which, for convenience's sake, we have been calling Yitro I, isn't really about just Yitro. In the larger sense, it is about Moses' early life: how he left Egypt as a young man, ran away to Midian, married, and first encountered God.[25] And the second narrative, what we've been calling Yitro II, likewise isn't really just about Yitro — it is about the early life of Moses' people: how they left Egypt, and then encountered God. At some level,

---

25 Indeed, the parallels between the stories probably stretch back earlier than we have seen, encompassing the entirety of Moses' early life; see above, footnote 23.

the first story seems to act as a kind of forerunner that blazes the trail for the latter.

Along the way, each story involves a marriage. One is personal, between a man and a woman; the other is national, between a people and her Heavenly paramour. Either way, the basics remain the same: A willingness to "be with" the one you love, to feel what they are feeling, to bear witness to their experience, to be moved to action, even, sometimes, to offer the kind of support a parent would offer, standing with the one you love when they feel outmatched or overwhelmed. These are the principles that emerge from Moses' first encounter with the Divine at a fiery bush, and later, from the nation's first encounter with God at a fiery mountain. Without these principles, love is ephemeral and fleeting, easily felt but easily lost. With them, love becomes a force that can transform our lives and the lives of those we love in deep and lasting ways.

YITRO I: How a Newborn Moses Is Saved from the Nile and Eventually Comes to Stand before God at Chorev	YITRO: How a Newborn Nation Is Saved from the Sea and Eventually Comes to Stand before God at Chorev
Moses saves shepherdesses threatened at a body of water; he then gives their thirsting sheep water to drink.	God saves an entire people, threatened at a body of water; God then gives them water to drink.
Yitro's daughters tell their father how Moses delivered them from the shepherds.	Moses tells Yitro how God delivered them from the Egyptians.
Yitro convenes a feast. Moses doesn't initially join the gathering.	Yitro convenes a feast, but Moses doesn't attend the gathering.
Moses takes Tziporah as his wife.	God takes Israel as His people.

YITRO I CONTINUES: Prologue to Burning Bush	YITRO II CONTINUES: Prologue to Revelation at Sinai
Leading sheep through the desert to Chorev (Sinai)	Leading God's sheep through the desert to Sinai
A bush is burning and is not consumed.	A mountain is burning and is not consumed.
God calls out to Moses.	God calls out to Moses.
Don't get too close.	Set up a perimeter; the people can't touch the mountain.

YITRO I: Dialogue at the Burning Bush	YITRO II: The Ten Commandments
I am the God of your fathers, who will take you out of Egypt	I Am the Lord Your God who took you out of Egypt
I am with you always	You should not have other Gods
What is My name? I am Eheya, I am YKVK	Do not take the Lord's name in vain
Turning blood into water is a sign of God's devotion to you, Israel	The Sabbath as a sign of your devotion to God
God will support Moses through his difficulties with his speech impediment	Honor your mother and father — they will be there to support you

Female Servitude… Wait, *What?*

וְכִי־יִמְכֹּר אִישׁ
אֶת־בִּתּוֹ לְאָמָה
לֹא תֵצֵא כְּצֵאת
הָעֲבָדִים:

When a man shall sell his daughter as a maidservant, she shall not leave servitude the way other servants leave servitude.

EXODUS 21:7

Female Servitude…
Wait, *What*?

I WANT TO TACKLE a topic that we don't often talk about: female servitude. The very notion of it seems almost barbaric in our day and age. However, convenient or not, the Torah *does* recognize the institution of servitude. Indeed, slavery was a fact of life in the ancient world; it took thousands of years and the advent of industrialization to finally rid most of the world of this institution. Seemingly, the Torah — written in a time in which slavery was simply a brute economic fact — seeks to make it humane rather than, perhaps futilely, ban it immediately and outright (see especially, Rambam, *Hilchot Avadim* 1:9; see also Kiddushin 21b, and the notion of *lo dibra Torah eleh keneged yetzer hara*).[1]

According to the Torah, in **Parshat Mishpatim,** a father has a right to sell his daughter into servitude. But not just any daughter. He is allowed to sell only his *little* daughter into servitude — any time before she reaches the age of twelve (see Rambam, *Hilchot Avadim* 4:1).

Now when you read that law, at first blush, it strikes you as just awful: *A father selling his little daughter into servitude? How beastly!* What's more,

---

1   It should also be noted that ancient slavery was not the same institution that existed in the last millennium in the Western world. It was a socioeconomic class that people — sometimes voluntarily, out of need — went in and out of.

This essay will focus, in particular, on the narrow issue of female servitude, as described in **Parshat Mishpatim**. As regards the broader issue of slavery, however, consider how the Torah introduces the laws of slavery in the book of Exodus: with, of all things, the law of how slaves *exit* servitude (they are to leave in their seventh year of service or in the Yovel year, whichever comes first [Exodus 21:2]). There are, of course, a lot of other issues one could have begun a discussion of slavery with: the rights of a master toward a servant, for example. The fact that the Torah chooses to begin its discussion of civil law with how slavery *ends* says something about its ultimate regard for the institution.

the whole thing doesn't even seem to make any economic sense. One can imagine an older girl — a teenager, maybe; a young adult — having real economic utility as a servant or a housemaid, but *a seven-year-old*? It just seems astonishingly… irrational. How are we to understand it?

So, I'd like to try something with you. Try to clear your mind about all this. Yes, slavery is a hot-button issue. Yes, we have an understandable revulsion against it, not to mention some skepticism about these verses that speak of this indentured little girl. But let's leave that baggage at the door momentarily while we take some time to actually look carefully at the text. I think if we do, we'll be rewarded for our efforts. We will discover a fascinating picture peeking out at us from just under the surface of the text.

Making Our Way through the Laws

This is how the Torah's discussion of female servitude opens:

Exodus 21:7

וְכִי־יִמְכֹּר אִישׁ
אֶת־בִּתּוֹ לְאָמָה
לֹא תֵצֵא כְּצֵאת
הָעֲבָדִים:

When a man shall sell his daughter as a maidservant, she shall not leave servitude the way other servants leave servitude.

Now what in the world does that puzzling expression mean? What "other servants" is the Torah referring to?[2] Given the context, one would guess: male servants. Which is to say that the verse seems to be asserting that female servants aren't supposed to leave their masters the way a male servant leaves. But the Gemara is puzzled by this, because, in fact, the Talmud shows that a female servant *does* leave exactly how a male servant leaves. For example, a male servant is allowed to serve only for six years; in the seventh year, he has to go free. Well, a female servant *also* has to go free in the seventh year. Likewise, a male servant leaves in Yovel, the Jubilee year that recurs every fifty years. Well, a female servant *also* leaves in the

---

2   The commentators are troubled by this. My interest here is to try to search for the most simple and basic understanding of the verse (cf. Rashi to Exodus 21:7, citing Arachin 29b; cf. Mechilta de-Rabbi Yishmael 21:7:1 and Kiddushin 20a).

Jubilee year.[3] So...in what way does a female servant leave servitude that's any different from other, male servants?

That's one problem. But let's not be daunted; let's move on, and continue reading the text.

The next thing the Torah tells us about the female servant is this:

אִם־רָעָה בְּעֵינֵי אֲדֹנֶיהָ אֲשֶׁר־לֹא [לוֹ] יְעָדָהּ וְהֶפְדָּהּ	If she is undesirable in the eyes of her master, such that he does not marry her during her term of servitude, he is to redeem her.	Exodus 21:8

This puzzling verse is taken by the Talmud (Kiddushin 14b, 16b) to mean that if the girl is so reprehensible in the eyes of her master that he chooses not to marry her, then he, the master, must give the father the opportunity to redeem his daughter at a prorated price. So, for example, if the father sold his daughter into servitude for a total of $6,000 for a full, six-year term, and now there remains only two years left in her term, then the master should allow the father to buy her back for $2,000, rather than the $6,000 for which she was initially sold. That's the opportunity the master is to give her father, should the master not marry her.

But if we stand back and survey the scene, this whole thing seems very puzzling. For the Torah just jumped into this whole idea of marriage in a very jarring way. The reader feels inclined to protest: *We were talking about servitude just a moment ago. Who said anything about marriage?*

But let's quiet that skeptical voice inside of you; we have more verses to read. Let's go on.

Treachery

The Torah goes on to say that, if the master chooses not to marry her,

לְעַם נׇכְרִי לֹא־יִמְשֹׁל לְמׇכְרָהּ בְּבִגְדוֹ־בָהּ׃	to a foreign nation he shall not have the right to sell her, since he dealt treacherously with her.	Exodus 21:8

---

3 See Mishnah Kiddushin 1:2.

Rambam (*Hilchot Avadim* 4:10)[4] interprets that business about a "foreign nation" figuratively. What it actually means, Rambam suggests, is that the master who doesn't marry the servant can't, in rejecting her, sell her to any other person — whether that new master might be from a foreign nation or a fellow Israelite.[5] But pay attention to the Torah's characterization of such a hypothetical sale. The text said: בְּבִגְדוֹ־בָה — he can't do this, *since he dealt treacherously with her.* But what does that mean? It seems rather harsh, wouldn't you say? All told, all that happened is that he bought her as a slave and he didn't up marrying her. Where is the treachery here?

But stay your beating heart; let's move on. Next, the text tells us:

Exodus 21:9

וְאִם־לִבְנוֹ יִיעָדֶנָּה כְּמִשְׁפַּט
הַבָּנוֹת יַעֲשֶׂה־לָּה:

If [the master] marries her off to his son, he has to treat her like a daughter.

And the Torah immediately clarifies this, given the fact that in those days polygamy was allowed:

Exodus 21:10

אִם־אַחֶרֶת יִקַּח־לוֹ שְׁאֵרָהּ
כְּסוּתָהּ וְעֹנָתָהּ לֹא יִגְרָע:

If [later on, the master or his son] decides to take another wife, he must not diminish her food, clothing, or intimate contact with her.

In other words, the master or his son — should they marry this girl — can't, upon taking another wife, in any way diminish the rights of this first wife, the servant girl. Anything to which she's entitled — be it the clothing he would give her, the food, or even the time he spends with her, which is

---

4   Underlying this interpretation is the notion that the word *am* can also, more colloquially, mean "tribe" or "family." See also Onkelos ad loc. and Mechilta de-Rabbi Shimon bar Yochai ad loc.

5   In other words, selling her to anyone would be as reprehensible as selling her to a foreign nation, and should just be avoided (see *HaKtav VehaKabalah* ad loc.).

to say, the moments of intimacy he has with her — he shouldn't dimin-ish any of that.[6]

And finally, we hear:

וְאִם־שְׁלָשׁ־אֵלֶּה לֹא יַעֲשֶׂה לָהּ...	And if the master doesn't do these three things...	Exodus 21:11

The Sages[7] take this to mean that if the master doesn't conform with one of the three general ideas discussed earlier, which is to say: (1) if he doesn't marry her, (2) if he doesn't give her in marriage to his son, or (3) if the father doesn't take the master up on the offer to redeem his daughter at a prorated price, then:

וְיָצְאָה חִנָּם אֵין כָּסֶף:	she shall go free, without having to pay any money.	Exodus 21:11

Again, the Sages add their explanation. They take this to mean that the girl goes free, automatically, when she reaches the age of twelve, even if her full, six-year term of servitude has not yet expired.

What Does It All Mean?

So there they are, the rather arcane laws of the female servant. What a strange list of precepts! It seems at first glance like a patchwork quilt of laws. How are we meant to understand them?

---

6 It is worth noting, parenthetically, that this verse, right here, is the source for a man's obligation in these three basic provisions of marriage: food, clothing, and intimate time together. It seems odd, when you think about it, that these basic ob-ligations of marriage — of any marriage, even between a high-born nobleman and a lady — should come from a verse describing this tangled case of a master marry-ing his servant girl.

7 Mechilta ad loc., summarized by Rambam (*Hilchot Avadim* 4:9).

I would like to suggest a theory to you. Let me preface it by asking you to consider a puzzling economic and social trend that seems to cut across most free-market societies. Why is it that, over time, the wealth gap in a society always seems to widen? Why is it that the rich tend to get richer and the poor tend to get poorer?

The reasons behind that trend aren't immediately apparent. Let's assume that the society is actually just and law-abiding. There is equal opportunity for all. There is a court system that upholds the laws and roots out corruption. So…why do these vast gaps in wealth continue to persist? Why can't the poor just pick themselves up by their bootstraps and get moving? Why do the poor inevitably get poorer? Why do the rich inevitably get richer? And, most of all: How should we, as a society, deal with these persistent realities?

The Roots of the Political Divide

It is here, of course, that the great political fault lines of a society begin to form. How should income inequality be addressed? For the most part, those with a liberal bent will say: *Let's redistribute the wealth. We will tax the rich and give the money to the poor. That will level the playing field.* And those of a conservative mindset will retort: *The playing field is already level. Everybody had equal opportunity. Fair is fair. It is unjust to simply take from the rich and give to the poor.*

Fine. That's how Democrats and Republicans might debate the issue. But long before America's great political divide, we had the Torah. Let's ask: How, if at all, does the Torah deal with this societal issue?

In the peculiar laws of female servitude you and I have been looking at, the Torah tries to address this issue of income inequality — and it does so not by looking at the mere symptoms of the problem, but by going directly to what it sees as one of its root causes. Which takes us back to the question I asked you above: Why is it that, even in a fair and just society, even in a society in which courts successfully enforce the law, still, the rich always seem to get richer and the poor always seem to get poorer?

What Makes Wealth Inequality So Pervasive?

The explanation for wealth disparity the Torah focuses upon lies outside the economic realm entirely. It lies in the social nature of humanity. For a

FEMALE SERVITUDE… WAIT, WHAT?   127

basic social truth animates our social lives: *We make friends with people who are like us.* The rich live among themselves, and they marry among themselves. The poor live among themselves, and they marry among themselves. Everyone socializes in their little corner of the room.

Why is it that people go to Harvard and Yale and Columbia? Sure, part of it is for the education. But you can get a great education online these days, and it's a lot cheaper. One of the prime, less talked-about reasons people go to the Ivy Leagues is for the social bonds, the friends you make. And, as you leave university, friends hire friends, and … *the rich get richer and the poor get poorer.*

In truth, the "old boy network" isn't evil or sinister; it is just the way people work. But still, what is the way out?

I think the Torah has a solution. It's not about redistributing wealth. It is about changing the social construct.

Rereading the Torah's Construct of Female Servitude

Consider this: Under what circumstances would a father resort to such a desperate measure? What would it take for a man to take the girl he raised, this child he loves, and … sell her?[8] Clearly, the Torah speaks of a man with his financial back to the wall. A man who is destitute. In desperation, he asks himself: *How can my daughter possibly have a better life?*

To get a little more granular about his thoughts: *Who is my daughter going to marry? We're poor. I have no money for a dowry, no money for anything.*

So the Torah gives him a chance. It creates a fiction called "female servitude"—an institution that, in fact, has little to do with servitude at all. The Torah gives a father the right to "sell his daughter" into service. *But to whom?* To the head of a well-off household that his father knows and trusts. In short, the father selects a family that he would want his daughter to marry into. And, when he does, she enters that household.

So you protest: *She's but a child; what can she actually do?* The answer: Not much, but that's not the point. She'll do light household work; she'll help set the table. The point is that she will grow up with them. They will get to know her from childhood. And, over time, as they get to know her

---

8   Indeed, Rambam (on Tosefta Arachin 5:7) writes that such extreme hardship is the only circumstance under which the father is ethically permitted to indenture his daughter (*Hilchot Avadim* 4:2).

and build trust with her — there is every expectation that they will take her in. Eventually, the master of the house will find someone in the household to marry her.

It is an unspoken social contract between these two men — a father, and a hoped-for benefactor.

How She Leaves

When a destitute father does this thing of last resort, when he sells his daughter into servitude,

Exodus 21:7	לֹא תֵצֵא כְּצֵאת הָעֲבָדִים:	she shall not leave servitude the way male slaves leave servitude.

In other words, she will leave in an entirely *new* way, in a way that's not open to male slaves: She will leave through marriage.[9] When a strong, able-bodied man enters slavery the arrangement is about work; it is about economics. When this little girl enters servitude, it's not about economics at all. It is about a hope, a hope that this girl will marry into a family she and her parents would never have anything else to do with. She will, in the end, become an equal of the nobility, in that she will eventually marry into their household.

The Torah continues:

Exodus 21:8	אִם־רָעָה בְּעֵינֵי אֲדֹנֶיהָ אֲשֶׁר־לֹא [לוֹ] יְעָדָהּ וְהֶפְדָּהּ	If she is undesirable in the eyes of her master, such that he does not marry her during her term of servitude, he is to redeem her.

---

9   Indeed, the Torah decrees that for the manservant, marriage during his term of service is, in essence, an obstacle to freedom. If he marries a Canaanite maidservant during his term of service, he might be put into a position where, come the expiration of his six-year term, he will not wish to go free, electing to stay in service so as not to break up his family life (see Ex. 21:1–6). In contrast to this, the Israelite girl who enters service as a child doesn't go out like he goes out. For her, marriage during her term of service isn't an obstacle; it is itself a way out of servitude. She has the option to marry into a family of means, and thereby to exit a life of poverty entirely.

Of course, the family into which she enters can't know for *sure* it will work out before she lives with them for a while. But on the other hand, they wouldn't have agreed to the initial arrangement unless everyone involved suspected there was a good shot at things actually working out. So... if things *don't* work out, meaning, as the Torah puts it, if she is *so* undesirable in the eyes of her master that he rejects her as a candidate for marriage — not for him, not for his sons, not for *anyone* in the household — well, should that be the case, then he has to at least give the father a chance to buy her back at a prorated price. The Torah sees no purpose in allowing her to continue to serve in the house once it becomes clear she is not going to marry into the household.

The Torah goes on, telling us that if the master decides against marriage,

לֹא־יִמְשֹׁל לְמָכְרָהּ בְּבִגְדוֹ־בָהּ׃   he shall not have the right to sell her [to outsiders], since he dealt treacherously with her.   Exodus 21:8

In other words, if the master *doesn't* marry her, and he *doesn't* marry her off to his son, and if the father isn't in a financial position to buy her back, then the master shouldn't think to himself that, having paid for her services, he has the right to sell her to someone else. He absolutely does *not* have that power. As the Torah says:

בְּבִגְדוֹ־בָהּ   he dealt treacherously with her.   Exodus 21:8

The master, in a way, broke faith with the girl's family. Yes, he's legally entitled not to marry her. But her father meant for her to join the master's family. If, for whatever reason, he or his son doesn't marry her, it would be the height of treachery to treat her like property and simply pass her off to someone else — to someone her own father had not selected for her to live with.

Erasing Servitude

The Torah continues, letting us know that if the master's son *does* marry her:

Exodus 21:9

כְּמִשְׁפַּט הַבָּנוֹת
יַעֲשֶׂה־לָּהּ:

Like a daughter shall [the master] treat her.

She is not a servant anymore: *She is your daughter-in-law. She is an equal.*

It is here that the Torah becomes explicit with its bold attempt in social engineering. Indeed, all this is a risky experiment. Especially in a world that still allows polygamy, it could all, potentially, go disastrously awry. For what if the master or son says to himself, *Sure, I'll marry this girl. I'll do it out of pity. She will be my little "servant-girl wife." But since I have the right to take more than one wife — and I can afford it, too — I'll also make sure to marry someone else as well, who is more my social equal. I'll marry my "movie-star wife," too.*

The Torah anticipates the problem:

Exodus 21:10

אִם־אַחֶרֶת
יִקַּח־לוֹ

If [later on, the master or his son] decides to take another wife

He dare not diminish the rights of his first wife. He may never treat her in any way inferior to his new wife. Instead,

Exodus 21:10

שְׁאֵרָהּ כְּסוּתָהּ וְעֹנָתָהּ לֹא
יִגְרָע:

he must not diminish her food, clothing, or intimate contact with her.

She must be treated as an equal. The Torah guards her rights.

The Magic of Retroactive Change

The Gemara (Kiddushin 19a) elaborates the general principle behind all these laws by letting us in on a fascinating legal truth. Normally, marriage is effectuated between a man and a woman when he gives her something of value, like a ring. The Gemara states, though, that in the above set of laws, when a master or his son ends up marrying this servant girl, he doesn't actually give her anything to effectuate the marriage. Why? The Gemara explains: It is because the original money that the master gave the father, *that*, retroactively, serves as the ring. It is the money for marriage.[10]

The Torah is saying, in effect, to the future husband of this girl: Once you choose to marry her, her status will have changed retroactively. Now, marriage is the only thing you must see; the servitude was but a mirage. Looking back, she was *never* your servant girl; this whole time, she was always your equal. Never look back and see her as having been anything else.

Beyond Band-Aids

The Torah, in this set of laws, is not attempting a mere Band-Aid solution to the problem of class. It is not trying to redistribute wealth in an after-the-fact attempt to put a thumb on the scales of economic advantage. And, on the other hand, it is not turning a blind eye to the problem, insisting that the playing field was equal, and that we don't therefore need to worry too much about the homeless in the streets. The Torah instead is going to the heart of the matter: It is addressing why, and in what sense, the playing field wasn't quite equal. *We are social creatures, and for good or for ill, we help those who are closest to us.* That doesn't make us bad, and it is not something we should hide from. But it is something that we can tinker around the edges with, and the Torah is doing just that. The Torah is trying to attack the issue of wealth inequality in a way that is both just and compassionate, in a way in which everyone wins. With no small measure of irony, the Torah is trying to use slavery, the most unequal institution on earth, to achieve the rarified goal of equality.

---

10 See Kiddushin 19a, *Ma'ot harishonot lekiddushin nitnu*, "The original money [from the sale of the maidservant] was given for [the purpose of] betrothal."

Finding Shelter in a World Not Your Own

וְצִפִּיתָ אתוֹ זָהָב טָהוֹר
מִבַּיִת וּמִחוּץ תְּצַפֶּנּוּ

You shall overlay it with pure gold,
inside and outside you shall overlay it.

EXODUS 25:11

Finding Shelter in a World Not Your Own

PARSHAT TERUMAH AND PORTIONS of **Parshat Tetzaveh** tell of how the *Mishkan*, the Tabernacle, was meant to be built. For the modern reader, those instructions can sometimes seem arcane and hard to follow. But deep in those blueprints something mysterious is afoot. In the pages that follow, I want to work with you to unearth a hidden pattern that lurks just beneath the surface of the text. If we can succeed in excavating it, we'll then try our hand at pondering what it might mean.

Inside, Outside

A good way to begin to see the pattern is to look at the way the Torah describes the construction of the Ark of the Covenant. The Ark, of course, is the holiest of the *Mishkan's* various utensils. It is where the tablets inscribed with the Ten Commandments were kept.

The Torah tells us that although the core of the Ark was supposed to be wood, both its interior and exterior were to be overlaid with gold:

וְצִפִּיתָ אֹתוֹ זָהָב טָהוֹר מִבַּיִת וּמִחוּץ תְּצַפֶּנּוּ

You shall overlay it with pure gold, inside and outside you shall overlay it.

Exodus 25:11

So now let's play a little game together: *Does that remind you of anything, anywhere else in the Torah?* Is there another structure that the Torah ordains shall be built in a similar way? A structure that, like the Ark, must be built out of wood, but then must be overlaid, inside and outside, with some other substance?

What is that other mystery structure?

As it turns out, it is another ark, at least in a manner of speaking: *Noah's* ark.[1]

God's Ark and Noah's Ark

Here is how the construction of Noah's ark was described in the book of Genesis:

עֲשֵׂה לְךָ תֵּבַת עֲצֵי־גֹפֶר קִנִּים
תַּעֲשֶׂה אֶת־הַתֵּבָה וְכָפַרְתָּ
אֹתָהּ מִבַּיִת וּמִחוּץ בַּכֹּפֶר:

Make yourself an ark of gopher wood; make it an ark with compartments, and cover it **inside and out with pitch**.

So Noah's big boat, like the Ark of the Covenant, was made of wood, and overlaid inside and outside with another substance. Moreover, the Hebrew words for the double overlay are precisely identical in both cases. Regarding both the Ark of the Covenant and Noah's lifesaving boat, the Torah states that the wood should be covered מִבַּיִת וּמִחוּץ, *inside and outside.*

Now of course, the substance used for the overlay was not identical by any means. It was pitch in the case of Noah, and gold in the case of the *Mishkan*. But, intriguingly, even though pitch and gold aren't the same in any way, they're not *unrelated* substances, like, say, apples and Cadillacs. Pitch and gold are actually *mirror images* of one another. Gold is bright, shiny, and reflects light. Pitch is dark, and it absorbs light. Gold is smooth and odorless; pitch is sticky and pungent. Gold is precious; pitch is almost worthless.

All told, an interesting set of correlations. And yet, if this were all, one not might make anything of it. Sure, the Ark of the Covenant and Noah's

---

1   In Hebrew, Noah's boat was known as a *teivah*, and the box that housed the Ten Commandments was known as an *aron*. Coincidentally, it just so happens that in English, the same word, "ark," denotes both structures: Noah's ark and God's Ark. For the balance of this discussion, I will refer to both of these structures as arks, playing somewhat whimsically on this coincidental feature of English translation. My arguments for the similarity between these structures, however, go far beyond the happenstance of English translation, as you will see later in this essay.

boat happen to be constructed in certain ways that are similar, and in certain ways that are diametrically different, but that could just be coincidental.

What would make you believe this correlation *wasn't* coincidental? Well, you'd have to see more. Is there more to these textual connections between the Ark and Noah's boat, or is that it?

As it happens, there's more.

Kofer

Let's look again at the verse which describes the pitch that covered Noah's ark. It states:

וְכָפַרְתָּ אֹתָהּ מִבַּיִת וּמִחוּץ
בַּכֹּפֶר׃

And you shall cover it, inside and outside, with pitch.

Genesis 6:14

Now, that word for "cover it," *vechafarta*, is spelled *kaf, peh, resh, tav* in Hebrew. Intriguingly, that exact sequence of letters — *kaf, peh, resh, tav,* in that same order — appears with reference to only one other item in the entire Torah. Where? You guessed it: with an article that was a component of God's Ark.

Yes, that's right: *kaf, peh, resh, tav* was, in Noah's case, a verb meaning "to cover." When it appears a second time, in connection to the *Mishkan,* it is a noun — כַּפֹּרֶת, *kaporet* — meaning "covering." *Kaporet* is the word the Torah coins to denote the solid gold covering that would be laid on top of the Ark in the Tabernacle (Exodus 25:19).

The Pattern

Tallying this up so far, we've got:

- Two wooden boxes
- *Mibayit umichutz* (inside and outside)
- Overlays that are exact opposites of one another
- *Kaporet, vechafarta*

The connections are starting to add up. But actually, there are even more of them — and I believe that, as one lays them out, they begin to form a pattern: A chiasm, or what we might call an ATBASH structure. I introduced these kinds of structures in the Genesis volume of this series. Just to refresh your memory, a chiasm is a literary structure that looks a bit like an arrow. The first element in a given section of text mirrors the last; the second element mirrors the second-to-last one; the third mirrors the third-to-last element, and so on, until one reaches the center of the structure:[2]

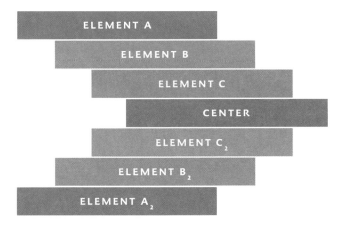

And, that's exactly, I think, what we have in these two pieces of text: a kind of chiasm spanning two texts that appear far apart, one in Genesis, the other in Exodus, the two texts that describe Noah's ark on the one hand, and the Ark of the Covenant on the other.

Let's see how this ATBASH structure starts to emerge. Start at the point I mentioned to you above: The fact that both Noah's ark and God's Ark needed to be covered, inside and out (מבית ומחוץ) with another substance:

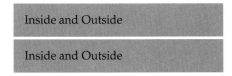

---

2   A chiasm can also be called an ATBASH pattern — *alef*, the first letter of the Hebrew alphabet, mirrors *tav*, the last letter; *bet* mirrors *shin*, and so on.

And now, let's explore the nearby text to see what else we find. Open a copy of Genesis, and flip over to chapter 6, verse 14, locate the מבית ומחוץ description that's given there of Noah's ark, and put a bookmark there. Then, open up a copy of Exodus, go to chapter 25, verse 11, find the מבית ומחוץ description of the Ark of the Covenant, and put another bookmark there. Now here's the tricky part: Start reading from each bookmark, in *opposite* directions — that is, working *backward* from the verse in Genesis and working *forward* from the verse in Exodus — and look for elements that pair up with one another. Yes, I know that sounds odd, but trust me, that's how you go about detecting a chiasm.[3]

If you don't happen to have a copy of Genesis and Exodus handy, don't worry. Just follow along with me here, and I'll lay it out for you.

Reading Backward, Reading Forward

So here we are in Exodus, chapter 25. We're right at those words *mibayit umichutz*, and you'll notice that shortly after this, we start reading about that cover for the Ark that we mentioned above: the כפרת, spelled *kaf, peh, resh, tav*:

Exodus 25:11, 17

וְצִפִּיתָ אֹתוֹ זָהָב טָהוֹר
מִבַּיִת וּמִחוּץ תְּצַפֶּנּוּ וְעָשִׂיתָ
עָלָיו זֵר זָהָב סָבִיב: ...
וְעָשִׂיתָ כַפֹּרֶת זָהָב טָהוֹר
אַמָּתַיִם וָחֵצִי אָרְכָּהּ וְאַמָּה
וָחֵצִי רָחְבָּהּ:

Overlay it with pure gold — overlay it **inside and out** — and make upon it a gold molding round about... You shall make **a cover** of pure gold, two and a half cubits long and a cubit and a half wide.

Now, as we mentioned before, the only other time in the Torah we find a word spelled exactly like that is back in the Noah story — but *where*, exactly, in the Noah story? Turns out it appears right *before* the words *mibayit umichutz* as describing Noah's ark:

---

3   A chiasm, remember, is a series of inverted literary pairs: ABCD in one text, pairs up with DCBA in the other. To see the paired elements in a text you suspect is a chiasm, it sometimes helps to start with the elements of a single pair, and to begin reading one text forward and the other backward.

Genesis 6:14   וְכָפַרְתָּ אֹתָהּ מִבַּיִת וּמִחוּץ   And you should **cover** it **inside and out**
בַּכֹּפֶר: with pitch.

So these are the first two elements in our pattern; together, they form a mirror image of sorts:

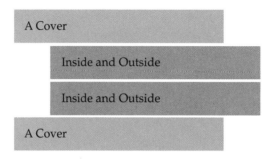

And of course, we haven't really proven the existence of any larger pattern quite yet. Because if we had only these two elements, we still might well chalk it all up to coincidence. To know for sure that we've got an honest-to-goodness chiasm on our hands, we'd have to see more.

So... *is* there more?

Well, I'm glad you asked. Let's continue reading Exodus and Genesis in opposite directions, and see what we find.

The Third Connection between the Arks

Let's pick up the thread on the Exodus side of the pattern. Just after the mention of the *kaporet* in Exodus (25:17), the text begins to speak of two angels known as cherubim. The text tells us they are to be fashioned out of gold, rising from the edges of the *kaporet*:

Exodus 25:19   וַעֲשֵׂה כְּרוּב אֶחָד מִקָּצָה   You should make a cherub from the gold
מִזֶּה וּכְרוּב־אֶחָד מִקָּצָה   of one edge, and another cherub from
מִזֶּה   the gold of the other edge.

Moreover, we are told that these cherubim are supposed to be *facing* one another. In the words of the text:

וּפְנֵיהֶם אִישׁ אֶל־ אָחִיו	The face of each should be toward the other.	Exodus 25:20

So to summarize, there's this mention of edges and faces in connection with these cherubim. Now, keeping that in mind, page over to Genesis, and take a look at the corresponding text there. When you do, you'll find a remarkable echo. For it turns out that right *before* the command *vechafarta,* to cover the ark with pitch, God used the following language to tell Noah that the end of humanity was near:

וַיֹּאמֶר אֱלֹהִים לְנֹחַ קֵץ כָּל־בָּשָׂר בָּא לְפָנַי כִּי־מָלְאָה הָאָרֶץ חָמָס מִפְּנֵיהֶם	And God said to Noah: The end [literally, **the edge**] of all flesh has come before Me, because the world is filled with corruption on their account [literally, **from their faces**].	Genesis 6:13

So there you have it: edge paired with faces once again. In Hebrew, the sense that God conveys to Noah is that humanity has reached "the edge," so to speak, of its time in this world; it is about to fall off that edge, as it were, into ruin.

All told, we now have three elements: (1) *mibayit umichutz* with each ark, (2) *kofer* with each ark, and (3) "edges" and "faces" with each ark. To see clearly how they are laid out in connection with one another, let's represent each with a different color:

GENESIS	וַיֹּאמֶר אֱלֹהִים לְנֹחַ קֵץ כָּל־בָּשָׂר בָּא לְפָנַי כִּי־מָלְאָה הָאָרֶץ חָמָס מִפְּנֵיהֶם וְהִנְנִי מַשְׁחִיתָם אֶת־הָאָרֶץ: עֲשֵׂה לְךָ תֵּבַת עֲצֵי־גֹפֶר קִנִּים תַּעֲשֶׂה אֶת־הַתֵּבָה וְכָפַרְתָּ אֹתָהּ מִבַּיִת וּמִחוּץ בַּכֹּפֶר:	And God said to Noah, "The end [edge] of all flesh has come before Me, because the world is filled with corruption on their account [from their faces]: I am about to destroy them with the earth. Make yourself an ark of gopher wood; make it an ark with compartments, and cover it inside and out with pitch. (Gen. 6:13–14)

Exodus

וְצִפִּיתָ אֹתוֹ זָהָב טָהוֹר
מִבַּיִת וּמִחוּץ תְּצַפֶּנּוּ
וְעָשִׂיתָ עָלָיו זֵר זָהָב סָבִיב:
וְיָצַקְתָּ לּוֹ אַרְבַּע טַבְּעֹת זָהָב
וְנָתַתָּה עַל אַרְבַּע פַּעֲמֹתָיו
וּשְׁתֵּי טַבָּעֹת עַל־צַלְעוֹ
הָאֶחָת וּשְׁתֵּי טַבָּעֹת עַל־
צַלְעוֹ הַשֵּׁנִית: וְעָשִׂיתָ בַדֵּי
עֲצֵי שִׁטִּים וְצִפִּיתָ אֹתָם
זָהָב: וְהֵבֵאתָ אֶת־הַבַּדִּים
בַּטַּבָּעֹת עַל צַלְעֹת הָאָרֹן
לָשֵׂאת אֶת־הָאָרֹן בָּהֶם:
בְּטַבְּעֹת הָאָרֹן יִהְיוּ הַבַּדִּים
לֹא יָסֻרוּ מִמֶּנּוּ: וְנָתַתָּ אֶל־
הָאָרֹן אֵת הָעֵדֻת אֲשֶׁר
אֶתֵּן אֵלֶיךָ: וְעָשִׂיתָ כַפֹּרֶת
זָהָב טָהוֹר אַמָּתַיִם וָחֵצִי
אָרְכָּהּ וְאַמָּה וָחֵצִי רָחְבָּהּ:
וְעָשִׂיתָ שְׁנַיִם כְּרֻבִים זָהָב
מִקְשָׁה תַּעֲשֶׂה אֹתָם מִשְּׁנֵי
קְצוֹת הַכַּפֹּרֶת: וַעֲשֵׂה
כְּרוּב אֶחָד מִקָּצָה מִזֶּה
וּכְרוּב־אֶחָד מִקָּצָה מִזֶּה
מִן־הַכַּפֹּרֶת תַּעֲשׂוּ אֶת־
הַכְּרֻבִים עַל־שְׁנֵי קְצוֹתָיו:
וְהָיוּ הַכְּרֻבִים פֹּרְשֵׂי כְנָפַיִם
לְמַעְלָה סֹכְכִים בְּכַנְפֵיהֶם
עַל־הַכַּפֹּרֶת וּפְנֵיהֶם אִישׁ
אֶל־אָחִיו אֶל־הַכַּפֹּרֶת יִהְיוּ
פְּנֵי הַכְּרֻבִים.

Overlay it with pure gold — overlay it inside and out — and make upon it a gold molding round about. Cast four gold rings for it, to be attached to its four feet, two rings on one of its side walls and two on the other. Make poles of acacia wood and overlay them with gold; then insert the poles into the rings on the side walls of the ark, for carrying the ark. The poles shall remain in the rings of the ark: they shall not be removed from it. And deposit in the Ark [the tablets of] the Pact which I will give you. You shall make a cover of pure gold, two and a half cubits long and a cubit and a half wide. Make two cherubim of gold — make them of hammered work — at the two ends of the cover. You should make a cherub from the gold of one edge, and another cherub from the gold of the other edge. Of one piece with the cover shall you make the cherubim at its two ends. The cherubim shall have their wings spread out above, shielding the cover with their wings. The face of each should be toward the other, the faces of the cherubim being turned toward the cover. (Ex. 25:11–20)

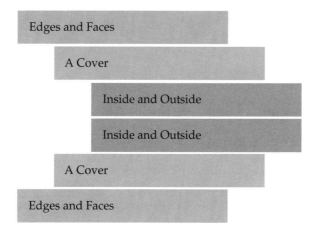

Edges and Faces

A Cover

Inside and Outside

Inside and Outside

A Cover

Edges and Faces

Dimensions

Now, as far as I can tell, that's as far *outward* as the chiasm extends. But I do think it extends farther *inward* than we've yet seen.[4] To see how, let's return to the initial pair we started with — the words *mibayit umichutz* in both Exodus and Genesis — and let's start moving *inward* from there.

First, let's look at Exodus.

Returning to *mibayit umichutz* in the Torah's discussion of the Ark's overlay, let's ask: What happens right before this? The text in Exodus that immediately precedes this speaks of the Ark's dimensions. Specifically, the Torah tells us about the length, width, and height of the Ark of the Covenant:

וְעָשׂוּ אֲרוֹן...אַמָּתַיִם וָחֵצִי אָרְכּוֹ וְאַמָּה וָחֵצִי רָחְבּוֹ וְאַמָּה וָחֵצִי קֹמָתוֹ:	You should make the Ark...two and a half cubits long, a cubit and a half wide, and a cubit and a half tall.	Exodus 25:10

Now, go to the corresponding text in Genesis, and let's see what we find right after *mibayit umichutz*. Fascinatingly, as if on cue (given the chiastic structure) — we find ourselves reading about the length, width, and height of Noah's ark:

---

4   By "inward," I mean that if we look at later points in Genesis, and earlier points in Exodus, we will find further correspondences, adding more pairs to the chiastic structure we've seen thus far.

Genesis 6:15   שְׁלֹשׁ מֵאוֹת אַמָּה אֹרֶךְ הַתֵּבָה
חֲמִשִּׁים אַמָּה רָחְבָּהּ וּשְׁלֹשִׁים
אַמָּה קוֹמָתָהּ׃

Three hundred cubits long, fifty cubits wide, and thirty cubits tall

So there we have it: Edges and faces. *Kofer. Mibayit umichutz.* And now, add to that … dimensions. The length, width, and height dimensions — in that same order — for each ark.

Here, then, are all four pairs that we've seen thus far:

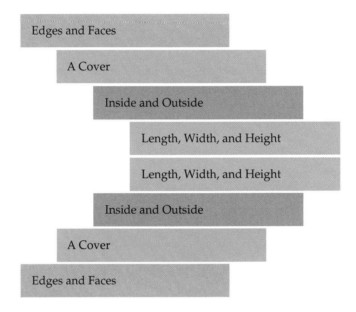

Edges and Faces

A Cover

Inside and Outside

Length, Width, and Height

Length, Width, and Height

Inside and Outside

A Cover

Edges and Faces

Clarity

And now, let's move inward one more step, and we will find a fifth matching pair: a pair comprised not of words, but of a common idea. To find it, keep reading — advancing *forward* in Genesis, and regressing *backward* in Exodus — and as you do, keep your eye out for the following idea: *That which makes the shape of things clear.*

Here are the two sets of text. Can you find the common element?

GENESIS

וַיֹּאמֶר אֱלֹהִים לְנֹחַ קֵץ כָּל־
בָּשָׂר בָּא לְפָנַי כִּי־מָלְאָה
הָאָרֶץ חָמָס מִפְּנֵיהֶם וְהִנְנִי
מַשְׁחִיתָם אֶת־הָאָרֶץ:
עֲשֵׂה לְךָ תֵּבַת עֲצֵי־גֹפֶר
קִנִּים תַּעֲשֶׂה אֶת־הַתֵּבָה
וְכָפַרְתָּ אֹתָהּ מִבַּיִת וּמִחוּץ
בַּכֹּפֶר: וְזֶה אֲשֶׁר תַּעֲשֶׂה
אֹתָהּ שְׁלֹשׁ מֵאוֹת אַמָּה
אֹרֶךְ הַתֵּבָה חֲמִשִּׁים אַמָּה
רָחְבָּהּ וּשְׁלֹשִׁים אַמָּה
קוֹמָתָהּ: **צֹהַר תַּעֲשֶׂה**
לַתֵּבָה וְאֶל־אַמָּה תְּכַלֶּנָּה
מִלְמַעְלָה וּפֶתַח הַתֵּבָה
בְּצִדָּהּ תָּשִׂים תַּחְתִּיִּם שְׁנִיִּם
וּשְׁלִשִׁים תַּעֲשֶׂהָ:

And God said to Noah, "The end [edge] of all flesh has come before Me, because the world is filled with corruption on their account [from their faces]: I am about to destroy them with the earth. Make yourself an ark of gopher wood; make it an ark with compartments, and cover it inside and out with pitch. This is how you shall make it: the length of the ark shall be three hundred cubits, its width fifty cubits, and its height thirty cubits. **A window you shall make for the ark, and terminate it within a cubit of the top. Put the entrance to the ark in its side; make it with bottom, second, and third decks."** (Gen. 6:13–16)

EXODUS

כְּכֹל אֲשֶׁר אֲנִי מַרְאֶה
אוֹתְךָ אֵת תַּבְנִית הַמִּשְׁכָּן
וְאֵת תַּבְנִית כָּל־כֵּלָיו וְכֵן
תַּעֲשׂוּ: וְעָשׂוּ אֲרוֹן עֲצֵי
שִׁטִּים אַמָּתַיִם וָחֵצִי אָרְכּוֹ
וְאַמָּה וָחֵצִי רָחְבּוֹ וְאַמָּה
וָחֵצִי קֹמָתוֹ: וְצִפִּיתָ אֹתוֹ
זָהָב טָהוֹר מִבַּיִת וּמִחוּץ
תְּצַפֶּנּוּ וְעָשִׂיתָ עָלָיו זֵר
זָהָב סָבִיב: וְיָצַקְתָּ לּוֹ
אַרְבַּע טַבְּעֹת זָהָב וְנָתַתָּה
עַל אַרְבַּע פַּעֲמֹתָיו וּשְׁתֵּי
טַבָּעֹת עַל־צַלְעוֹ הָאֶחָת
וּשְׁתֵּי טַבָּעֹת עַל־צַלְעוֹ
הַשֵּׁנִית: וְעָשִׂיתָ בַדֵּי
עֲצֵי שִׁטִּים וְצִפִּיתָ אֹתָם
זָהָב: וְהֵבֵאתָ אֶת־הַבַּדִּים
בַּטַּבָּעֹת עַל צַלְעֹת הָאָרֹן

Just as I, God, show you the pattern of the Tabernacle and the pattern of all its furnishings—so shall you make it. They shall make an ark of acacia wood, two and a half cubits long, a cubit and a half wide, and a cubit and a half high Overlay it with pure gold—overlay it inside and out—and make upon it a gold molding round about. Cast four gold rings for it, to be attached to its four feet, two rings on one of its side walls and two on the other. Make poles of acacia wood and overlay them with gold; then insert the poles into the rings on the side walls of the ark, for carrying the ark. The poles shall remain in the rings of the ark: they

EXODUS
CONT.

לָשֵׂאת אֶת־הָאָרֹן בָּהֶם. טו
בְּטַבְּעֹת הָאָרֹן יִהְיוּ הַבַּדִּים
לֹא יָסֻרוּ מִמֶּנּוּ: וְנָתַתָּ אֶל־
הָאָרֹן אֵת הָעֵדֻת אֲשֶׁר
אֶתֵּן אֵלֶיךָ: וְעָשִׂיתָ כַפֹּרֶת
זָהָב טָהוֹר אַמָּתַיִם וָחֵצִי
אָרְכָּהּ וְאַמָּה וָחֵצִי רָחְבָּהּ:
וְעָשִׂיתָ שְׁנַיִם כְּרֻבִים זָהָב
מִקְשָׁה תַּעֲשֶׂה אֹתָם מִשְּׁנֵי
קְצוֹת הַכַּפֹּרֶת: וַעֲשֵׂה
כְּרוּב־אֶחָד מִקָּצָה מִזֶּה
וּכְרוּב־אֶחָד מִקָּצָה מִזֶּה
מִן־הַכַּפֹּרֶת תַּעֲשׂוּ אֶת־
הַכְּרֻבִים עַל־שְׁנֵי קְצוֹתָיו:
וְהָיוּ הַכְּרֻבִים פֹּרְשֵׂי כְנָפַיִם
לְמַעְלָה סֹכְכִים בְּכַנְפֵיהֶם
עַל־הַכַּפֹּרֶת וּפְנֵיהֶם אִישׁ
אֶל־אָחִיו אֶל־הַכַּפֹּרֶת יִהְיוּ
פְּנֵי הַכְּרֻבִים:

shall not be removed from it. And deposit in the Ark [the tablets of] the Pact which I will give you. You shall make a cover of pure gold, two and a half cubits long and a cubit and a half wide. Make two cherubim of gold — make them of hammered work — at the two ends of the cover. You should make a cherub from the gold of one edge, and another cherub from the gold of the other edge. Of one piece with the cover shall you make the cherubim at its two ends. The cherubim shall have their wings spread out above, shielding the cover with their wings. The face of each should be toward the other, the faces of the cherubim being turned toward the cover. (Ex. 25:9–20)

In Exodus, right before discussing the Ark's dimensions, the text tells us that we must build all the utensils in the Tabernacle…

Exodus 25:9   כְּכֹל אֲשֶׁר אֲנִי מַרְאֶה אוֹתְךָ   just as I, God, show you

And now, turn to our Genesis section of text. There, right *after* the discussion of dimensions, we hear, of all things, about a *window*:

Genesis 6:16   צֹהַר תַּעֲשֶׂה לַתֵּבָה   A window[5] shall you make for the ark

---

5   I've translated *tzohar* here as "window." There is a debate, though, among the Sages as to whether it was in fact a window or another source of light. According to some, it was a gemstone that would miraculously light up during the day and become dim at night, thus replacing the natural light of the sun (see Bereishit Rabbah 31:11).

Without any windows, during the storm raging outside, the ark would be dark inside. Those inside the ark would be unable to see anything. The function of the window was to let at least some light stream in from the outside, illuminating the shape and boundaries of things inside the ark.[6]

So, if we compare and contrast the two texts, we get this: In Noah's case, the shape of things inside a building was made clear to its inhabitants through a window. And in the case of the *Mishkan*, the shape of things inside a building was made clear to its builders, inasmuch as God showed those who were to build it what everything was to look like.[7] That conceptual similarity — *how you know what everything looks like* — becomes the fifth element in our emerging chiasm:

---

6   See previous footnote. According to some commentators, the *tzohar* was a shining gemstone that could light up the ark from the inside. Presumably, these interpreters would assert that during a dark storm a window could hardly be counted upon to bring sufficient light into the ark on its own.

7   What does it mean for God to "show you" what the implements of the Tabernacle looked like? Rashbam suggests it means that in addition to the written descriptions transmitted to Moses and written down in the Torah, God also showed Moses pictorially what the implements were to look like (see also *Ibn Ezra*). Rashi, however, seems to imply that the text is instead referring to the written instructions for construction.

GENESIS

וַיֹּאמֶר אֱלֹהִים לְנֹחַ קֵץ כָּל־
בָּשָׂר בָּא לְפָנַי כִּי־מָלְאָה
הָאָרֶץ חָמָס מִפְּנֵיהֶם וְהִנְנִי
מַשְׁחִיתָם אֶת־הָאָרֶץ: עֲשֵׂה
לְךָ תֵּבַת עֲצֵי־גֹפֶר קִנִּים
תַּעֲשֶׂה אֶת־הַתֵּבָה וְכָפַרְתָּ
אֹתָהּ מִבַּיִת וּמִחוּץ בַּכֹּפֶר:
וְזֶה אֲשֶׁר תַּעֲשֶׂה אֹתָהּ
שְׁלֹשׁ מֵאוֹת אַמָּה אֹרֶךְ
הַתֵּבָה חֲמִשִּׁים אַמָּה רָחְבָּהּ
וּשְׁלֹשִׁים אַמָּה קוֹמָתָהּ:
צֹהַר תַּעֲשֶׂה לַתֵּבָה וְאֶל־
אַמָּה תְּכַלֶּנָּה מִלְמַעְלָה
וּפֶתַח הַתֵּבָה בְּצִדָּהּ תָּשִׂים
תַּחְתִּיִּם שְׁנִיִּם וּשְׁלִשִׁים
תַּעֲשֶׂהָ:

And God said to Noah, "The end [edge] of all flesh has come before Me, because the world is filled with corruption on their account [from their faces]: I am about to destroy them with the earth. Make yourself an ark of gopher wood; make it an ark with compartments, and cover it inside and out with pitch. This is how you shall make it: the length of the ark shall be three hundred cubits, its width fifty cubits, and its height thirty cubits. A window you shall make for the ark, and terminate it within a cubit of the top. Put the entrance to the ark in its side; make it with bottom, second, and third decks. (Gen. 6:13–16)

EXODUS

כְּכֹל אֲשֶׁר אֲנִי מַרְאֶה
אוֹתְךָ אֵת תַּבְנִית הַמִּשְׁכָּן
וְאֵת תַּבְנִית כָּל־כֵּלָיו וְכֵן
תַּעֲשׂוּ: וְעָשׂוּ אֲרוֹן עֲצֵי
שִׁטִּים אַמָּתַיִם וָחֵצִי אָרְכּוֹ
וְאַמָּה וָחֵצִי רָחְבּוֹ וְאַמָּה
וָחֵצִי קֹמָתוֹ: וְצִפִּיתָ אֹתוֹ
זָהָב טָהוֹר מִבַּיִת וּמִחוּץ
תְּצַפֶּנּוּ וְעָשִׂיתָ עָלָיו זֵר
זָהָב סָבִיב: וְיָצַקְתָּ לּוֹ
אַרְבַּע טַבְּעֹת זָהָב וְנָתַתָּה
עַל אַרְבַּע פַּעֲמֹתָיו וּשְׁתֵּי
טַבָּעֹת עַל־צַלְעוֹ הָאֶחָת
וּשְׁתֵּי טַבָּעֹת עַל־צַלְעוֹ
הַשֵּׁנִית: וְעָשִׂיתָ בַדֵּי
עֲצֵי שִׁטִּים וְצִפִּיתָ אֹתָם
זָהָב: וְהֵבֵאתָ אֶת־הַבַּדִּים
בַּטַּבָּעֹת עַל צַלְעֹת הָאָרֹן
לָשֵׂאת אֶת־הָאָרֹן בָּהֶם.
בְּטַבְּעֹת הָאָרֹן יִהְיוּ הַבַּדִּים

Just as I, God, show you the pattern of the Tabernacle and the pattern of all its furnishings—so shall you make it. They shall make an ark of acacia wood, two and a half cubits long, a cubit and a half wide, and a cubit and a half high Overlay it with pure gold—overlay it inside and out—and make upon it a gold molding round about. Cast four gold rings for it, to be attached to its four feet, two rings on one of its side walls and two on the other. Make poles of acacia wood and overlay them with gold; then insert the poles into the rings on the side walls of the ark, for carrying the ark. The poles shall remain in the rings of the ark: they shall not be removed from it. And deposit in the Ark [the tablets of] the Pact which I will give you. You

EXODUS
CONT.

לֹא יָסֻרוּ מִמֶּנּוּ: וְנָתַתָּ אֶל־
הָאָרֹן אֵת הָעֵדֻת אֲשֶׁר
אֶתֵּן אֵלֶיךָ: וְעָשִׂיתָ כַפֹּרֶת
זָהָב טָהוֹר אַמָּתַיִם וָחֵצִי
אָרְכָּהּ וְאַמָּה וָחֵצִי רָחְבָּהּ:
וְעָשִׂיתָ שְׁנַיִם כְּרֻבִים זָהָב
מִקְשָׁה תַּעֲשֶׂה אֹתָם מִשְּׁנֵי
קְצוֹת הַכַּפֹּרֶת: וַעֲשֵׂה
כְּרוּב־אֶחָד מִקָּצָה מִזֶּה
וּכְרוּב־אֶחָד מִקָּצָה מִזֶּה
מִן־הַכַּפֹּרֶת תַּעֲשׂוּ אֶת־
הַכְּרֻבִים עַל־שְׁנֵי קְצוֹתָיו:
וְהָיוּ הַכְּרֻבִים פֹּרְשֵׂי כְנָפַיִם
לְמַעְלָה סֹכְכִים בְּכַנְפֵיהֶם
עַל־הַכַּפֹּרֶת וּפְנֵיהֶם אִישׁ
אֶל־אָחִיו אֶל־הַכַּפֹּרֶת יִהְיוּ
פְּנֵי הַכְּרֻבִים:

shall make a cover of pure gold, two
and a half cubits long and a cubit
and a half wide. Make two cherubim
of gold—make them of hammered
work—at the two ends of the cover.
You should make a cherub from the
gold of one edge, and another cherub
from the gold of the other edge. Of
one piece with the cover shall you
make the cherubim at its two ends.
The cherubim shall have their wings
spread out above, shielding the cover
with their wings. The face of each
should be toward the other, the
faces of the cherubim being turned
toward the cover.
(Ex. 25:9–20)

Edges and Faces

A Cover

Inside and Outside

Length, Width, and Height

Shape of Things Becomes Clear

Shape of Things Becomes Clear

Length, Width, and Height

Inside and Outside

A Cover

Edges and Faces

The Center

I think there may well be still more pairs in this ATBASH pattern spanning Genesis and Exodus, but for now, let's skip forward a bit and get to what all this seem to be leading to — the central element in the chiasm. Remember, every chiastic structure, inasmuch as it is built from mirrored, converging pairs, naturally leads the reader from its edges toward its core. At the center one usually finds something *central*, some sort of climactic element, an idea around which everything else in the chiasm revolves.

Now, to be sure, our chiasm is somewhat unusual, insofar as one half of the text comes from the book of Genesis and the other from the book of Exodus. So in our case, what I'm calling "the center" is not a single sentence in the middle but the innermost pair in the pattern — the pair created by the latest reference in Genesis and the earliest reference in Exodus.

With that in mind, let's try to find the center now; let's keep *advancing* in the book of Genesis, and keep *going backward* in the book of Exodus, until we locate the last pair we can find.

So here we are in Exodus, and so far we've been looking at verses that detail the building of the Ark. But now, we are going to look at the text that appears *just before* this, which actually doesn't speak of the *Mishkan* at all, but of Moses' forty days and nights atop Mt. Sinai:

Exodus 24:18

וַיָּבֹא מֹשֶׁה בְּתוֹךְ הֶעָנָן וַיַּעַל אֶל־הָהָר וַיְהִי מֹשֶׁה בָּהָר אַרְבָּעִים יוֹם וְאַרְבָּעִים לָיְלָה:

And Moses entered the cloud and ascended the mountain; and Moses was on the mountain for forty days and forty nights.

Right after this, in Exodus, the Torah tells of the command, addressed to each person in Israel, to give of himself to help build the Tabernacle:

Exodus 25:1–2

וַיְדַבֵּר יְקֹוָה אֶל־מֹשֶׁה לֵּאמֹר: דַּבֵּר אֶל־בְּנֵי יִשְׂרָאֵל וְיִקְחוּ־לִי תְּרוּמָה מֵאֵת כָּל־אִישׁ אֲשֶׁר יִדְּבֶנּוּ לִבּוֹ

And God said to Moses: "Speak to the Children of Israel, and let them bring Me gifts; from each person, according to what his heart moves him."

All in all, then, what do we have here in Exodus? We have a very particular time period that Moses is atop that mountain (forty days and forty nights), and then we hear of gifts the people should give to create the Tabernacle, gifts known as *terumah*.

So far so good. Now, page on over to Genesis, and we will see a mirror of that emerge.

You'll recall that in Genesis, our pattern had thus far focused on verses that describe the construction of the ark. But as we continue reading in Genesis, the verses move on to describe the onset of the Great Flood itself. And as we look at those verses, we encounter this:

וַיְהִי הַגֶּשֶׁם עַל־הָאָרֶץ אַרְבָּעִים יוֹם וְאַרְבָּעִים לָיְלָה:	The rain fell on the earth [for] forty days and forty nights.	Genesis 7:12

Forty Days, Clouds, and Arks

Remarkable: In Exodus, six pairs or so into our chiasm, we came across a forty-day-and-forty-night time period in which Moses was atop the mountain. And now, in the corresponding text in Genesis, six pairs or so into our chiasm, we find the Torah speaking of *another* forty-day-and-forty-night period. And intriguingly, the latter period is a kind of thematic mirror image of the former…

- **Ascending into clouds, descending from clouds.** In Exodus, those forty days and nights take place just as Moses *ascends* a mountain, and enters, of all things … a *cloud*. And in Genesis, we read of rain that, for forty days and nights, *descends* toward Noah from — where else? — *clouds*.
- **Shelter in an ark.** In Exodus, during a period of forty days and nights, Moses receives tablets that would need to be sheltered in an Ark. And, in Genesis, during a period of forty days and nights, Noah needs to shelter *himself* … in a very different kind of ark.

And let's address one more issue: In Exodus, right after we were told of Moses' forty days and forty nights atop the mountain, we heard of the idea of *terumah* — those gifts the people were to bring to help construct the *Mishkan*. In Genesis, is there anything that corresponds to that? Do the forty days and forty nights of Genesis somehow get paired with the idea of *terumah*, too?

As a matter of fact, they do — but in a clever, surprising kind of way. Because you have to ask yourself exactly what *terumah* means. In the context in which the word appears in Exodus, we translated it as "gifts." The *terumah* consisted of various items that people donated, from their own possessions, to help construct the *Mishkan*. But *terumah* actually has a more literal meaning than this. It comes from the word *leharim*, which means *to lift up*.

And, wouldn't you know it, if we look in Genesis, right after we hear of rain descending from the clouds for forty days and forty nights — we hear about what that rainfall did, once it became floodwaters on the ground.

Genesis 7:17

וַיְהִי הַמַּבּוּל אַרְבָּעִים יוֹם עַל־הָאָרֶץ וַיִּרְבּוּ הַמַּיִם וַיִּשְׂאוּ אֶת־הַתֵּבָה וַתָּרָם מֵעַל הָאָרֶץ:

The Flood continued forty days on the earth, and the waters increased and raised the ark so that it **rose** above the earth.

The rainfall lifted up the ark.

THE THEMES OF THE CHIASM

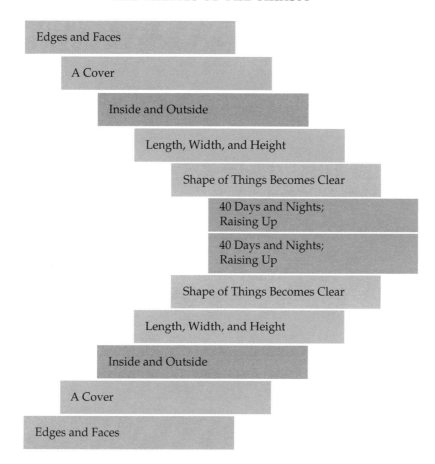

We seem, then, to have arrived at the center of an extended ATBASH structure, hidden in the text. The structure spans the books of Genesis and Exodus, and seems to connect the construction of two arks — Noah's and God's — entwining the two in its web of mirrored pairs. What are we to make of this remarkable structure in the text? And what are we to make of its center?

To Live in a World Unlike Your Own

In order to understand the purpose of this chiasm, and its center, let's consider a question we've been assiduously avoiding until now, a basic, fundamental question that underlies everything we've seen in the last few pages of this essay. *Broadly speaking, how would you describe the relationship, if any, between the two arks we have been talking about — the Ark of the Covenant on the one hand, and Noah's ark on the other?*

Sure, there is a chiasm, a literary structure, that seems to connect them. But why *should* they be connected? Is there anything, conceptually, that links the ark in which Noah took refuge to the Ark which housed the Ten Commandments?

I think there is.

Remember how, in some of the earlier pairs of our chiasm, we saw an indication that the two arks were somehow…inverses of one another? We saw that with respect to their overlays — for example, pitch and gold being quite the mirror image of one another. I want to suggest that perhaps, broadly speaking, the two arks really *are* mirrors of one another. Not just in their appearance, but in their function, too.

Noah's ark floated on the waves. That meant it would keep its inhabitants above the surface of a world that was so unlike their own, a water world. And in so doing, it would keep them safe. And later in history…the inverse would take place. With the building of the *Mishkan*, God would come to dwell in *our* world, a world very unlike the Heavenly abode that is native to the Divine.[8] And when that would occur, safety would once again become a prime concern.

To explain: When the Divine Presence comes to a world not its own, as wonderful as that is, danger is potentially afoot. The sheer power and brilliance of the Divine could potentially dominate, and perhaps obliterate, the world it is visiting.[9] The Ark of the Covenant, at some level, existed perhaps to create a kind of buffer between the Divine and man's world, assuring the safety of the latter in the presence of the former.

The Talmud (Sotah 35a) seems to take this idea even further. It teaches that the Ark which housed that Divine Presence would keep itself above the surface of the world. As strange as it sounds, the Ark of the Covenant, like Noah's ark before it…would "float," as it were.

---

8   See Psalms 115:16: הַשָּׁמַיִם שָׁמַיִם לַיקֹוָה וְהָאָרֶץ נָתַן לִבְנֵי־אָדָם, "The heavens belong to God, and the earth He gave to mankind."

9   For example, in the aftermath of the Golden Calf (Ex. 33:2–3), even after the people win a reprieve and God tells them He will still allow them to come into the Land of Israel, He warns the people that an angel will need to escort the people into the land. It would be too dangerous, the Almighty tells Moses, for God to allow His Presence to dwell directly among the people. God's Presence is treasured, but its power can be overwhelming.

Buoyancy

Indeed, the Talmud (Sotah ibid.) teaches that the Ark of the Covenant, as a vehicle for God's Presence in the world, would appear to possess an almost miraculous power. It says, for example, that people didn't really carry the Ark. On the contrary, נשא ארון את נושאיו, *the Ark itself would bear aloft those who carried it.* According to the Talmud, it was as if God's Ark were buoyant. In their telling, it floated off the surface of the earth — almost, if you think about it, *like Noah's ark did.*

The center of our chiasm, I want to suggest, tells of buoyancy for each of the two arks — and perhaps, of the mechanics through which that buoyancy was achieved. For Noah's ark, buoyancy came from the water. As one of the verses at the center of our chiasm states:

| וַיִּרְבּוּ הַמַּיִם וַיִּשְׂאוּ אֶת־הַתֵּבָה וַתָּרׇם מֵעַל הָאָרֶץ׃ | The waters were great, and they lifted the ark up above the earth. | Genesis 7:17 |

But for the Ark of the Covenant, buoyancy came… *from what?* Seemingly, the answer would come in the corresponding verse on the Exodus side of the chiasm. Yet that verse states just:

| וְיִקְחוּ־לִי תְּרוּמָה מֵאֵת כָּל־אִישׁ אֲשֶׁר יִדְּבֶנּוּ לִבּוֹ | Take for Me gifts [*terumah*, a "lifting up"] from every person whose heart wishes to give. | Exodus 25:2 |

In fact, in those very words lies the secret we have been searching for. That verse described how the raw materials from which the Ark, and the *Mishkan* that housed it, would be constructed. And, as I mentioned above, in that verse, *terumah* has a double meaning. Its plain meaning is "gifts," and its literal meaning is *that which lifted up* — a meaning that corresponds thematically to the water *that lifted up* Noah's ark.

I'd like to suggest that both these meanings — *gifts* and *lifting up* — merge to become one. The *gifts* of the people — that which they volunteered to donate to the *Mishkan* and to the Ark that was its centerpiece — given of a free spirit, caused a kind of *lifting up.* In a deep way, the force that elevated the raw material of the *Mishkan* and made it special and worthy of being consecrated, that distinctive quality which made its centerpiece, the Ark, literally lift itself up off the ground, came from the simple and pure desire, on the part of humans, to…give a gift to the Divine. It came from the hearts of the people. For indeed, look at how the *terumah* was brought:

Exodus 25:2

דַּבֵּר אֶל־בְּנֵי יִשְׂרָאֵל וְיִקְחוּ־לִי תְּרוּמָה מֵאֵת כָּל־אִישׁ אֲשֶׁר יִדְּבֶנּוּ לִבּוֹ תִּקְחוּ אֶת־תְּרוּמָתִי:

Tell the Israelite people to bring Me gifts; you shall accept gifts for Me from every person whose heart so moves him.

Terumah was given from the heart. Each person delivered what he or she most desired to bring to God. Thus, perhaps the mysterious power of the Ark reflected a profound truth: A gift you give from the heart, something you use to make a place in your world for someone you love, may *look* like a mere material object — just a rose, just a card — but when given from the heart, it is more than a material item. It rises above the material. It dances on air. It can invest everything around it with a lightness of being. A gift from the heart has the power to bring a little bit of God's world into our own, and to keep that "place within a place" safe among us.

THE CHIASM AS A WHOLE

וַיֹּאמֶר אֱלֹהִים לְנֹחַ קֵץ כָּל־
בָּשָׂר בָּא לְפָנַי כִּי־מָלְאָה
הָאָרֶץ חָמָס מִפְּנֵיהֶם וְהִנְנִי
מַשְׁחִיתָם אֶת־הָאָרֶץ:
עֲשֵׂה לְךָ תֵּבַת עֲצֵי־גֹפֶר
קִנִּים תַּעֲשֶׂה אֶת־הַתֵּבָה
וְכָפַרְתָּ אֹתָהּ מִבַּיִת וּמִחוּץ
בַּכֹּפֶר: וְזֶה אֲשֶׁר תַּעֲשֶׂה
אֹתָהּ שְׁלֹשׁ מֵאוֹת אַמָּה
אֹרֶךְ הַתֵּבָה חֲמִשִּׁים אַמָּה
רָחְבָּהּ וּשְׁלֹשִׁים אַמָּה
קוֹמָתָהּ: צֹהַר תַּעֲשֶׂה
לַתֵּבָה וְאֶל־אַמָּה תְּכַלֶּנָּה
מִלְמַעְלָה וּפֶתַח הַתֵּבָה
בְּצִדָּהּ תָּשִׂים תַּחְתִּים שְׁנִיִּם
וּשְׁלִשִׁים תַּעֲשֶׂהָ:

* * *

וַיְהִי הַגֶּשֶׁם עַל־הָאָרֶץ
אַרְבָּעִים יוֹם וְאַרְבָּעִים
לָיְלָה: בְּעֶצֶם הַיּוֹם הַזֶּה בָּא
נֹחַ וְשֵׁם־וְחָם וָיֶפֶת בְּנֵי־נֹחַ
וְאֵשֶׁת נֹחַ וּשְׁלֹשֶׁת נְשֵׁי־
בָנָיו אִתָּם אֶל־הַתֵּבָה: הֵמָּה
וְכָל־הַחַיָּה לְמִינָהּ וְכָל־
הַבְּהֵמָה לְמִינָהּ וְכָל־הָרֶמֶשׂ
הָרֹמֵשׂ עַל־הָאָרֶץ לְמִינֵהוּ
וְכָל־הָעוֹף לְמִינֵהוּ כֹּל
צִפּוֹר כָּל־כָּנָף: וַיָּבֹאוּ אֶל־
נֹחַ אֶל־הַתֵּבָה שְׁנַיִם שְׁנַיִם
מִכָּל־הַבָּשָׂר אֲשֶׁר־בּוֹ רוּחַ
חַיִּים: וְהַבָּאִים זָכָר וּנְקֵבָה
מִכָּל־בָּשָׂר בָּאוּ כַּאֲשֶׁר צִוָּה
אֹתוֹ אֱלֹהִים וַיִּסְגֹּר יְקֹוָק
בַּעֲדוֹ: וַיְהִי הַמַּבּוּל אַרְבָּעִים
יוֹם עַל־הָאָרֶץ וַיִּרְבּוּ הַמַּיִם
וַיִּשְׂאוּ אֶת־הַתֵּבָה וַתָּרָם
מֵעַל הָאָרֶץ:

And God said to Noah, "The end [edge] of all flesh has come before Me, because the world is filled with corruption on their account [from their faces]: I am about to destroy them with the earth. Make yourself an ark of gopher wood; make it an ark with compartments, and cover it inside and out with pitch. This is how you shall make it: the length of the ark shall be three hundred cubits, its width fifty cubits, and its height thirty cubits. A window you shall make for the ark, and terminate it within a cubit of the top. Put the entrance to the ark in its side; make it with bottom, second, and third decks. (Gen. 6:13–16)

* * *

The rain fell on the earth forty days and forty nights. That same day Noah and Noah's sons, Shem, Ham, and Japheth, went into the ark, with Noah's wife and the three wives of his sons—they and all beasts of every kind, all cattle of every kind, all creatures of every kind that creep on the earth, and all birds of every kind, every bird, every winged thing. They came to Noah into the ark, two each of all flesh in which there was breath of life. Thus they that entered comprised male and female of all flesh, as God had commanded him. And the Lord shut him in. The Flood continued forty days on the earth, and the waters increased and raised the ark so that it rose above the earth. (Gen. 7:12–17)

וַיָּבֹא מֹשֶׁה בְּתוֹךְ הֶעָנָן
וַיַּעַל אֶל־הָהָר וַיְהִי
מֹשֶׁה בָּהָר אַרְבָּעִים יוֹם
וְאַרְבָּעִים לָיְלָה: וַיְדַבֵּר
יְקֹוָה אֶל־מֹשֶׁה לֵּאמֹר: דַּבֵּר
אֶל־בְּנֵי יִשְׂרָאֵל וְיִקְחוּ־לִי
תְּרוּמָה מֵאֵת כָּל־אִישׁ
אֲשֶׁר יִדְּבֶנּוּ לִבּוֹ תִּקְחוּ אֶת־
תְּרוּמָתִי: וְזֹאת הַתְּרוּמָה
אֲשֶׁר תִּקְחוּ מֵאִתָּם זָהָב
וָכֶסֶף וּנְחֹשֶׁת: וּתְכֵלֶת
וְאַרְגָּמָן וְתוֹלַעַת שָׁנִי
וְשֵׁשׁ וְעִזִּים: וְעֹרֹת אֵילִם
מְאָדָּמִים וְעֹרֹת תְּחָשִׁים
וַעֲצֵי שִׁטִּים: שֶׁמֶן לַמָּאֹר
בְּשָׂמִים לְשֶׁמֶן הַמִּשְׁחָה
וְלִקְטֹרֶת הַסַּמִּים: אַבְנֵי־
שֹׁהַם וְאַבְנֵי מִלֻּאִים לָאֵפֹד
וְלַחֹשֶׁן: וְעָשׂוּ לִי מִקְדָּשׁ
וְשָׁכַנְתִּי בְּתוֹכָם: כְּכֹל
אֲשֶׁר אֲנִי מַרְאֶה אוֹתְךָ
אֵת תַּבְנִית הַמִּשְׁכָּן וְאֵת
תַּבְנִית כָּל־כֵּלָיו וְכֵן תַּעֲשׂוּ:
וְעָשׂוּ אֲרוֹן עֲצֵי שִׁטִּים
אַמָּתַיִם וָחֵצִי אָרְכּוֹ וְאַמָּה
וָחֵצִי רָחְבּוֹ וְאַמָּה וָחֵצִי
קֹמָתוֹ: וְצִפִּיתָ אֹתוֹ זָהָב
טָהוֹר מִבַּיִת וּמִחוּץ תְּצַפֶּנּוּ
וְעָשִׂיתָ עָלָיו זֵר זָהָב סָבִיב:
וְיָצַקְתָּ לּוֹ אַרְבַּע טַבְּעֹת זָהָב
וְנָתַתָּה עַל אַרְבַּע פַּעֲמֹתָיו
וּשְׁתֵּי טַבָּעֹת עַל־צַלְעוֹ
הָאֶחָת וּשְׁתֵּי טַבָּעֹת עַל־
צַלְעוֹ הַשֵּׁנִית: וְעָשִׂיתָ בַדֵּי
עֲצֵי שִׁטִּים וְצִפִּיתָ אֹתָם
זָהָב: וְהֵבֵאתָ אֶת־הַבַּדִּים

Moses went inside the cloud and ascended the mountain; and Moses remained on the mountain forty days and forty nights. The Lord spoke to Moses, saying: Tell the Israelite people to bring Me gifts; you shall accept gifts for Me from every person whose heart so moves him. And these are the gifts that you shall accept from them: gold, silver, and copper; blue, purple, and crimson yarns, fine linen, goats' hair; tanned ram skins, dolphin skins, and acacia wood; oil for lighting, spices for the anointing oil and for the aromatic incense; Lapis lazuli and other stones for setting, for the ephod and for the breast piece. And let them make Me a Sanctuary that I may dwell among them. Just as I, God, show you the pattern of the Tabernacle and the pattern of all its furnishings—so shall you make it. They shall make an ark of acacia wood, two and a half cubits long, a cubit and a half wide, and a cubit and a half high. Overlay it with pure gold—overlay it inside and out—and make upon it a gold molding round about. Cast four gold rings for it, to be attached to its four feet, two rings on one of its side walls and two on the other. Make poles of acacia wood and overlay them with gold; then insert the poles into the rings on the side walls of the ark, for carrying the ark. The poles shall remain in the rings of the ark: they

בַּטַּבָּעֹת עַל צַלְעֹת הָאָרֹן
לָשֵׂאת אֶת־הָאָרֹן בָּהֶם. טו
בְּטַבְּעֹת הָאָרֹן יִהְיוּ הַבַּדִּים
לֹא יָסֻרוּ מִמֶּנּוּ: וְנָתַתָּ אֶל־
הָאָרֹן אֵת הָעֵדֻת אֲשֶׁר
אֶתֵּן אֵלֶיךָ: וְעָשִׂיתָ כַפֹּרֶת
זָהָב טָהוֹר אַמָּתַיִם וָחֵצִי
אָרְכָּהּ וְאַמָּה וָחֵצִי רָחְבָּהּ:
וְעָשִׂיתָ שְׁנַיִם כְּרֻבִים זָהָב
מִקְשָׁה תַּעֲשֶׂה אֹתָם מִשְּׁנֵי
קְצוֹת הַכַּפֹּרֶת: וַעֲשֵׂה
כְּרוּב־אֶחָד מִקָּצָה מִזֶּה
וּכְרוּב־אֶחָד מִקָּצָה מִזֶּה
מִן־הַכַּפֹּרֶת תַּעֲשׂוּ אֶת־
הַכְּרֻבִים עַל־שְׁנֵי קְצוֹתָיו:
וְהָיוּ הַכְּרֻבִים פֹּרְשֵׂי כְנָפַיִם
לְמַעְלָה סֹכְכִים בְּכַנְפֵיהֶם
עַל־הַכַּפֹּרֶת וּפְנֵיהֶם אִישׁ
אֶל־אָחִיו אֶל־הַכַּפֹּרֶת יִהְיוּ
פְּנֵי הַכְּרֻבִים:

shall not be removed from it. And deposit in the Ark [the tablets of] the Pact which I will give you. You shall make a cover of pure gold, two and a half cubits long and a cubit and a half wide. Make two cherubim of gold—make them of hammered work—at the two ends of the cover. You should make a cherub from the gold of one edge, and another cherub from the gold of the other edge. Of one piece with the cover shall you make the cherubim at its two ends. The cherubim shall have their wings spread out above, shielding the cover with their wings. The face of each should be toward the other, the faces of the cherubim being turned toward the cover.

(Ex. 24:18–20)

Clothes That Speak Volumes, and Volumes... That Speak of Clothes

וְנָשָׂא אַהֲרֹן אֶת־מִשְׁפַּט בְּנֵי־יִשְׂרָאֵל עַל־לִבּוֹ לִפְנֵי יְקֹוָה תָּמִיד:

Aaron shall carry the *mishpat* of the Israelites over his heart, before God always.

EXODUS 28:30

Clothes That Speak Volumes, and Volumes…That Speak of Clothes

AS A CONVERSATION STARTER on **Parshat Tetzaveh**, I'd like to play a free-association game with you. I'll run a Hebrew term by you that is loosely associated with **Parshat Tetzaveh**, and you tell me what that term recalls for you:

Ketzot hachoshen.

Well, if you spent any time in a major yeshivah studying Talmud, chances are you'd associate that phrase immediately with a classic work of halachic analysis written hundreds of years ago. The *Ketzos*, as it is affectionately known in yeshivah circles, is one of the most incisive and mind-bendingly original commentaries on the *Shulchan Aruch*, one of the central and nearly universally accepted codes of Jewish law.[1] The *Ketzos* is widely studied to this day by advanced yeshivah students across the world.

Here's a second phrase for you: *choshen mishpat.*

Again, if you've been to yeshivah for any length of time, you'd associate that phrase with a halachic work. *Choshen Mishpat* is one of the four major sections of the *Shulchan Aruch*.[2] It examines monetary and civil law, addressing questions of ownership, theft, and damages.

And now, here's one more for you: the *tur.*

Well, the *Tur*, as any rabbi or student of Jewish law will tell you, is one of the first great law codes in Jewish history, written in the fourteenth

---

1 The *Ketzot HaChoshen* was authored by R. Aryeh Leib Heller (c. 1745–1812). It is a commentary on the section of *Shulchan Aruch* that deals with laws of damages and financial transactions.

2 The *Shulchan Aruch* was authored by R. Yosef Karo in 1563. He borrowed the names of the four major sections of his work (including *Choshen Mishpat*) from an earlier halachic work known as the *Tur*.

century by Rabbi Yaakov ben Asher.[3] It predates, and is actually the template for, the *Shulchan Aruch* itself. The *Tur* is divided into four major sections, known as the *Arba'ah Turim*.

Not Books, but Clothes

OK, so that concludes our free-association game. But I have news for you: Despite the fact that most of us yeshivah-trained folks would associate these three terms with books, the *original choshen mishpat*, the *original tur*, and the *original ketzot hachoshen* actually had nothing to do with books at all. They actually had to do with … *clothes*.

Long before the *Ketzot HaChoshen, Choshen Mishpat*, or *Tur* ever came to be known as titles for three great halachic works, they were the names of various clothes, or clothing accessories, of the Kohen Gadol. I must say that, as a young yeshivah student, this came as something of a surprise to me. I was used to studying more Talmud than Bible, and so, when I first noticed these phrases in **Parshat Tetzaveh**, I almost felt like asking why God named priestly vestments after famous law codes. But of course, the reverse was true: It was the authors of the law codes who were naming their works after the Torah's descriptions of priestly clothing. Why would they have done that?

Justice and Clothes

The answer is that the Torah itself seems, curiously, to associate these clothes with the notion of judgment — principally, the *choshen*. The *choshen* was, of course, a breastplate the Kohen Gadol would wear. It would, in turn, have four rows — *turim* — of precious stones inlaid upon it. On the corners of the *choshen* — the *ketzot hachoshen* — there were rings, and cords would loop through those rings to keep the *choshen* fastened to the shoulder plates of the Kohen Gadol's garments (see Exodus 28). But here's the thing: The *choshen* is not *just* a *choshen*, a simple breastplate. There's a mysterious adjective added to the Torah's description of this *choshen*:

---

3   He was the son of Rabbeinu Asher, the famed halachic scholar known as the Rosh.

וְעָשִׂיתָ חֹשֶׁן מִשְׁפָּט   And you shall make [for the Kohen   Exodus 28:15
Gadol] a breastplate of judgment.

What a strange thing to call a piece of clothing a "breastplate of judgment." How is one supposed to even wrap one's mind around that? Is the Kohen Gadol, the wearer of this breastplate, an ancient version of some modern superhero? A captain of the Justice League, as it were, sporting a shield on his chest that symbolizes Truth, Justice, and the Israelite Way? It seems so odd. The Kohen Gadol doesn't fight crime; he is not a prosecutor. Why would he wear a breastplate of "judgment"?

As it happens, the Torah actually does offer something of an explanation for this. But its explanation, if we can call it that, does little to dispel the mystery associated with the breastplate. If anything, it deepens the mystery still further. The Torah tells us that, by wearing the *choshen mishpat*...

וְנָשָׂא אַהֲרֹן אֶת־מִשְׁפַּט בְּנֵי־   Aaron shall carry the *mishpat* of the   Exodus 28:30
יִשְׂרָאֵל עַל־לִבּוֹ לִפְנֵי יְקֹוָה   Israelites over his heart, before God,
תָּמִיד: always.

So we now know something of what this judgment — or, in Hebrew, this *mishpat* — is about. The *choshen* represents the "*mishpat* of the Children of Israel." And the Kohen Gadol is supposed to wear the *choshen* so that when he enters into the holy sections of the *Mishkan*, this "judgment of Israel" is constantly right there with him, when he is present before God. Which leads me to ask you, dear reader: How excited are you by the symbolic meaning of this *choshen*? How much do you like being judged? How thrilled are you to know that *this* is what the Kohen Gadol is wearing over his heart each time he goes before God?

The whole thing sounds rather frightening. Does the *choshen* allude to some kind of divine judgment, some sentence that the Heavenly Court hands down about Israel? If so, why would the High Priest be instructed to walk around before God and *constantly* "remind" the Almighty about what that sentence is? Again, it feels less than reassuring. It makes you want to ask Aaron and his children to maybe take a few weeks off and vacation somewhere. The less time they have in close quarters with God, reminding Him about our *mishpat*, the better.

And while we're at it, think about all these books that, later in history, get named after the *choshen mishpat* and its various accouterments. Why did respected sages, over the generations, give such names to these works? Are they, too, meant to remind God of all of Israel's judgments? It sounds like the *last* thing anyone would want to remind God of. Why name perfectly fine books after such scary things?

What Does "the Mishpat of X" Really Mean?

I want to suggest to you that perhaps we have been misunderstanding this phrase, "the *mishpat* of the Children of Israel." Our assumption has been that it connotes some sort of Heavenly judgment or sentence handed down about Israel. But perhaps we are being too hasty in making such a supposition. Maybe it means something else.

How might we discern what the phrase really means? Well, to do that, one would probably have to look at how the Torah uses that phraseology elsewhere. And while the exact phrase "the *mishpat* of the Children of Israel" doesn't appear elsewhere in the Torah, the Torah does speak elsewhere of the *mishpat* of other people, and such cases seem to have a certain connotation that I think we can pin down.

To illustrate, let's begin with the immediately preceding instance in which the Torah speaks of the "*mishpat* of X" (where X is a person or a group of people). That appears just a few chapters earlier in — of all places — the parshah of the Torah devoted to *mishpatim*, namely, **Parshat Mishpatim**. There, just after the Ten Commandments are given, the Torah lays out dozens of what the Torah calls *mishpatim*, or in English, "laws." And one of those *mishpatim* just happens to address *the process of applying mishpat itself*. It is a meta-law, as it were. This law tells of the *mishpat* of one group in particular: the *mishpat* of the poor, the destitute, the disadvantaged. The Torah admonishes us:

Exodus 23:6 — לֹא תַטֶּה מִשְׁפַּט אֶבְיֹנְךָ בְּרִיבוֹ: — You shall not incline the judgment of your poor in his cause.

The language of the verse is instructive. The Hebrew *tateh* literally means "to incline." In this context, it seems to mean that we must ensure that the *mishpat* of the poor lies straight and even, which is to say, it needs to be fair. The destitute among us need to be able to advance their *riv*, their cause or complaint, on a level playing field.[4]

Now, who would you say this admonition is addressed to? The answer would have to be that the Torah is addressing those who are in charge of the justice system itself, or, more narrowly, it is addressing the judge adjudicating any given poor person's case.[5] The Torah is telling the judge that he has to be fair even to the poor; he can't conveniently offer the benefit of the doubt to the richer or more powerful litigant. To do so would be to illegitimately *incline mishpat* against the poor.

Note, then, that the word *incline* is exquisitely accurate. Think of the image it evokes here. In one's mind's eye, the rich litigant is higher up the socioeconomic ladder than his lowly, poor adversary. Which means that were you to draw a line from one litigant to the other, it wouldn't be flat. The line would be a diagonal, which is to say, it will *incline*. That picture is a perfect metaphor for how the justice system might "naturally" treat cases involving litigants from vastly different socioeconomic classes. The rich fellow is powerful and well connected. His adversary has little weight or established reputation in the community. If society is not on its guard, then even a judge with the best of intentions may find himself naturally, even subconsciously, favoring the strong litigant, the more respected and seemingly upstanding member of his community. Thus, before you know it, the line that represents justice, the line that is supposed to lie straight and even, becomes ever so slightly inclined. It is a diagonal now.

As such, the Torah instructs every judge to be especially vigilant. *Lo tateh mishpat*: Don't incline the line of judgment by virtue of your natural biases; don't "diagonalize" it against the poor.

---

4   Most classical commentators read the verse as mandating protection for the poor (see Rabbi Yosef Bechor Shor, Chizkuni ad loc., Rashi to Sanhedrin 36b, s.v. לא תטה, in line with the similar expression in Deut. 24:17). Earlier sages, however, have actually read this verse as an injunction against inclining the case in the pauper's favor (see Mechilta 23:6, Talmud Yerushalmi Pe'ah 4:7).

5   See *Ibn Ezra* ad loc.

Two Inclinations

So let's pause for a moment and just add up what we have now.

Here is a law that instructs us about someone's *mishpat*. It tells us not to incline the law of the destitute as they seek to press their case in the courts, expressing that with the words: *lo tateh mishpat evyoncha berivo*, do not incline the "*mishpat* of your poor" in his cause. Then, just a few chapters later, the Torah once more speaks of someone's *mishpat*: it tells us that the Kohen Gadol must wear the "*mishpat* of Israel" over his heart. The question I want to put before you is this: Might the former phrase teach us something about the latter? Can it help explain what the "*mishpat* of Israel" might mean, or why the High Priest might be required to quite literally wear "the *mishpat* of Israel" upon him as he enters the holy places of the Sanctuary?

I think it does. To see how, let's look a little more closely at that first law, the one that warns the judge how to treat a destitute person in court. Recall the verb there: *Lo tateh mishpat* — we must not "incline" his *mishpat*; we shouldn't "tilt" it, so to speak. This is the first time the Torah speaks of someone's *mishpat*. Now, glance at the next time the Torah speaks of someone's *mishpat*, where we encounter the *choshen mishpat* worn by the Kohen Gadol. Ask: Do we find anything there that reminds you of this *lo tateh* idea?

As it turns out, we do. For here is what the Torah tells us about the Kohen Gadol's *choshen mishpat*:

Exodus 28:28

וְיִרְכְּסוּ אֶת־הַחֹשֶׁן מִטַּבְּעֹתָו
[מִטַּבְּעֹתָיו] אֶל־טַבְּעֹת
הָאֵפֹד בִּפְתִיל תְּכֵלֶת...
וְלֹא־יִזַּח הַחֹשֶׁן מֵעַל
הָאֵפֹד:

The breastplate [i.e., the *choshen*] shall be held in place by a cord of blue from its rings, to the rings of the ephod — so that the breastplate...doesn't get moved from [its rightful place] on the ephod.

The Torah tells us that this breastplate, this *choshen*, of the Kohen Gadol, which bears the "*mishpat* of the Children of Israel," has to *lay straight*; it can't be allowed to come loose so that it wobbles and becomes tilted one way or the other. To this end, the Torah tells us that the *choshen* needs to be securely fastened to the ephod (apron) of the Kohen Gadol by cords.

The upshot of all this is a striking confluence. Fascinatingly, the *mishpat* of the Children of Israel, like the *mishpat* of the poor, can't be allowed to tilt.[6]

Two Iterations of the Same Law

The more you look at them, the more these two back-to-back instances of "the *mishpat* of X" seem to be talking about two versions of the same idea. The only difference between them, perhaps, is that the former concerns the *mishpat* of an individual, and the latter, the *mishpat* of an entire nation. In the first situation, a judge holds the welfare of a relatively weak person in his hands. In the second, perhaps, a judge holds the welfare of a relatively weak community — namely, the nation of Israel — in his hands. In the first case, the judge is human. In the second case, the Judge is…divine.

The Torah seems to be saying that the Kohen Gadol should wear the *choshen* representing the *mishpat* of Israel for a reason: to remind the judge of the perils of inclined judgment. But while the Torah reminds an earthly judge of the perils of inclined judgment, astoundingly, in the case of a needy community, the Torah seems to bid the Kohen Gadol to "remind" the Judge in heaven of much the same.

---

6   For the purposes of discerning the meaning of the "*mishpat* of Israel" with respect to the Kohen Gadol's clothes, the "*mishpat* of the destitute" in court is the closest comparable instance, appearing just a few chapters earlier in the book of Exodus. There are, though, other examples of the "*mishpat* of X" in the Torah — and, as it happens, they reinforce the argument we have been making here about the connotations of the phrase. In case after case, the "*mishpat* of X" seems to be a phrase that demands fair treatment for the naturally disadvantaged. For example, the Torah ordains that if someone takes a maidservant as a wife for his son, she cannot be treated unfairly because of her servant status; rather, כְּמִשְׁפַּט הַבָּנוֹת יַעֲשֶׂה לָּהּ, he must act with her as he would in the *mishpat* of daughters (Exodus 21:9). Or, if a man illegitimately wishes to revoke the rights of his firstborn child, he cannot do so. Instead, לוֹ מִשְׁפַּט הַבְּכֹרָה, the true firstborn, even if he or his mother has fallen out of favor with the father, possesses the "*mishpat* of the firstborn" (Deut. 21:17). The Torah even issues an additional warning to judges not to tilt *mishpat* with respect to other vulnerable people: לֹא תַטֶּה מִשְׁפַּט גֵּר יָתוֹם, do not incline the "*mishpat* of the stranger or the fatherless" (Deut. 24:17). The phrase "*mishpat* of X" somehow almost always seems to make an appearance in the Torah's text when justice is at risk of tilting away from the powerless.

This idea seems to be reinforced by the fact that the *choshen* contains not just the *mishpat* of Israel but the names of Israel, too. The *choshen* contains precious stones inlaid upon it, stones that represent the tribes of Israel — and the verse picks up on that, telling us the following:

Exodus 28:29

וְנָשָׂא אַהֲרֹן אֶת־שְׁמוֹת בְּנֵי־
יִשְׂרָאֵל בְּחֹשֶׁן הַמִּשְׁפָּט עַל־לִבּוֹ
בְּבֹאוֹ אֶל־הַקֹּדֶשׁ לְזִכָּרֹן לִפְנֵי־
יְקֹוָה תָּמִיד:

Aaron shall carry the names of the Children of Israel on the breastplate of *mishpat* over his heart, whenever he enters the Sanctuary, as a remembrance before God, constantly.

The Torah seems to be saying that the Kohen Gadol should wear the *choshen* representing the names of Israel and their *mishpat* for a reason: So that when he enters the holy Sanctuary, and comes into the proximity of the Divine Presence, the *choshen* is there along with him. God should remember our names, and should remember our fragility in the face of His power.

Indeed, everyone is an *evyon*, poor and outmatched, when standing before the Master of the Universe.[7] The Kohen Gadol is asking the Judge of us all to be careful with that strength. In essence, every time the Kohen Gadol enters the inner chamber of the *Mishkan*, God's holy place, he bears with him a plea: *You, God, are strong, and Israel is weak. They have needs, and You have the power to address those needs. Hear out their pleas and consider carefully what they ask of You. Don't allow Your strength to intimidate them or silence them. Allow them an even playing field as they make their case before You.*

Moreover, the verse suggests something poignant about the Kohen Gadol's attitude in all this:

Exodus 28:30

וְנָשָׂא אַהֲרֹן אֶת־מִשְׁפַּט בְּנֵי־
יִשְׂרָאֵל עַל־לִבּוֹ לִפְנֵי יְקֹוָה
תָּמִיד:

Aaron shall carry the *mishpat* of the Israelites **over his heart**, before God, **always**.

---

7   In this connection, bear in mind that our Sages also read the term *evyon* as implying someone who is bereft of good deeds (Mechilta ad loc.). It is not just a term that reflects those of fragile financial circumstances; it can also connote fragility of merit.

It is not just anywhere that Aaron shall place "the *mishpat* of the Children of Israel," the pleas and yearnings of his people, as well as the names of Israel, when he goes before God. He shall bear their plight before the Divine, *right over his heart*. He is our emissary. And, as our emissary, our pleas, hopes, and dreams must mean something personally to him. He must take that heartfelt care with him, *always* — he must literally wear it — every time he goes into the *Mishkan*'s inner chamber to encounter the Divine.

Shoulders and Heart: Stones Meet Stones

We can fill out the picture still further. Note how it is that the *choshen mishpat* of the Kohen Gadol is to be held in place. According to the Torah, it was fastened to the ephod, the apron of the Kohen Gadol, by means of two sky-blue pieces of string. On one end, these strings would be fastened to rings on the side of the *choshen*, and on the other end, they would be fastened to a second set of rings resting on the shoulders of the Kohen Gadol's garments. There, on the Kohen Gadol's shoulders, where the string met the rings, two precious, rectangular stones would sit:

וְלָקַחְתָּ אֶת־שְׁתֵּי אַבְנֵי־שֹׁהַם וּפִתַּחְתָּ עֲלֵיהֶם שְׁמוֹת בְּנֵי יִשְׂרָאֵל:	You shall take two precious lazuli stones and engrave on them the names of the Children of Israel.	Exodus 28:9
וְשַׂמְתָּ אֶת־שְׁתֵּי הָאֲבָנִים עַל כִּתְפֹת הָאֵפֹד אַבְנֵי זִכָּרֹן לִבְנֵי יִשְׂרָאֵל וְנָשָׂא אַהֲרֹן אֶת־שְׁמוֹתָם לִפְנֵי יְקֹוָה עַל־שְׁתֵּי כְתֵפָיו לְזִכָּרֹן:	And you shall attach the two stones to the shoulder pieces of the ephod, as stones for remembrance of the Israelite people. And Aaron shall carry their names upon his two shoulders, for remembrance before God.	Exodus 28:12

Think about where these names of Israel are positioned. The Kohen Gadol is to approach God with the names of Israel on his heart *and* on his shoulders. He is to both *feel* Israel's plight, and bear that weight on his shoulders — as if he were assuming their burden as his own.

Moreover, consider the fact that when the Kohen Gadol enters the holiest place in the Sanctuary, bearing these two rectangular stones on his shoulders, it is then that he finds himself face-to-face with … *two other rectangular stones*. For indeed, in the Holy of Holies, the room is empty save the Ark, and in that Ark, were … two rectangular, stone tablets:

Exodus
25:21–22

וְאֶל־הָאָרֹן תִּתֵּן אֶת־הָעֵדֻת
אֲשֶׁר אֶתֵּן אֵלֶיךָ: וְנוֹעַדְתִּי לְךָ
שָׁם וְדִבַּרְתִּי אִתְּךָ מֵעַל הַכַּפֹּרֶת
מִבֵּין שְׁנֵי הַכְּרֻבִים

Into the Ark place the [Tablets of] the Covenant that I will give you. There I will meet with you, and speak with you, over the covering of the Ark, between the two cherubim.

Intriguingly, the two stones that adorned the Kohen Gadol's shoulders had the *names* of the tribes of Israel inscribed upon them. And the two stone tablets in the ark had *laws* inscribed upon them, the ten laws that introduce the myriad *mishpatim* of the Torah.[8] It is almost as if one set of stones were ours and the other set were God's. On *our* tablets are that which we wish God to remember: our names, tied with delicate thread to our *mishpat*, the case we want to make before the Heavenly Throne. That case embodies our hopes, dreams, and needs that are brought before God, and it is placed over the Kohen Gadol's heart. On God's tablets are the laws that He wishes *us* to remember. Like in any good relationship, each party bears a responsibility to take care with what is important to the other. We are to remember what is dear to the Almighty, and the Almighty is to remember what is dear to us.

Who Looks at What?

There is, indeed, one more of the Kohen Gadol's vestments that seems to powerfully reinforce the idea we have just spoken of, that God and Israel must remember what is dear to the other. It is the *tzitz*:

---

8   Indeed, the words of the Ten Commandments appear in the text immediately before the long list of *mishpatim*. The former comprises the bulk of chapter 20 of the book of Exodus; the latter, chapter 21 and on.

וְעָשִׂיתָ צִּיץ זָהָב טָהוֹר וּפִתַּחְתָּ עָלָיו פִּתּוּחֵי חֹתָם קֹדֶשׁ לַיקֹוָה: וְשַׂמְתָּ אֹתוֹ עַל־פְּתִיל תְּכֵלֶת

You shall make a frontlet of pure gold [to adorn the Kohen Gadol's forehead], and engrave on it the seal inscription: "Holy to the Lord." And suspend it on a cord of *techelet* blue.

Exodus 28:36–37

The *tzitz* was a gold plate adorning the Kohen Gadol's forehead. But isn't it intriguing that ordinary, non-Kohanim wear something as a matter of course that reminds us of the *tzitz*, too? Consider this: The *tzitz* was tied around the Kohen Gadol's forehead with a cord of *techelet* blue. What do ordinary people wear that has the same colored threads?

דַּבֵּר אֶל־בְּנֵי יִשְׂרָאֵל וְאָמַרְתָּ אֲלֵהֶם וְעָשׂוּ לָהֶם צִיצִת עַל־ כַּנְפֵי בִגְדֵיהֶם לְדֹרֹתָם וְנָתְנוּ עַל־צִיצִת הַכָּנָף פְּתִיל תְּכֵלֶת: וְהָיָה לָכֶם לְצִיצִת וּרְאִיתֶם אֹתוֹ וּזְכַרְתֶּם אֶת־כָּל־מִצְוֹת יְקֹוָה וַעֲשִׂיתֶם אֹתָם

Speak to the Children of Israel and instruct them to make for themselves *tzitzit* — fringes — on the corners of their garments throughout the ages; let them attach a cord of blue to the fringe at each corner. This shall be *tzitzit* for you; look at it and recall all the commandments of the Lord and observe them.

Numbers 15:38–39

The *tzitzit* bear a striking phonetic similarity to the Kohen Gadol's *tzitz*. The *tzitzit* are fringes with *techelet*-blue thread that adorn the *bottom* of our clothes. And the *tzitz*, a gold plate held in place by *techelet*-blue thread at the very *top* of the Kohen Gadol's clothing, seems like a kind of counterpoint to that. According to the verse, the *tzitz* was engraved with the words "holy to God." And intriguingly, the Torah suggests that the *tzitzit* charge us with making those very same words — holy to God — a reality:

לְמַעַן תִּזְכְּרוּ וַעֲשִׂיתֶם אֶת־ כָּל־מִצְוֹתָי וִהְיִיתֶם קְדֹשִׁים לֵאלֹהֵיכֶם:

In order that you remember, and do, all My mitzvot — and thereby become **holy unto God.**

Numbers 15:40

Most striking of all, of course, is the alliteration: *tzitzit* and *tzitz*. *Ibn Ezra* suggests that both seem to derive from the same Hebrew word: *metzitz* — which in Song of Songs appears to mean "to gaze at."[9] I'd like to spend a moment pondering the following thought with you: How does the idea of gazing at something figure into both these articles of clothing?

With the *tzitzit,* the answer to that question seems clear: *Tzitzit* are meant for us humans to gaze at. They are on our clothes, where we can see them all the time — and the text tells us they are meant to help us remember God's laws, His mitzvot:

Numbers 15:39	וְהָיָה לָכֶם לְצִיצִת וּרְאִיתֶם אֹתוֹ וּזְכַרְתֶּם אֶת־כָּל־מִצְוֹת יְקֹוָה וַעֲשִׂיתֶם אֹתָם וְלֹא־תָתוּרוּ אַחֲרֵי לְבַבְכֶם וְאַחֲרֵי עֵינֵיכֶם אֲשֶׁר־אַתֶּם זֹנִים אַחֲרֵיהֶם:	That shall be your *tzitzit*; look at it and recall all the commandments of God and observe them, so you won't go after your own heart and your own eyes, that you might follow them to go astray.

But what of the apparent counterpoint to the *tzitzit,* the Kohen Gadol's *tzitz*? The links between the two garments suggest that, perhaps, it too was meant to be gazed at. But the question is: By *whom*? For the *tzitz* is positioned on the one place on its wearer's body — his forehead — where it is literally impossible for him to ever view it. So who was supposed to see the *tzitz*?

The answer, apparently, is the one who *encounters* the Kohen Gadol. When the Kohen Gadol, alone, enters the confines of the Holy of Holies, daring to approach the Divine Presence ensconced over the Ark of the Covenant — it is then, perhaps, that the *tzitz* attains its purpose. It is then that it is meant to be gazed at … by the Divine Being Himself.

We humans have our *tzitzit.* But reciprocally, perhaps God has a version of *tzitzit,* too: the Kohen Gadol's *tzitz.* Each serves as a kind of reminder, for after all, we have a responsibility and God has a reciprocal responsibility. We are meant to gaze at our *tzitzit* and remember the divine laws we are meant to keep. For by keeping those laws, we can hope to refine ourselves; *we can hope to become more holy.* And as for God, He is to look

---

9   See Song of Songs 2:9.

at the Kohen Gadol's *tzitz* and remember, too — that we are *trying* to become holy, as mortal and as earthly and as flawed as we are.

A Wordless Plea

The *choshen mishpat* and the *tzitz* both serve as reminders. Through them, the Kohen Gadol humbly and wordlessly addresses God on behalf of those who've sent him. He asks the Almighty to remember that, if He, God, is the giver of laws, of *mishpatim*, then we, the ones who are trying to live up to those laws, have a kind of *mishpat*, too. We have a *mishpat* in the other sense of the word: a case to present before the Heavenly Throne. We have hopes, dreams, and needs that we want the Almighty to take seriously.

Through these vestments, the Kohen Gadol asks God to remember that He is strong and we are frail, that we are easily intimidated in His Presence, and that He should remember our needs, even if we find ourselves speechless and unable to effectively present our *mishpat* before Him. Most of all, perhaps, the Kohen Gadol's clothes send a message not only to God but to us, His people. They tell us something both astounding and comforting: that the "line" of Heavenly justice will never be inclined against us, such that it's an uphill struggle for us just to be treated fairly. Poignantly, the very same God who adjures the judge to be careful with the weak empowers the Kohen Gadol to ask the same of Him, in all His dealings with us.

We no longer have a Kohen Gadol, nor a *choshen mishpat* that he would bear over his heart. But we still have books that remind us of that *choshen*. Indeed, millennia after we received those stone tablets from God, and committed ourselves to keep the Ten Commandments and the rest of His laws, great minds of our nation composed halachic works elaborating the intricacies of those laws and showing how they might apply to novel cases and new circumstances. The authors named these volumes after the Kohen Gadol's *choshen*. And these works, so named, bear testimony to the fact that we, the nation of Israel, have remembered and continue to treasure those *mishpatim* that are so dear to our Maker. These books, like the vestments for whom they were named, speak volumes. They implicitly make an argument to the Master of the Universe: Please continue to remember our *mishpat*, for we remember Yours.

Moses' Benevolent Chutzpah

וַיְחַל מֹשֶׁה אֶת־פְּנֵי יְקֹוָה
אֱלֹהָיו וַיֹּאמֶר לָמָה יְקֹוָה
יֶחֱרֶה אַפְּךָ בְּעַמֶּךָ

Moses entreated God, and he said:
"Why, God, should You be angry
with Your people?"

EXODUS 32:11

Moses' Benevolent Chutzpah

1 NO EXIT

IN THE ENTIRE TORAH, what would you say is the most astounding thing that Moses ever says?

For my money, it is something that occurs in **Parshat Ki Tisa**, in the story of the Golden Calf. There Moses is, standing atop Mt. Sinai. He has just received the Ten Commandments from the Almighty. And then, God tells him about what is happening at the bottom of the mountain. A disaster is unfolding below: In his absence, the people are worshipping a calf of their own making. The Almighty tells Moses that He is prepared to destroy the people, and to start over with just him.

Imagine you were Moses at that moment. It looks like the end is near. You are desperate to win a reprieve for the nation. What would you say?

I'm not quite sure what I would say — but seemingly, it would be anything other than what Moses actually *does* say. Here is how the Torah records Moses' response to God at that moment:

וַיְחַל מֹשֶׁה אֶת־פְּנֵי יְקוָה אֱלֹהָיו וַיֹּאמֶר לָמָה יְקוָה יֶחֱרֶה אַפְּךָ בְּעַמֶּךָ	Moses entreated God, and he said: "Why, God, should You be angry with Your people?"	Exodus 32:11

At face value, this seems to be the most outrageous defense one could possibly advance. How could Moses possibly suggest that God somehow lacks sufficient grounds to be "angry at His people"? Here the people are, standing at Mt. Sinai; they have witnessed divine revelation. They are supposed to be readying themselves to accept the Torah... and what are they doing instead? Dancing around a golden calf, an idol they fashioned with their own hands. So now, here comes Moses to defend them,

179

and he has the chutzpah to declare to God, "Why should You be angry with Your people?" What is he *talking* about?

I think finding an answer to this question is important not just because it would shed light on a single, puzzling verse; it is important because it stands to transform the way we understand the choices Moses made in what may have been the most difficult test of his leadership. So, in service of trying to gain some needed insight here, I'd like to suggest that we go back and look at the surrounding verses more carefully. Let's read some more of the back-and-forth between Moses and God, and see what jumps out at us.

Ominous Signs

The conversation between Moses and God really begins here:

Exodus 32:7

וַיְדַבֵּר יְקֹוָה אֶל־מֹשֶׁה לֶךְ־רֵד
כִּי שִׁחֵת עַמְּךָ אֲשֶׁר הֶעֱלֵיתָ
מֵאֶרֶץ מִצְרָיִם:

God said to Moses: "Go down, because your people, that you took out of Egypt, have corrupted themselves."

There are a couple of things to notice in that verse. In particular, God's words contain two signs that things look very bleak for the nation. The first is the word *shichet,* as in "the people have *corrupted* themselves." That word has a short but terrible history in the Five Books of Moses. It was, notably, the word that foreshadowed the Great Flood:

Genesis 6:12

וַיַּרְא אֱלֹהִים אֶת־הָאָרֶץ וְהִנֵּה
נִשְׁחָתָה כִּי־הִשְׁחִית כָּל־בָּשָׂר
אֶת־דַּרְכּוֹ עַל־הָאָרֶץ:

God looked upon the land — and indeed it was **corrupt**; because all flesh had **corrupted** its way upon the land.

The last time a group of people were described this way, it was the end of the line for them. Now, God seems to be setting the stage for the possibility that it might well be the end of the line for, if not the entire world, at least the nation of Israel.

The second ominous sign lies in the way God identifies the people as the nation "Moses took out of Egypt" — as if, somehow, God had little to do with it:

לֶךְ־רֵד כִּי שִׁחֵת עַמְּךָ
אֲשֶׁר הֶעֱלֵיתָ מֵאֶרֶץ
מִצְרָיִם:

"Go down, because **your people**, Moses, the ones that **you took out** of Egypt, have corrupted themselves."

Exodus 32:7

One might imagine Moses responding: *What do you mean the people that "I took out of Egypt"? You had quite a hand in the Exodus too!* But in describing them as He does, God seems to be disassociating Himself from the nation, as if, somehow, they're not His anymore… That's ominous, because it seems like the kind of thing you would need to do in preparation for destroying someone or something precious to you. It is nearly unfathomable to destroy someone you are still connected with. How, indeed, would one bear the pain? So…a would-be destroyer tends to pull back, to disassociate with the victim. And that seems to be exactly what the Almighty is doing.

So, all told, these are ominous signs. But now, keep on reading. Because in the next verses, what these signs merely imply starts to becomes quite explicit, indeed.

An Indictment and…a Pause

The Almighty goes on to detail the nature of Israel's crime:

סָרוּ מַהֵר מִן־הַדֶּרֶךְ אֲשֶׁר
צִוִּיתִם עָשׂוּ לָהֶם עֵגֶל מַסֵּכָה
וַיִּשְׁתַּחֲווּ־לוֹ וַיִּזְבְּחוּ־
לוֹ וַיֹּאמְרוּ אֵלֶּה אֱלֹהֶיךָ
יִשְׂרָאֵל אֲשֶׁר הֶעֱלוּךָ מֵאֶרֶץ
מִצְרָיִם:

They have quickly left the path that I have commanded them; they made a molten calf, they have worshipped it, they have sacrificed before it, and they have said, "This is your god, O Israel, who has taken you out of Egypt."

Exodus 32:8

If we put this in today's legal terms, we might call that an indictment. Which allows us to notice something intriguing about what happens next:

Exodus 32:9

וַיֹּאמֶר יְקֹוָה אֶל־מֹשֶׁה רָאִיתִי אֶת־הָעָם הַזֶּה וְהִנֵּה עַם־קְשֵׁה־עֹרֶף הוּא:

God said to Moses, "I have seen these people, and behold, they are stiff-necked people."

It is striking that the verse prefaces God's words with a new *vayomer*, meaning: "And God said." God has been speaking this whole time, so why add this? The new *vayomer* has the effect of creating a break between what God said before, and what God is going to say now. It suggests that God paused, as it were, before going further… in effect giving Moses a chance to speak.

But he didn't take the opportunity. Why not?

The Defense Rests

By pausing, God, acting essentially as a prosecutor, gave Moses the opportunity to rebut the charge He was leveling against the people. Except Moses, the defense attorney, didn't do that. He was silent. The reason would have to be that there was nothing that could possibly be said in the people's defense. Dancing around the calf at the foot of Sinai was simply inexcusable; there was no way around it. So, after that pause — and Moses' silence — the Almighty begins speaking again. The prosecution laid out its case, the defense had nothing to say, so now it is time for a new phase of the unfolding trial: the handing down of a verdict.

Exodus 32:9

וַיֹּאמֶר יְקֹוָה אֶל־מֹשֶׁה רָאִיתִי אֶת־הָעָם הַזֶּה וְהִנֵּה עַם־קְשֵׁה־עֹרֶף הוּא:

And God said to Moses: "I have seen these people…they are a stiff-necked people."

In Hebrew, *oref* is the back of the neck. To be a stiff-necked people means not just that you are stubborn and unchanging. It means that you've turned around and are walking away. It means you are consistently showing nothing but the back of your neck to the one you used to be talking to. No matter how hard they plead to continue the conversation, you are having none of it. You are impervious to them.

What is the one thing most likely to cause a gracious parent to decide this is not the time for grace, and to choose, instead, to deal sternly with a child? It would be this. God's judgment that the people are "stiff-necked" is bitter, indeed; it suggests that Israel has its mind made up and is not going to change. Which leads to what the Almighty says next, the bitterest pill of all:

וְעַתָּה הַנִּיחָה לִי וְיִחַר־אַפִּי בָהֶם וַאֲכַלֵּם וְאֶעֱשֶׂה אוֹתְךָ לְגוֹי גָּדוֹל:	Now, leave Me alone and let My anger flare against them and I will utterly destroy them and I will make you into a great nation.	Exodus 32:10

God tells Moses that it is over between Him and the people. I will start over with you, instead.[1]

What Now?

So let's sum this up. There's an indictment, followed by a moment to mount a defense — except that no defense is forthcoming. After that, the Almighty convicts the people, as it were, and hands down a sentence.

It seems like it is all over. Everything is signed, sealed, and delivered. But somehow, Moses didn't get the memo. For some reason, he doesn't accept that it's over.

---

1   Indeed, God's words to Moses precisely echo the words He spoke to the very first founding father of Israel, Abraham: לֶךְ־לְךָ מֵאַרְצְךָ וּמִמּוֹלַדְתְּךָ וּמִבֵּית אָבִיךָ אֶל־הָאָרֶץ אֲשֶׁר אַרְאֶךָּ: וְאֶעֶשְׂךָ לְגוֹי גָּדוֹל, "Go for yourself, from your native land and from your father's house, to the land that I will show you. And *I will make you into a great nation.*" Clearly, Moses has the opportunity to become a kind of Abraham, founder of a people. It is an opportunity that Moses will decline.

Instead, Moses finally begins to speak. But how *can* he? He was given the chance to say something in defense of the people and he passed on that chance. Which means he essentially admitted that there *was no defense*, so what is there left to say? Nevertheless, Moses speaks. He seems to sense an opening; a possibility that has just opened up, right now. But what is it?

An Opening

The opening came in the very last words God said. Listen to the wording of the verdict that God handed down. As final as it sounds, there is something decidedly un-final about it:

Exodus 32:10   וְעַתָּה הַנִּיחָה לִי וְיִחַר־אַפִּי Now, leave Me alone and let My anger
בָהֶם flare against them.

Rashi suggests that Moses inferred something from God's words. *If You're asking me to "leave You alone" and You'll destroy them*, it seems reasonable to wonder: What happens if I don't "leave You alone"? Does that mean You might not destroy them?

It certainly sounds that way. And with that in mind, Moses proceeds to "not leave God alone." Except that doing so is harder than it looks. Because…what, really, could Moses say to God in that moment?

Let's consider the options.

We already saw that Moses was fresh out of options when it came to actually defending the people's actions. There is simply no reasonable defense. So, Ramban suggests, that leaves another possibility — which, on the face of it, sounds like maybe it would work. Generally, when one is guilty of a sin, even a great sin, a heartfelt admission of guilt, coupled with a real apology can work wonders. The only problem is: In this case, Moses wasn't in a position to do this. He couldn't offer a heartfelt apology on behalf of the nation, because the people, at the foot of the mountain, were still in the middle of worshipping the calf. An apology in those circumstances is laughable (see Ramban to Exodus 32:11).

To meaningfully apologize on behalf of the people, Moses would first have to go to the bottom of the mountain, speak to the nation, and somehow get them to see the error of their ways. The problem with that, Ramban remarks, is that by the time Moses reaches the bottom of the mountain, there's likely to be nothing left of the people anymore. Remember, God had said to Moses, *Hanichah Li*, "Leave Me alone and I will destroy them." So, while those words create a sliver of an opportunity for Moses, they also close off the possibility of immediately working toward a long-term solution involving contrition and apology. There is simply no time for that right now.[2] Moses *has* to stay at the top of the mountain. He has to keep talking. But he can't defend the people, and he can't apologize for them. So… *what can he possibly say?*

Two Kinds of "Why"

As it turns out, Moses comes up with an ingenious solution. It entails saying the most outrageous thing of all:

לָמָה יְקֹוָה יֶחֱרֶה אַפְּךָ בְּעַמֶּךָ	Why, God, should You be angry with Your people?	Exodus 32:11

We asked before how he could possibly say that. Did the Almighty really lack reasons to be angry with His people just now? But to see what Moses was actually saying, you need to abandon the English translation for a moment, and look a bit more carefully at the original Hebrew.

In the question "Why, God, should You be angry with Your people?" the Hebrew word for "why" happens to be לָמָה, *lamah*. But what you need to know is that in Hebrew, that's not the only word for why. You can also ask why using the Hebrew word מַדּוּעַ, *madua*.

---

2 Later in the story, Moses *does* offer a confession and apology on behalf of the people. He goes down to the bottom of the mountain, destroys the calf, talks with the people, and comes back up again, at which point, he admits the sin and begs God's forgiveness. But he is only able to do so once the immediate crisis passes. His challenge right now is: What can Moses say, right now, at the top of the mountain — without leaving the presence of God — to buy the time necessary to get the people to see the error of their ways, and then to possibly rectify things later with an apology? (see Ramban to Exodus 32:11).

Now why would a single language have two words for "why"? There must be a difference between them. Let's explore what it is.

The Scientific "Why"

Madua, related to the modern Hebrew word *mada* (knowledge, or science), is what we might call the scientific "why." It is, I would suggest, fundamentally directed toward the past. It asks: *What happened in the past to cause the present state of affairs?*

So, for example, when Joseph, languishing in prison, notices that his cellmate is looking rather glum, he says: מַדּוּעַ פְּנֵיכֶם רָעִים הַיּוֹם, "Why do you look so crestfallen today?" (Genesis 40:7). The word for "why" there is *madua*, because Joseph is implicitly asking about the past: *What happened to get you so down?*

Similarly, when a bush that was burning but was not consumed caught Moses' eye, he stopped and asked, in genuine wonder: מַדּוּעַ לֹא־יִבְעַר הַסְּנֶה, "Why is the bush not burning?" (Exodus 3:3). The Hebrew word for "why" is likewise *madua*, because the question, in essence, was: How did things get to be this way? What is it about this bush that causes it not to burn?

But *madua* is not the only kind of "why" that one can quest after. One can also lodge a different kind of query altogether. One can ask: לָמָה (*lamah*), too.

What does *lamah* mean?

It's All in the Contraction

Lamah, I would suggest, is a contraction of ל-מה, *le* and *mah*. The prefix ל means "to" or "for," and מה means "what," yielding למה, *lamah* — as in: "to what end?" or "for what purpose?" The point here is that *lamah* doesn't ask about the past; it asks about the future. It doesn't care what *happened* to bring about the present state of affairs. It cares about what *will happen* in the future. What will a given course of action achieve? To what end are you acting? For what purpose? These are *lamah* questions.

Coming back to Moses now, at the time of the Golden Calf — when he asked God "why" he should be angry with His people, he didn't ask *madua*. He wasn't asking what happened, in the past, to make You, God, angry. The answer to that would have been obvious: *The people are dancing around a calf. We all get why You are angry.* No. Moses was asking *lamah,* a future-oriented question. He was asking: *"To what end* are You angry with Your people"? What is the purpose of this anger? What will it achieve?

Moses' Benevolent Chutzpah

To further discern what exactly Moses meant with this *lamah* question, take note, as well, how Moses chooses to refer to the people of Israel, upon whose behalf he is trying to intercede:

לָמָה יְקֹוָה יֶחֱרֶה אַפְּךָ בְּעַמֶּךָ	Why, God, should You be angry with **Your people?**	Exodus 32:11

We pointed out before that God, in His indictment of the people, had seemed to disclaim them. The Almighty had distanced Himself from the Israelites, declaring that "Moses' people had corrupted themselves." Now, Moses seems to push back: *Don't say they are "my" people, God. They are, actually Your people.*

When Moses says this, he isn't just engaging in an empty rhetorical gesture. He takes pains to substantiate his words; to show the Almighty that what he's saying is actually true. This, in fact, is the whole point of what Moses says next:

אֲשֶׁר הוֹצֵאתָ מֵאֶרֶץ מִצְרַיִם בְּכֹחַ גָּדוֹל וּבְיָד חֲזָקָה:	[Your people,] whom **You** took out of Egypt with great strength and a mighty arm.	Exodus 32:11

God simply can't credibly disassociate Himself from the people. He just took them out of Egypt with miraculous signs and wonders — *with great strength and a mighty arm.* The way the people escaped Egypt left little doubt as to who was responsible for Israel's exit from there. Sure, Moses was the "man on the ground," using his staff to orchestrate the plagues, but he wasn't the power behind the plagues. In choosing to use signs and wonders, God makes the divine identity of the ultimate Author of the Exodus …

unmistakable. Moses is thus saying to God: You publicly claimed this people as Your own. You *can't* say they're "not Yours" anymore.

Given this, what will happen if You now choose to destroy them? Moses goes on to explain exactly what he meant with his *lamah* question. *Here's what will happen* if you destroy them:

Exodus 32:12

לָמָה יֹאמְרוּ מִצְרַיִם לֵאמֹר
בְּרָעָה הוֹצִיאָם לַהֲרֹג אֹתָם
בֶּהָרִים וּלְכַלֹּתָם מֵעַל פְּנֵי
הָאֲדָמָה

Why should You cause Egypt to say that You took them out in bad [faith]; [that] You took them out to kill them on the mountaintops and to destroy them from upon the face of the earth?

Egypt will say that You were treacherous, that the entire Exodus was conducted in bad faith. You *pretended* to love the people when You took them out of slavery, but in the end, You betrayed them and got rid of them.[3] *Like it or not, God… You've tied Your destiny to theirs.*

---

3   As if to say: *Egypt will never understand the truth!* The truth, Moses is arguing, is quite literally unbelievable — and therefore there is great risk that it simply *won't* be believed. For it wasn't the case that the people were worshipping a golden calf at just *any* moment in their travels through the desert. No; the people were gathered at the foot of Mt. Sinai, waiting to receive the Torah. The Master of the Universe was, for the first time in history, coming into the world. And He was making the people a glorious offer that seemingly just can't be refused: *I'll make you a treasured nation; a kingdom of priests and a holy nation.* And right then, the people…*go dancing around a calf?*

A betrayal like that is beyond comprehension. Egypt would never believe it, for indeed, in this case, the truth is stranger than fiction. So Egypt would disregard the reports, and instead concoct what they'd see as a more plausible story for the people's demise. *It looked like the Almighty cared about them, but in the end, He lost interest, and just got rid of them.* And in making that argument, they would, in effect, be accusing God of acting in bad faith. This, I would suggest, is the meaning of Moses' words to God: בְּרָעָה הוֹצִיאָם, literally: "in bad" He took them out, i.e., in bad faith.

What Will Your Friends Say?

Moses then continues, making the reciprocal point. *It is not just Your ene-mies who won't understand. Let's talk about what Your friends will say:*

זְכֹר לְאַבְרָהָם לְיִצְחָק וּלְיִשְׂרָאֵל עֲבָדֶיךָ אֲשֶׁר נִשְׁבַּעְתָּ לָהֶם בָּךְ אַרְבֶּה אֶת־זַרְעֲכֶם כְּכוֹכְבֵי הַשָּׁמָיִם	Remember Your servants [the forefathers]: Abraham, Isaac, and Jacob. [After all,] You swore to them that "I will multiply your descendants like the stars of the heaven."	Exodus 32:13

Again, Moses is asking what purpose divine anger will serve. To this end, he points out that God had promised the forefathers that their children would be "like the stars of the heaven," virtually innumerable, when they entered the Land. So if God goes through with this threat to destroy the people, and start over with Moses…how will the forefathers regard this? If, in the end, only a small band of Moses' immediate family enters Canaan, will God's servants, the forefathers, see this as the fulfillment of His prom-ise to them? Not likely. *Where are the promised multitudes?*

Moses' question puts forward the ultimate *lamah*: What end will Your anger really serve?

Winning When Your Hand Has No Cards

How does one stop the Most Powerful Being in the universe from doing what He says He wants to do, when He has justifiable grounds to do it? Obviously, a mere mortal lacks the power to oppose God. At the end of the day, there is only one force that could *possibly* box God in. And that would be…God Himself.

You made certain decisions, God. You chose to bring the people out with signs and wonders, and You chose to swear to the forefathers that You would bring their descendants into the land "like the stars of the heavens." Those ac-tions have consequences — consequences that even You cannot escape.

Having articulated the essence of his argument, Moses concludes with a plea:

שׁוּב מֵחֲרוֹן אַפֶּךָ וְהִנָּחֵם עַל־ Turn back from Your anger; renounce
הָרָעָה לְעַמֶּךָ: the terrible [decree] against Your people.

Lamah, indeed: You have every right to be angry. But where will that anger lead? Destroying the people can't be an option anymore. Your own reputation won't allow for it.

Moses, from Sinai's summit, mounted what was perhaps the first known filibuster in recorded history. Circumstances required him to stay there and speak, but there was nothing he could possibly say. So, he found a way to say the impossible, and somehow, it worked. He found a way to save the people when seemingly no such path existed at all.

Buying Time

What did Moses do here?

In essence, he bought time. Time for him to go down the mountain. Time to destroy the calf and talk the people back to their senses. Time to slowly, carefully, craft a reconciliation between the people and the God they seemingly had all but rejected. The following chapters in the book of Exodus tell the story of that slow reconciliation process. But the greatness of Moses' actions in those first moments atop the mountain, in his initial interaction with God just as Israel was worshipping the calf, was that he found a way to buy that time in the first place.

In order to buy the time the people and God would need to patch things up between them, Moses mounted a clever argument; there is no doubt about that. But it was not principally in the *cleverness* of his argument that his heroism lies. It wasn't just that Moses found an ingenious, intellectual solution to a bedeviling puzzle. Something else was going on here, too. Moses' heroism here was a function not just of his mind but of his character. Fate was calling forth from Moses more than mere tactical brilliance.

What was that "something else"? Let's take a moment to explore it.

Let's take one more dive into the language of Moses' back-and-forth with God. This time, as we read, let's ask, together: *Where have we heard any of this before?*

Echoes of Apocalypse

Well, let's start with that word *shachet* we were talking about above. We saw before how it echoes the way God talked about mankind right before the Great Flood. But as it turns out, that word is really just the tip of the proverbial iceberg. *Many* words and phrases in the story we've just looked at echo aspects of the Great Flood. Here are just a few of them:

Listen to the language the text uses to describe how Moses begins to plead with God:

וַיְחַל מֹשֶׁה אֶת־פְּנֵי יְקֹוָה אֱלֹהָיו	And Moses implored the Lord, his God.	Exodus 32:11

That verb *vayechal* — take a moment to note its spelling: *vav, yod, chet, lamed*. Now, would you care to hazard a guess as to how many times in the Torah we've seen those letters, in that order, form a word before? It turns out that happens only twice before this. And each of the times it happens, the word that is formed appears in connection with ... Noah:

וַיָּחֶל עוֹד שִׁבְעַת יָמִים אֲחֵרִים וַיֹּסֶף שַׁלַּח אֶת־הַיּוֹנָה מִן־הַתֵּבָה:	He waited another seven days, and again sent out the dove from the ark.	Genesis 8:10
וַיָּחֶל נֹחַ אִישׁ הָאֲדָמָה וַיִּטַּע כָּרֶם:	Noah, the tiller of soil, began to plant a vineyard.	Genesis 9:20

Noah "waits" (ויחל) before sending out a bird; and Noah "begins" (ויחל) to plant a vineyard. In each case, the meaning of the word differs from its third use, with Moses, where the word means "to entreat." Nevertheless, its spelling is the same.

That's connection number two. Still might be a coincidence. But here's number three: How many biblical characters do you know of who ever lived…in an ark?

Well, you might say, there *was* another person who found shelter from threatening waters in a little boat. That would be Moses, when, as an infant, his life was threatened while he lay helpless in a little box among the reeds of the Nile's shoreline.

And note, by the way, that it is not only the *idea* of an "ark," or a "life-saving boat," that reappears with Moses. The exact language reappears, too. Each ark is known in Hebrew as a *teivah*:

Exodus 2:3	וְלֹא־יָכְלָה עוֹד הַצְּפִינוֹ וַתִּקַּח־לוֹ תֵּבַת גֹּמֶא וַתַּחְמְרָה בַחֵמָר וּבַזָּפֶת וַתָּשֶׂם בָּהּ אֶת־הַיֶּלֶד וַתָּשֶׂם בַּסּוּף עַל־שְׂפַת הַיְאֹר׃

When she could hide him no longer, she got a wicker **ark** for him and caulked it with tar and pitch. She put the child into it and placed it among the reeds by the bank of the Nile.

These are the only two contexts in the entire Five Books of Moses where that word ever appears.

Let's continue. Here's another trivia question for you: How many people in the Torah ended up spending forty days and forty nights in an extreme environment, with no outside access to food? That would be Noah, cooped up in the ark while it rained incessantly…and Moses, when, alone atop Mt. Sinai, he encountered God:

Exodus 34:28	וַיְהִי־שָׁם עִם־יְקֹוָה אַרְבָּעִים יוֹם וְאַרְבָּעִים לַיְלָה לֶחֶם לֹא אָכַל וּמַיִם לֹא שָׁתָה

And he was there with the Lord forty days and forty nights; he ate no bread and drank no water.

Finally, here's one more language connection, which I'll phrase for you in terms of a riddle: *How many people in the Torah do you know of who…end up sending birds away from them?*

Noah did, famously, several times — first a raven, and then a dove (Genesis 8:7–8). But intriguingly, Moses *also* did — at least in a manner of speaking. For Moses' wife just happened to be named…Tziporah — the Hebrew word for "bird." And look what the Torah tells us about her:

וַיִּקַּח יִתְרוֹ חֹתֵן מֹשֶׁה אֶת־צִפֹּרָה אֵשֶׁת מֹשֶׁה אַחַר שִׁלּוּחֶֽיהָ׃	Moses' father-in-law, Yitro, took Tziporah, wife of Moses, after her having been sent away.[4]	Exodus 18:2

Starting Over

So let's posit, for a moment, that these language echoes aren't just the products of mere accident. Let's say the Torah really wants its readers to be hearing echoes of Noah, even as they peruse the story of Moses. The next question to ask is: *Why?* What is it about Moses' story that is so very-"Noah-like"?

And it is here, in the answer to that question, that we come to the great, overarching thematic parallel between the two stories. It isn't just about the *shachet*, the *vayachel*, the arks, the forty days and nights, or even the sending away of birds. It is about something much larger. It is about a grand bargain. A bargain proposed by God to a man…only twice in human history:

I'll destroy everyone, and start over with you.

---

4 Note, as well, that the Hebrew verb for the "sending" of Noah's birds and Moses' wife, Tziporah, is identical:it is שלח, as in וַיְשַׁלַּח אֶת־הָעֹרֵב (Gen. 8:7).

Other connections abound as well. For example: The Torah describes God's destruction of humanity during the flood using the term מחה, as in אֶמְחֶה אֶת־הָאָדָם אֲשֶׁר־בָּרָאתִי מֵעַל פְּנֵי הָאֲדָמָה, "I will **wipe out** from the earth the men whom I created." Likewise, Moses tells God that it will not do for Him to destroy all of Israel and to spare him alone; if You'll try to do that, Moses says, מְחֵנִי נָא מִסִּפְרְךָ אֲשֶׁר כָּתָבְתָּ, "**Wipe me out** from the book You've written!"

Curiously, as well, the newly dry land upon which Noah treads when he exits the ark is known as *charavah*. And the mountain Moses treads upon? It is *Chorev* — a name seemingly derived from the same root.

God's history with Noah is the background against which we need to read the story of Moses and God after the Golden Calf. The people of Israel, like the inhabitants of Noah's world, had committed crimes so great that the Creator was willing and ready to wipe them out. In each case, the Heavenly Judge had issued an indictment. In each case, a single human found himself unable to articulate a defense. In each case, a verdict was reached, and a sentence handed down. And in each case, a single man was being offered a bargain: *Everyone else is lost. Let Me start over with you.*

God struck that bargain with a man named Noah. And he tried to strike it again with a man named Moses. Only this time...the man said no.

Just Be a Noah to Me

The contrast between the two men is highlighted dramatically by a searing double entendre that haunts the words God uses to propose the bargain to Moses. Listen carefully to them:

Exodus 32:10	וְעַתָּה הַנִּיחָה לִּי וְיִחַר־אַפִּי בָהֶם וַאֲכַלֵּם וְאֶעֱשֶׂה אוֹתְךָ לְגוֹי גָּדוֹל:

Now leave Me alone and let My anger flare against them, and I will utterly destroy them, and I will make you into a great nation.

Focus on those opening words, *Now leave Me alone.* Forget the English translation now, and look at the Hebrew. What do you see?

הניחה לי

How do you spell that word meaning "leave Me alone"? Lurking right there, in the middle of that word, is nothing less than...*Noah's name*:

הניחה לי

The double entendre adds depth and meaning to what's going on. The plain and direct way to read the words is that the Almighty told Moses to "just leave Him alone," and that He would destroy the people. But a secondary way to read the words adds another layer of meaning. God was also saying, in effect: *And now, Moses...*הניחה לי.

Hanicha Li—just be a Noah to Me.

It is as if God were saying to Moses: *Noah left Me alone when I told him I'm going to destroy the world. Why don't you leave Me alone, also?*

Except that Moses, as we saw above, discerned an important implication in God's words. There was an opening there. *Overtly, You are telling me to leave You alone. But covertly, what are You saying? You are implying that I have a say in the matter. You are implying if I don't listen to You; if I don't leave You alone, then maybe You won't destroy. In effect, then, You are asking me...not to leave You alone.* So I won't.

This, indeed, is exactly how Rashi understands the inference that Moses made here.[5] God's words taken at face value displayed nothing but the finality of judgment. But hidden within them could be discerned the still-glowing embers of divine compassion. Moses was attentive to that, and responded to it.

A Simple Twist of Fate

With all this in mind, consider one last connection between the stories of Moses and Noah. It lies in the way the exchange between Moses and God at the top of the mountain finally ends. After the Almighty asks Moses to leave Him alone, and Moses declines, after Moses invokes the likely reaction of Egypt and Israel's forefathers to news that the nation has been destroyed — after all that, we get this:

וַיִּנָּחֶם יְקֹוָה עַל־הָרָעָה אֲשֶׁר דִּבֶּר לַעֲשׂוֹת לְעַמּוֹ:	And God regretted having said He would bring destruction upon His people.[6]	Exodus 32:14

So now I have a question for you: When is the only other time in the Torah that we ever encounter that phrase — *vayinachem Hashem*, "and God regretted"?

In all Five Books of Moses, it appears elsewhere only once. That lone other occurrence is — maybe you guessed it by now — in the case of the Great Flood. Here is the language the Torah uses to describe God's decision to wipe out humanity with that flood:

---

5   See Rashi to Exodus 32:10. Cf. Shemot Rabbah 42:9; cf. also Berachot 32a.

6   Alternatively, "And God renounced the destruction He said He would bring upon His people." The word *vayinachem* is tricky to translate. Rashi (to Gen. 6:6) suggests the word conveys a change of mind or in perspective.

Genesis 6:5–6

וַיַּ֣רְא יְהֹוָ֔ה כִּ֥י רַבָּ֛ה רָעַ֥ת
הָאָדָ֖ם בָּאָ֑רֶץ וְכׇל־יֵ֙צֶר֙
מַחְשְׁבֹ֣ת לִבּ֔וֹ רַ֥ק רַ֖ע כׇּל־הַיּֽוֹם׃
וַיִּנָּ֣חֶם יְהֹוָ֔ה כִּֽי־עָשָׂ֥ה אֶת־
הָֽאָדָ֖ם בָּאָ֑רֶץ וַיִּתְעַצֵּ֖ב
אֶל־לִבּֽוֹ׃

The Lord saw how great was man's
wickedness on earth, and how every plan
devised by his mind was nothing but evil
all the time. **And God regretted** having
made man on earth, and His heart was
saddened.[7]

Interestingly, although the words are the same in each instance — "God
regretted" — the meaning of the words is completely inverted. In Genesis,
God regrets the decision to bring man into existence, and He decides instead to *destroy*. In Exodus, God regrets the decision to destroy, and instead, chooses to *maintain* the existence of the nation He founded.

Given how parallel the stories of Noah and Moses run, it would seem
almost as if fate had decreed that the latter story would need to end with
words borrowed from the former. And indeed it does. The fateful words
through which God decided to destroy humanity would reappear in the
story of Moses. But *how* those words would reappear — what their *meaning* would be — that was yet to be determined. And in the end, their meaning flipped. The words that in Genesis were used to destroy, in Exodus …
were used to save:

---

7   The parallels between the two texts are actually somewhat more extensive than
the repetition of the single phrase *vayinachem Hashem*. There are at least three in-
terconnected elements:

God Relents about the Destruction of Israel	God Decides upon the Destruction of Humanity
וַיִּנָּ֣חֶם יְהֹוָ֑ה עַל־הָ֣רָעָ֔ה אֲשֶׁ֥ר דִּבֶּ֖ר לַעֲשׂ֥וֹת לְעַמּֽוֹ׃ (שמות לב:יד)	וַיַּ֣רְא יְהֹוָ֔ה כִּ֥י רַבָּ֛ה רָעַ֥ת הָאָדָ֖ם בָּאָ֑רֶץ וְכׇל־יֵ֙צֶר֙ מַחְשְׁבֹ֣ת לִבּ֔וֹ רַ֥ק רַ֖ע כׇּל־הַיּ֑וֹם׃ וַיִּנָּ֣חֶם יְהֹוָ֔ה כִּֽי־עָשָׂ֥ה אֶת־הָֽאָדָ֖ם בָּאָ֑רֶץ וַיִּתְעַצֵּ֖ב אֶל־לִבּֽוֹ׃ (בראשית ו:ה-ו)

וַיִּנָּחֶם יְקֹוָק עַל־הָרָעָה אֲשֶׁר
דִּבֶּר לַעֲשׂוֹת לְעַמּוֹ׃

And God regretted having said He would bring destruction upon His people.

Exodus 32:14

What was the difference?

The difference was Moses. Moses somehow manages to create a different ending in his story. At the time of the flood, God had assumed the role of Heavenly Judge; He had made up His mind, informed Noah of what was to happen, and it seemed there was no way to change that fate. So, silently, Noah waited for the rain to come.

Later, Moses would encounter a similar moment in history. When God told Moses about the impending destruction of Israel, Moses, like Noah, was at least temporarily forced into silence. The Judge had spoken. Defense seemed impossible. It seemed there was no way out. It seemed like all you could do was leave God alone, stand aside, and watch the destruction to come.

And yet, when God asked Moses to leave Him alone, to "be a Noah" to Him, Moses refused. Moses simply would not accept the inevitability of the situation. He wouldn't accept that God was *only* a Judge in Heaven; God's compassion was still there to be found, even in this darkest of times. It *had* to be. So Moses entreated God:

וַיְחַל מֹשֶׁה אֶת־פְּנֵי יְקֹוָק אֱלֹהָיו   Moses **entreated** Hashem, his God.

Exodus 32:11

Moses turned "waiting" — one form of *vayechal* — into a different form of the word, into a different phenomenon entirely. He started talking with nothing to say, and somehow, he found the words to keep talking. By the time he was done, the words *vayinachem Hashem* would ring out once more, but their meaning would be reversed. God would change His mind about destruction. Moses had created a path to salvation, almost out of sheer force of will.

It is ironic, indeed, that the man who opposed God so forcefully in this story of the Golden Calf should, at the end of his life, come to be known as "the servant of God." But maybe that's what it *means* to be a servant of God: to defend His people even when they've lost the right, according to strict divine justice, to continue to exist; to hear a divine command insisting that You leave God alone, and discern in that command something else…a hidden opportunity to *not* leave God alone.

The line between service of God and defiance of God is a very thin one indeed. Moses walked that tightrope successfully. And we, the children of those he saved, are forever in his debt.

3   MOSES' FINEST HOUR

In conclusion, I want to suggest to you that the story we've been looking at — this interaction Moses has with God just as God tells him the people are worshipping a golden calf at the foot of the mountain — isn't just another one of the many interactions Moses has with God in the forty-year journey from Egypt to the Promised Land. No. This is different. There is something climactic about what is happening here.

I want to argue that this, to quote Winston Churchill, was Moses' finest hour. His whole life was leading up to this. It was, perhaps, the moment for which he was chosen.

Indeed, consider this: Why *did* God select Moses, of all people, to lead the Israelites out of Egypt? There's no question he was a reluctant candidate. At the Burning Bush, Moses proffered many reasons why he *shouldn't* be the one to go to Pharaoh on Israel's behalf. And yet, the Almighty didn't take no for an answer. He didn't simply move on to select someone else. He sticks with Moses, tenaciously, as if he were the only viable candidate. Apparently, no one else will do. I think it is worth wondering: What *was* it about Moses that made him the ideal candidate — the *only* candidate — for the job?

While the Torah doesn't tell us outright, it does suggest an answer to this question. The answer comes in the form of the vignettes the Torah chooses to tell us about Moses, just before he was chosen. Those stories would seem to be his résumé, as it were — the "bullet points" that convinced God that Moses' was the only one for The Job.

What was in that résumé?

A Common Denominator

We know several things about Moses before God appears to him at the Burning Bush. We know, first of all, that he faced almost certain death, as an infant, by the shores of the Nile where he was saved by the daughter of Pharaoh. The princess could have seen herself as a mere bystander and not responded to the cries of the child in the reeds — but she didn't do that. She saved him, at great personal risk to herself.

After that episode, we hear that when he grows up, he performs a version of what his adoptive mother did: He finds himself confronted by the sight of an Israelite slave who was being beaten by an Egyptian, and he intercedes. He kills the aggressor and saves the victim. In doing this, he surely knows that he is in effect saying goodbye to his own life of comfort and privilege in the palace. But he does it anyway, to save someone who had no one else to turn to for help.

Shortly after this, Moses witnesses another altercation — this time between two Israelites. Again, he intercedes to save the victim, forcing him to flee Egypt. And finally, after he runs away to Midian to escape arrest by Pharaoh's agent, he does it again: He stands up against a gang of shepherds who were harassing a group of shepherd girls — Yitro's daughters.

The common denominator of all these episodes? *Moses consistently puts himself at risk to save others who are in danger.* Factor out everything else, and it is this that remains. It doesn't matter who the victim is, Israelite or gentile. And it doesn't matter who the aggressor is, Israelite or gentile. He always intercedes to save those in peril, no matter how powerful the aggressor. He never remains a mere bystander.

Immediately after we hear about all these stories involving Moses, we hear about God selecting him, at the Burning Bush, to lead Israel out of slavery. I would submit that's not a coincidence. In telling us these stories, the Torah is telling us why he was chosen: *Moses is willing to go against any aggressor, no matter how powerful, to save someone in danger.*

A Refusal to Stand By

Why would *that* particular quality be so important for Israel's leader to possess?

The answer might have something to do with … the Golden Calf. Even at the Burning Bush, at the very inception of Israel's national life — the omniscient God is aware of what their darkest moment might be like. There could come a moment in this people's future when they might do something so reprehensible as to lose the right to continue to be God's people. *And what then?*

Maybe *that* is the moment Moses was chosen for. The moment where, for Israel to survive, its leader would have to face the justified anger of the most powerful Being of all: the Master of the Universe Himself.

As he would in all those previous episodes in his life, Moses refused to be a bystander. He took God's command to stand aside and heard in it something else: *the possibility that he could disobey the command, and destruction might not come.* In order to have the gall to do this, Moses would have to call on nothing less than the experience of his own life. Moses, who in his own life displayed compassion over and over again, would need to believe in the authenticity of that compassion so deeply that he saw in it not just a quirk of his own personality, but a deep reflection of His Maker. *Even when you couldn't see it, God was compassionate, too. He had to be.*

And so, Moses took a risk. He said no. He risked defying God in order to stand with Israel. And in that moment, he reached out to touch his destiny. He became the leader he was always meant to be.

A Peculiar Kind of Rest

שֵׁשֶׁת יָמִים תֵּעָשֶׂה
מְלָאכָה וּבַיּוֹם הַשְּׁבִיעִי
יִהְיֶה לָכֶם קֹדֶשׁ שַׁבַּת
שַׁבָּתוֹן לַיקֹוָה

On six days work may be done, but on the seventh day you shall have a Sabbath of complete rest, holy to God.

EXODUS 35:2

A Peculiar Kind of Rest

PARSHAT VAYAKHEL SPEAKS BRIEFLY about Sabbath rest before going on to detail the construction of utensils used in the Tabernacle. That juxtaposition of topics may seem to be of only marginal interest, but, as we shall soon see, the Sages of the Talmud saw something profound in it. I want to explore with you what it is that I think they understood. I'd like to begin by telling you about a scene I witnessed recently when I happened to attend a weekend away at a hotel along with a group of other observant Jews.

A Perilous Choice

A large extended family had checked in to celebrate *sheva brachot* for their daughter. As it happens, the father of the bride had, unfortunately, taken ill and was confined to a wheelchair. As one might well imagine, that made getting around the hotel, especially on the Sabbath, a bit of a challenge. The guest rooms were on different floors than the banquet hall, and because observant Jews generally refrain from using electricity on the Sabbath, this rendered the elevators pretty much useless to the family.[1]

What to do, then, with the wheelchair-bound father of the bride? Well, there's always the stairs, but needless to say, long staircases are not very friendly terrain for wheelchairs. So, five burly sons and sons-in-law devised another plan. They wheeled Dad to the top of a large staircase, hoisted him (still strapped into the chair) carefully aloft, and slowly started making a stair-by-stair descent.

---

1 Halachah makes certain exceptions around the edges of Sabbath observance for those who have fallen ill. So, from a technical standpoint, our wheelchair-bound dad might have found a way to use make use of the hotel elevators, within the confines of Jewish law. Nevertheless, he and his children evidently felt uncomfortable with that option, and opted, for better or for worse, to take the stairs instead.

When they were about halfway down the staircase, another hotel guest caught sight of this hair-raising spectacle. Aghast, he pointed to the elevator and exclaimed to the descending wheelchair bearers, sweating and out of breath, that they could much more easily use *that*. At which point, one of the bearers of the wheelchair politely replied: "Thanks very much, sir, but we can't use the elevator today. This is our Sabbath. You see, it is our day of *rest*."

With that, he and the others hoisted Dad aloft again and continued carrying him down the stairs, prompting the bewildered guest to remark: "Folks, if this is your day of rest, I'd hate to see what your days of *work* look like!"

The guest's exclamation perfectly captures a broad and obvious difficulty: *Why do we observe the Sabbath the way we do?* We seem to have such a strange understanding of what "rest" means. Lighting a match or making a small furrow in the ground, not to mention pressing the button on an elevator, is somehow deemed a violation of "Sabbath rest." But schlepping a wheelchair-bound person up and down a flight of stairs is evidently perfectly consistent with Sabbath rest. It seems so counterintuitive.

How Hard Was It for God to Create the World?

A clue to answering this puzzling question can be found if we entertain some big-picture theological questions around the notion of Sabbath rest. For starters: If the Sabbath we observe commemorates God's rest after six days of work creating the universe — why *did* God feel so compelled to "rest" after those first six days? Yes, creating a universe sounds like hard work, at least from a human standpoint. But from a divine standpoint, *how hard could it really have been?* God is an all-powerful Being; was He really "tired" afterward? Was He seeking a breather to gather His strength before moving on to other tasks? The notion of God "needing" rest is preposterous. So why did the Almighty bother resting at all?

Rosa Parks Day

Moreover, whatever the answer to that question is, why do we go to the trouble of building a whole big holiday around the notion of God's rest? It also seems counterintuitive. Seemingly, the Sabbath commemorates

God's creation of the world: God created the world in six days and rested on the seventh, and to remember God's authorship of creation, we rest just like He did. But if it is creation we are remembering, why do we memorialize that by *resting*?

The strength of this question becomes evident if we take it out of the realm of the theological and bring it down to earth a bit. Imagine you were a town council member, and the township was debating ways to commemorate a new holiday on the town calendar: Rosa Parks Day. The holiday is supposed to commemorate Rosa's heroic stand against segregation, when the civil rights icon refused to move to the back of a segregated bus. The town council wants to commemorate her historic act, and is considering ways to do so. What symbolic activity could townsfolk engage in on Rosa Parks Day to remember what she did?

A few folks on the council propose that it would be nice to ask people to ride buses around town on this day, and for everyone to stand in the front of the bus while doing so, just like Rosa did. Other council members nod their heads in agreement. But then some newly elected councilperson raises his hand and suggests something else: "I know," he says. "Let's all…take naps on Rosa Parks Day."

Naps? Why should anyone take naps? So he explains: "You see, Rosa was very tired when she came back from her bus ride — so when she came home, she immediately went to take a nap. So…we should all nap too, just like Rosa did."

And now imagine his suggestion carried the day. That would be startling, a truly odd way to commemorate Rosa's act of civil disobedience. But aren't we doing something every bit as strange every week when we observe the Sabbath as we do? *We rest because that's what God did after creation.* But isn't God's rest really besides the point? If anything, we should *create* like God did! Every six days or so, we should all…make paper-mache globes or something, to symbolically reenact God's creation of the world. Why do we *rest*?

The Secret of Rest

Evidently, we aren't just remembering that God created the world. As the verse itself seems to suggest, we are remembering, every week, a composite idea: that God *first* created the world and *then* He rested. The emphasis is on the latter notion every bit as much as the former. God's rest is essential, not incidental, to what we are celebrating and remembering. There is something sacred about God's rest.

I want to suggest that creativity — or at least the kind of creativity God engaged in when He created the world — absolutely *requires* rest afterward and that this rest is to be treated as a treasured thing. Let's explore why this might be so.

What Do You Do When You Want to Create a World?

When in six primal days, God fashioned the world, what is it that He was principally doing? He was creating. But what does that entail?

Well, creativity, in the context of the genesis of the universe, wasn't just a matter of making something out of nothing. It *was* that, to be sure, at least at the very beginning — but it was more, too. God was taking that which *was*, and molding it into something more complex and sophisticated. He was taking electrons and protons and molding them into hydrogen atoms. He was taking water and causing species of marine life to arise from it (Genesis 1:20). He was taking earth and fashioning from it the body of a human being (2:7). In a word, God was performing… *melachah*, the kind of transformative work you do when you want to create a world.

Genesis 2:2	וַיְכַל אֱלֹהִים בַּיּוֹם הַשְּׁבִיעִי מְלַאכְתּוֹ אֲשֶׁר עָשָׂה וַיִּשְׁבֹּת בַּיּוֹם הַשְּׁבִיעִי מִכָּל־מְלַאכְתּוֹ אֲשֶׁר עָשָׂה:	On the seventh day God finished the *melachah* that He had been doing, and He ceased on the seventh day from all the melachah that He had done.

Humans also engage in *melachah*. Any time a person kindles a flame, or plows, or weaves — no matter how easily and routinely he or she does it — they master the world around them and mold it to suit their liking in ways an animal could never do. In fact, one might even argue that the more routinely people engage in these actions, the more our mastery over nature is evident. When man takes the raw material of the world around him and molds it, when he brings it into higher states of being in accordance with his will — he imitates his Heavenly Creator.[2]

All told, God's activity during the six days of creation actually had very little in common with dragging a heavy table around the house, or a wheelchair up a flight of stairs. But it had everything to do with striking a match, or even kindling the modern kind of fire we call electricity — the kind of "fire" those sons-in-law were thinking about resisting when they avoided using the elevator.[3] Indeed, dragging a table just moves an object from point A to point B. This might be *avodah,* the more generic Hebrew word for "work," but it is not *melachah.* Which is to say, it might make you tired, but it doesn't transform the world in any way. Igniting fire, though, as routine as it seems, is different. *Melachah* mimics the kind of creativity God involved Himself in when He created the world — hence, it is forbidden on the Sabbath. Indeed, technology as we know it begins with the mastery of a kind of fire — taking electricity and converting it, transforming it into controlled voltage, power that allows us to charge our phones, turn on lights, and yes, take elevators, too.

This specialized kind of activity, *melachah,* demands rest. Not the kind of rest that is a mere means to an end, like the break that helps you recoup your energy so you can engage in another bout of work. No, it demands the kind of rest that is *an end in and of itself.* Indeed, if we are to take the words of our Friday night prayers seriously, God deemed the rest which replaced His *melachah* to be so important that, astonishingly, it could rightly be called the very purpose of creation itself:

---

2   For a beautifully rendered articulation of this idea, see Dayan Dr. I. Grunfeld's *The Sabbath: A Guide to Its Understanding and Observance,* 5th ed. (Jerusalem: Feldheim, 2013).

3   Pressing a button on the elevator connects two circuits that create a flow of electricity, a flash of electrons, that sends the elevator up or down. Modern halachic decisors have classified this as a subcategory of one of two types of *melachah*: the prohibition against kindling fire or the prohibition against building (others suggest the *melachah* of *makkeh bepatish*; for a discussion of the various views, see *Chazon Ish, Orach Chaim* 50:9).

Sabbath
evening prayer

אַתָּה קִדַּשְׁתָּ אֶת יוֹם הַשְּׁבִיעִי
לִשְׁמֶךָ, תַּכְלִית מַעֲשֵׂה שָׁמַיִם
וָאָרֶץ.

You made the seventh day holy for Your name, it being the very purpose of the making of heaven and earth.

The Death of Creativity

Why is rest from creativity so precious? Why is it that even the most all-powerful Creator — the kind of Being who would never get tired — would insist on engaging in rest after performing *melachah*?

The answer is: we get something profound by resting after *melachah*. Paradoxically enough, stopping and resting after creating something is, in a way, the most creative act of all. Because…consider what happens when a creator *doesn't* stop. When unabated creativity continues indefinitely, it eventually ceases to be constructive. As a matter of fact, it eventually destroys itself.

The examples are everywhere. The artist who always has one more brushstroke to add; the editor who constantly needs to rearrange sentences one more time; the parent who can't let go, who always wants to "fix" his child, no matter how established or grown up that child becomes. All of these things are acts of creativity gone bad. They can cause the object of creation to simply collapse under its own weight. At some point, a creator needs to let go, to be at rest. When he does, he sets his creation free and makes it independent. When he doesn't, he compromises the very thing he is trying to make perfect.

Deciding to be at rest isn't easy. A creator finds it hard to let go, because that seems like the end. And in a way, it is. Letting go of something I made engenders a natural sense of mourning. The wondrous act of making something is over, and what has emerged is separate from me now. But that, really, is cause for celebration. For when I finally let go, what I've created stands independently in the world, able to go about its business and fulfill its destiny. It is for this reason that resting is really the final, creative, act; it grants independence to the thing I've created. *It is that which makes it "something else," rather than being just my puppet.*

Rest Is When Relationship Becomes Possible

Indeed, the moment of letting go is important not just for the thing being created; it is also important for the creator of that thing. For it is now that I, the creator, can truly *relate* to what I've brought forth. So long as I'm tinkering with something, I'm not relating to it or establishing a connection with it. Only once I've let go of the thing I've created can I now appreciate it *for what it is in itself*, right now — not for what I can still try to make it into.

It is this kind of rest that the Almighty inaugurated into the world on the first Sabbath. As the sixth day came to a close, the Almighty made a conscious, fateful decision to stop tinkering with the universe and with the humans He created within it. He looked at His handiwork and declared: *"Indeed, it is very good."* This proclamation signaled God's willingness to stop making the universe better, to stop fixing it, and to begin the process of relating to it for what it is.

The Almighty stopped not because the work was over. The work of improving things is never "over." But He pulled back and left that work in the hands of mankind. It was now up to us to pick up the mantle of *melachah* — to imitate the Divine by becoming earthly creators. In the words of the verse, our charge would be to "guard the world and to work it,"[4] to leave to the next generation a world better than the world we were given. Indeed, God, in His benevolence, decided to share with humans — these new, earthly creators — the capacity for *melachah*, but along with that capacity He taught us something about *melachah*, and it amounts to this: the act of creation is seductive, and if one is not careful, it can become all-consuming. *If you wait to rest for the moment your creations are complete, you will never rest.* So God also shared with us…the gift of the Sabbath, the imperative to step back from incessant *melachah*. Through it, man learns to emulate his Creator, and to crown creativity with rest.

The Magic of Rest

In truth, it is not just the world around us that we learn to appreciate through rest; it's the people in that world as well. We all have our top five ways we would like to change our spouse to suit our needs. And most of us, at least in subtle ways, try to make these wishes known…as gently as

---

4   In Hebrew the verse says לְעָבְדָהּ וּלְשָׁמְרָהּ (Gen. 2:15).

possible, of course. But again, as long as you are in the process of tinkering, of trying to improve him or her, you are not in the business of relating. To let go is to make a powerful statement: I love you, and I want to relate to you — right now, for the person you are *now*, not just for what I might eventually make you into.

In letting go, we are finally able to appreciate the world for what it is, not just for what it can do for us. On the Sabbath, we escape the relentless drive to endlessly fiddle at the edges, and we taste the deliciousness of pure being.

An "Apartment" in Our Everything

וַיֹּאמֶר מֹשֶׁה אֶל־בְּנֵי יִשְׂרָאֵל רְאוּ קָרָא יְקֹוָה בְּשֵׁם בְּצַלְאֵל בֶּן־אוּרִי בֶן־חוּר לְמַטֵּה יְהוּדָה:

And Moses said to the Israelites: "See, God has singled out by name Bezalel, son of Uri son of Hur, of the tribe of Judah."

EXODUS 35:30

211

An "Apartment" in Our Everything

Note to Reader: This essay can be read alone, but it further develops some ideas laid out in our previous essay on Parshat Vayakhel, "A Peculiar Kind of Rest." I'd recommend reading that essay first, then moving on to this one.

The Sabbath and the *Mishkan*

In our last essay on **Parshat Vayakhel**, we began to explore the enigma of Sabbath rest. But an important question remains, and I'd like to raise it with you:

Let's accept that *melachah*, for the purpose of Sabbath laws, is loosely defined as "creative labor," the kind of transformative, creative activity we described in the previous essay. All well and good. But now let's get down to the brass-tacks question: What particular activities actually count as "creative labor"? And it is here that we find something surprising. The Sages of the Talmud, in order to answer this question, turned to a section of the Torah entirely unrelated to the Sabbath. For some reason, they used the Torah's laws for constructing the *Mishkan*, the Tabernacle, to develop their paradigm for the types of creative labor prohibited on the Sabbath.[1]

In essence, the Rabbis said: If you want to understand what you're not allowed to do on the Sabbath, just look at what the people of Israel did when constructing the *Mishkan*. The people colored material with dyes, so coloring material with dye is prohibited on the Sabbath. The people engaged in weaving when constructing the *Miskhan*, so weaving is prohibited on the Sabbath… and so on, and so on. The Sages ultimately delineated thirty-nine different types of activities that are prohibited on the Sabbath, all deriving in some way from what the Israelites did when they

---

1   See Mechilta de-Rabbi Yishmael 35:1, Talmud Yerushalmi Shabbat 7:2, Shabbat 70a.

constructed the Tabernacle. So the question I want to ask you is: *Why?* What did the Sages see in the Tabernacle's construction that made them think this should be used as a kind of blueprint for… Sabbath labor, of all things?

Now, at the technical, halachic level, the answer to this question is not hard to answer. Indeed, the Sages themselves tell us of the technical rationale behind their reasoning: the Talmud, in tractate Shabbat,[2] states that in **Parshat Vayakhel** the Torah juxtaposes verses that command us to construct the Tabernacle with verses that command us to observe the Sabbath. First, the Torah speaks to us about keeping the Sabbath:

Exodus 35:1–2

אֵלֶּה הַדְּבָרִים אֲשֶׁר־צִוָּה יְקֹוָה
לַעֲשֹׂת אֹתָם: שֵׁשֶׁת יָמִים
תֵּעָשֶׂה מְלָאכָה וּבַיּוֹם הַשְּׁבִיעִי
יִהְיֶה לָכֶם קֹדֶשׁ שַׁבַּת שַׁבָּתוֹן
לַיקֹוָה

These are the things that God has commanded you to do: On six days work may be done, but on the seventh day you shall have a Sabbath of complete rest, holy to the Lord.

And immediately after this, the Torah tells us of the need to construct the utensils that would be used in the Tabernacle:

Exodus 35:4–5, 10–11

זֶה הַדָּבָר אֲשֶׁר־צִוָּה יְקֹוָה
לֵאמֹר: קְחוּ מֵאִתְּכֶם תְּרוּמָה
לַיקֹוָה...וְכָל־חֲכַם־לֵב בָּכֶם
יָבֹאוּ וְיַעֲשׂוּ אֵת כָּל־אֲשֶׁר צִוָּה
יְקֹוָה: אֶת־הַמִּשְׁכָּן אֶת־אָהֳלוֹ
וְאֶת־מִכְסֵהוּ

This is the thing that God has commanded: Take from among you gifts to the Lord… And let all among you who are skilled come and make all that the Lord has commanded: the Tabernacle, its tent, and its covering.

From that alignment of verses, the Sages inferred a connection between the Sabbath laws and the construction of the *Mishkan*.[3] And there it is,

---

2   Shabbat 49b.

3   Indeed, it almost seems as if the Torah *itself* is connecting the laws, inasmuch as each set of laws is introduced with virtually the same phrase: ־אֵלֶּה הַדְּבָרִים אֲשֶׁר צִוָּה יְקֹוָה לַעֲשֹׂת אֹתָם, "These are the things that God has commanded you to do."

simple as that: as far as legalities are concerned, this is why prohibited Sabbath *melachah* is modeled after what we did when building the *Mishkan*, case closed.

But the question I'm asking is not technical or halachic in nature; it's conceptual: *What in the world does the construction of the Tabernacle really have to do with the observance of the Sabbath?* Conceptually, these sets of requirements just seem…utterly different and unconnected to one another, almost as if they were apples and Cadillacs. It seems bizarre, then, that the Sages would derive the laws of one from the other. Why do they do it? What, if anything, are we to understand from it?

I believe this question is a fundamental one, and its answer is equally fundamental. The solution to the problem I've just raised will help us understand not just the nature of Sabbath labor, but a great many other things, too — including some of the most basic questions one can raise about what it means to be a Jew. As a matter of fact, what I'd like to do with you next is raise some of those basic questions — the kinds of basic questions about Judaism that somehow they never really taught you much about in yeshiva — the kind that, maybe, you dread having to answer should your own kids ever bring them up. Let's take a moment to articulate some of these basic mysteries, and then I'll try to show you how the Rabbis' derivation of Sabbath labor from the *Mishkan* might help us grapple with them.

Thinking about the Big Things

What would you say are some of the most basic mysteries of Judaism? By "basic," I mean the kinds of mysteries that are more about the forest than the trees. Sure, any given aspect of Judaism might be mysterious, but I'm talking about "basic" mysteries, things that might seem bewildering to someone coming from the outside, trying to figure out what this thing called Judaism is really all about.

And of course, Judaism, like any religion, contains lots of mysteries — even basic ones. Many are philosophical or theological in nature: How can we humans have free will if God knows what we will choose? Why do bad things happen to good people? What, exactly, happens to our souls when we die? But I'm not talking about those kinds of mysteries. I'm not sure we are meant to find solutions to those questions, at least not in our short time here on earth. Sure, one day, maybe, after 120 years, the Lord Almighty might just grant us answers to existential questions like these. But in the meantime, it feels like we are meant to live with the mystery.

That being said, there are other kinds of mysteries, more down-to-earth ones, that I think we are meant to devise answers to: mysteries that affect how we really live life, or understand the Torah that is supposed to guide us on that journey. What would you say are your candidates for your top three mysteries of this kind?

Here are three that would make it to the top of my list…

Does Judaism Have a Mission Statement?

What, really, is the point of life, according to Judaism?

To explain: our religion seems to be organized around a lot of rules and laws — 613 of them, to be exact. So here's a question to consider: Do all those laws more or less coalesce around a goal that we are trying to achieve? A goal that we might be able to nail down, say, in a sentence or two? In other words, spiritually speaking, what are we humans trying to do in this-here world? Is our goal just "keep all the rules you can; who-ever dies with the 'most rules kept' wins"? Or is there some sort of over-arching goal that all these laws are pointing to, some objective we could actually wrap our minds around that life beckons us to achieve?[4]

And by way of clarification: Can we articulate this goal in a way that's not hopelessly vague? Sure, one might say: Our overarching spiritual goal in life is that…"we should all try to be good" or "we should try to fulfill the will of God" or "we should try to be holy." And surely, that's not "wrong." But it feels vague. What exactly does it mean to "be good" or "do the will of God" or "be holy"? If we could get just a little more specific about it, that would help. If life is a journey, what spiritual destination are we hop-ing to arrive at?

---

4   Judaism speaks to the individual and it also speaks to the community of Israel as a whole. So this question really applies to both realms. Broadly speaking, does Judaism define goals for us to strive for? And if it does, how are the spiritual goals of the individual related to the spiritual goals of the nation?

The Laws We Don't Understand

Here's another question at the top of my list: As I mentioned, Judaism asks us to observe many laws, but a fair amount of them seem inscrutable, which is to say that the rationale for observing them is not made available to us by the Torah. This class of laws is even given a name by our tradition: *chukim*. If there are reasons for *chukim*, these remain shrouded in mystery.[5] Many, but not all, *chukim* have to do with service in the Beit HaMikdash or the Tabernacle. Certain items can become *tamei* or *tahor*, ritually pure or impure; other items can attain consecrated status (become *kodesh*). But ideas such as "purity" and "impurity" and "consecration" seem metaphysical and foreign to us. So a very practical question I would pose is this: As a spiritually striving person, *how should I motivate myself to keep sets of laws whose rationale I am completely in the dark about?*

Does the Torah Have a Plot?

Finally, to round out my list, here is a third basic mystery:

What would you say the "plot" of the Torah is?

The Torah, as we've discussed, is comprised of many laws. But it also contains lots of stories. Leaving aside the laws, for now, would you say that the "story" sections of the Torah coalesce into a single narrative? Do they unite to tell a single, overarching, story? If so, what would you say the "plot" of that story is?

It might be, of course, that no such arc exists. It might be that the stories of the Torah amount to a collection of short, stand-alone vignettes, loosely organized around chronology: First we hear a bit about Adam and Eve, the first humans; then, some alarming stories about a flood and a tower-building project that got out of hand; then we hear a bit about Abraham. Eventually, we get a recalcitrant Pharaoh and the drama of the

---

5   The distinction between rational and ritual commandments is originally made by the Sages in Yoma 67b and is restricted to pork, *shatnez*, *chalitzah*, *taharat hametzorah*, and *se'ir le'azazel*. Rambam, at the end of *Sefer Avodah* (*Hilchot Me'ilah*), expands this to include all *korbanot* and ritual impurity, whereas Rabbi Saadiah Gaon (*Emunot VeDeot* 3:2) restricts it to only certain parts of sacrifice. I am using the term *chukim* loosely as a kind of shorthand for mitzvot whose rationale seems inscrutable.

Ten Plagues. Eventually, the people leave Egypt and wander in the desert for a while, and all sorts of interesting things happen to them. All in all, a lot of interesting drama, but not necessarily any common theme or story that binds it all together.

On the other hand, perhaps there *is* a large, epic story that is being told. And if a larger story is out there, it goes without saying that we should try to figure out what it is.

Now, before we go any further, I want to take a stab at answering this very last question. And I want to show you that developing a coherent answer to the question is actually not as easy as it might seem. The reason the answer is elusive, as a matter of fact, is partly because of... *Parshat Vayakhel itself.* Let me show you what I mean:

Homecoming

If I had to take a stab at identifying a larger theme that binds the "story sections" of the Torah together, I'd say it would be... *homecoming.*[6] Here's how I would wend that theme through the Torah's various vignettes, so that a large, encompassing narrative emerges:

The Torah begins with the story of the first two humans, who were granted by God the privilege of living in a very special place — God's summer home on earth, as it were: the Garden of Eden. They called this garden... *home.* But before long, the humans sinned, and they had to leave. Their descendants colonized the rest of the planet, making it their new "home" — but soon enough, they corrupted their new environment. It got so bad that they were eventually evicted from *that* home, too: an inconvenient deluge forced everyone off the planet, quite literally, and only Noah and his descendants survived.

Eventually, God established a relationship with a family born of those descendants, the children of Israel, and the Almighty promised them a new home, the land of Canaan. For a short while, the patriarch of the family, Jacob, lived in that land, but soon enough, these children cast their brother in a pit, and before long they found themselves exiled from that home, as they took up residence in Egypt. There, they were eventually

---

6   A somewhat similar theory is advanced by Ramban, in his introduction to the book of Exodus.

enslaved. After some time, God took them out of there, seeking, once again, to bring them … *home.*

This saga more or less continues throughout the Five Books of Moses, and it pretty much covers most of the stories in the book. But here's the rub: it covers only *most* of the stories. Not all of them. In particular, there is a specific, inconvenient hole in my theory — and it comes right smack in the middle of the book …

The Middle of the Book

You see, here's the problem with my little homecoming theory: It more or less works as a description of Genesis, the first half of Exodus, the second half of Numbers, and Deuteronomy. But there's a whole other part of the Torah that it emphatically does *not* describe, namely, the whole middle part of the book. The second half of Exodus, all of Leviticus, and the first part of Numbers deal with something else entirely, something that doesn't seem to fit: *the story of the construction of the Tabernacle and its inauguration into service.*

If the Torah really is a big "homecoming" story, why does it devote all those chapters to an entirely unrelated account of this sacred building that the Israelites were constructing as they made their way through the wilderness? It seems like an unconscionable distraction from the main point of things. And truthfully, if it had been just a chapter here or there, tucked away at the edges, we might perhaps overlook it. But it's not. The Tabernacle episodes — the giving of its blueprints, its construction, its consecration, its service — all this occupies chapter upon chapter of text, smack in the middle of the Torah. Why is it all there? And why is it so prominent?

To summarize, then, here is what I'm wondering: Does the existence of this major "Tabernacle" section right in the middle of God's book completely blow to pieces the homecoming theory I suggested above? Or can the "homecoming" theory survive?

How the Homecoming Theory Survives

I want to suggest that not only does the homecoming theory *survive* the existence of the Tabernacle chapters, but it actually flourishes because of them. But to understand why, we need to understand more about this apparent digression in the middle of the Torah. We need to take a closer look at the Tabernacle and its story. Once we do, we shall be in a position, I believe, not just to understand more precisely the larger, overarching plot of the Torah's stories, but possessing this key, we will also be able to better respond to the other two "basic mysteries" I outlined above: How should I motivate myself to keep laws of the Torah I don't understand, and, most broadly, is there a simple but compelling way I can articulate the larger, spiritual goal the Torah wants me to strive for?

We will get back to these "three big mysteries" about Judaism and the Torah soon enough, but for the meantime, let's clear our mind of them and dive into the Tabernacle and try to understand its place in the Torah. How, exactly, are we going to do that? Well, we are going to return to the very first question I started with at the beginning of this essay: Why does our understanding of Sabbath labor derive from, of all things, the way the *Mishkan* was built?

Let's try to investigate that now.

Building an Apartment for the One You Love

In our last essay — if you haven't read it yet, may I recommend you take a few moments to do just that — we identified *melachah* as "acts of creative labor," taking the world and changing it, molding it to suit your will. These, we said, were the kinds of acts God was performing when He created the universe in the original, primal six days, and these were the kinds of acts He rested from on the original seventh day.

Having established this, let's talk a little more about God's creative labor during those first six days. Let's even go back to the very beginning — to the very first act of creation God performed in the book of Genesis. Let me ask you a question about that act: *How did it change the status quo?*

First There Was Nothing…

The answer seems as plain as day. That act and the ones following it ushered the universe into existence. It was the most dramatic change of the status quo one could possibly imagine: *Before that, there was absolutely nothing. And then, after creation, there was everything!*

That's what you'd think, right? And truthfully, that statement is accurate…but only from a certain point of view. Only from…*mankind's* point of view. It's *not* true from God's point of view. Because sure, if you're a person, someone who lives in this tidy little world of space and time, with stars and planets and all those good things, then yes, you can say: "Before creation there was nothing, and afterward, there was something." But you wouldn't put it that way if you were God. As a matter of fact, if you were God, you might be a little insulted at the notion that "first, there was nothing, and then there was something." *First there was nothing? What do you mean, "First there was nothing"? Wasn't I there?*

If anything, from God's standpoint, the reverse is true: Before creation, there was…*everything!* God was doing just fine living in His own tremendous, mysterious, realm. He was lacking nothing, which is to say, God's existence was a perfect "everything" in its own right. So how then did creation change that status quo? Well, you'd have to say that, from God's point of view, creation was…almost a kind of diminishment. Before, there was nothing else besides the Divine, nothing that was really separate from Him. But with creation, that suddenly changed. The act of creation was like carving out a space in your world for something…that *wasn't* you. The Kabbalists called this idea *tzimtzum* — almost a contraction of the Divine, so to speak: God making space in existence for something else besides Him.[7]

The Universe and the Advent of Love

Let's take this line of thinking a bit further. Ask yourself: *Why* would God do this? Why would He willingly "diminish Himself," so to speak?

Well, to solve that little mystery, consider this: God isn't the only being who diminishes Himself to make room for another. People do it too, when they have children. Think about the process of having a child. One's whole body — nose, ears, eyes, lungs, heart, and kidneys — all of that is there to nourish…*your* life. Yet one part of the human body *isn't* there for you, but for someone else. It is the womb. A womb is a space within a woman that strangely isn't there for her. The womb is a space for another, an environment perfectly calibrated to nourish the being you want to create.

---

7   See R. Chaim Vital, *Etz Chaim, sha'ar* 1, part 2.

Why, then, did God contract Himself, as it were, to make room for someone else? We can get an inkling of the answer, perhaps, by considering why we willingly have children. The answer, I would suggest, is love. To some extent, contraction of our sense of self is the great price that love always demands of us: *make room in your world for someone else.* If that is true for us, it is no less true for God.

The Almighty wanted to create a being, a child, another separate being possessed of free will with whom God could form a relationship. But that being, which we call mankind, couldn't exist in God's world. It had to have an environment of its own. So God went about crafting that environment, this nifty little place designed to nourish us, this place we call ... the universe.[8]

Who Was the First Being to Keep Laws?

The environment God would craft for us required a great deal. It required the creation of space and time itself. And just stop to think about how ... *selfless* all this was. God doesn't need space; God doesn't need time. He lives outside these constructs. And setting up the environment was hardly a simple matter. It required the creation of subatomic particles, and the bringing into being of the simplest of atoms, hydrogen. These hydrogen atoms would aggregate into massive clouds, and the clouds would collapse through the force of their own gravity — and when they did, friction would ignite their thermonuclear furnaces, and the clouds would become stars. The stars would burn and burn — and when they collapsed, the resulting supernovas would create carbon, zinc, gold, and all the other

---

8   The notion of the universe as a kind of womb "within" God may sound fanciful, but it is an ancient idea with strong roots in our tradition. The Midrash (Bereishit Rabbah 68:9) memorably expressed this idea in an elegant little aphorism. Why, they say, do we sometimes refer to God as *HaMakom*, "the Place"? Because, the Sages say, "He is the Place of the world, but the world is not His place."

The Sages are dancing here with the mystery of "where" God is to be found. All told, the Sages' analogy portrays two environments, one nested in the other. We exist in the universe, an environment that nurtures us. But *that* all exists entirely within another environment, surrounding it, nurturing it, holding it, and allowing for it ... and that outer environment is nothing other than the Creator. Hence, the universe is like God's womb.

heavy elements. These would eventually be brought together by gravity to form planets. And, those planets — at least one of them — would need to be further calibrated to sustain human life.

All this was made possible by a delightful confluence of laws — principles we call "the laws of physics." And those laws needed to be perfectly calibrated, and perfectly adhered to. A nuclear strong force would need to exist in perfect ratio to a nuclear weak force. Gravity, electromagnetism, Planck's constant, the three laws of thermodynamics — all these things would need to be held in perfect balance in order for the environment to actually work. The laws could not be violated or the whole environment would come crashing down.

God Himself didn't need any of that. God doesn't need planets and stars. But God paid attention to those laws, for one reason. Because God knew that the being that He wanted to love required them in order to exist. And so, after setting up that wondrous environment, and meticulously observing the laws that made it all possible — the final thing God made on that sixth, primal day was the child, the being itself that God would love:

וַיִּבְרָא אֱלֹהִים אֶת־הָאָדָם בְּצַלְמוֹ   And God created mankind, in His image.   Genesis 1:27

In the Image of God

Strange. God has this "child," as it were, and the Torah insists that this child — mankind — is "like God" in some fundamental way. But how? God is unfathomable. We have forms, bodies. God doesn't. So we don't really "look" like God in any way...because God doesn't "look like" anything at all. In what way, then, are we made "in His image"?

Well, maybe the answer to that is simple. Maybe the Torah doesn't expect us to know more about God than what the Torah itself has told us about Him until this point in time. What would the reader of the Torah, having made his or her way through most of Genesis, chapter 1, think about God? What would the reader know about Him? And the answer to that is clear. Because while there is much that is inscrutable about the Almighty, the one thing that we can say with confidence about Him — the one thing we've seen, over and over, during these six days of creation — is that God is … a *Creator*. Indeed, that's all He's really been doing these last six days. So, if at the culmination of day six, we hear that God created someone "just like" Him — perhaps that means, He brought into being *a creator*, "just like Him."

Indeed, humans *are* creators, "just like" God. As we talked about in our last essay on **Parshat Vayakhel**, we, like God, are practitioners of *melachah*. Indeed, man *must* practice *melachah* if he has any hope of bringing to fruition the blessing God confers upon him. For this is what God says to man, at the end of the sixth day, just after declaring that he has been made in the image of God:

Genesis
1:27–29

וַיִּבְרָא אֱלֹהִים אֶת־הָאָדָם
בְּצַלְמוֹ בְּצֶלֶם אֱלֹהִים בָּרָא
אֹתוֹ זָכָר וּנְקֵבָה בָּרָא אֹתָם:
וַיְבָרֶךְ אֹתָם אֱלֹהִים וַיֹּאמֶר
לָהֶם אֱלֹהִים פְּרוּ וּרְבוּ וּמִלְאוּ
אֶת־הָאָרֶץ וְכִבְשֻׁהָ וּרְדוּ בִּדְגַת
הַיָּם וּבְעוֹף הַשָּׁמַיִם וּבְכָל־חַיָּה
הָרֹמֶשֶׂת עַל־הָאָרֶץ:

And God created man in His image, in the image of God He created him; male and female He created them. God blessed them and God said to them, "Be fertile and increase, fill the earth and master it; and rule the fish of the sea, the birds of the sky, and all the living things that creep on earth."

How, indeed, is man to actualize this blessing to master the earth, to rule over all other living things? Bears are more powerful than people. So how did it come to be that people have bears in their zoos, rather than bears having people in *their* zoos? The answer is: *melachah*. Over time, we conceived of ideas and we actualized them with our hands. We imagined tools, and we built them: spears, bows and arrows, guns, cages. And so, even though no human being on his own is a match for an individual bear on a lonely mountain road, still, humans *collectively* managed to master bears — and lions and tigers, too — through *melachah*.

Big Creator, Little Creator

So God practices *melachah*, and man is a practitioner of *melachah*, too. God is the Master of the Universe, and in our own little ways, we master the world, too. God is responsible for making the universe through *melachah*. Man, already *in* the universe, uses *melachah* to innovate within it. God authors the laws of physics. Man uses the laws of physics to tinker at the edges.

So at one level, to be a *tzelem Elokim*, a being created in the image of God, is to be possessed with the Godlike ability to create. But I want to suggest that being "in the image of God" is ever so slightly more than that, too. I want to suggest to you that perhaps the title *tzelem Elokim* doesn't describe just our capacity, but our *destiny*.

Perhaps we are ultimately meant to do something special with our creativity. Perhaps we are meant to do with this power…exactly what God did with it. Perhaps to actualize the meaning of being a *tzelem Elokim*, man needs to create not just *like* God created, but to actually create *what* God created, or at least a miniature version of it. Perhaps man's destiny is to do with *melachah* what God did with it: *create a space in his everything for the one that he loves.*

All of which helps us answer the great three "basic mysteries" of Judaism we outlined above.

The Center of the Torah

Let's come back now to the mystery we began to wrestle with earlier. We had wondered about the mysterious middle part of the Torah, which revolves almost exclusively around the construction of the *Mishkan*, its dedication, and its service. All of that had seemed so out of place. The main plotline of God's book was otherwise all about coming home. Why the digression?

But maybe it is not a digression at all. This, too, is about coming home.

After all, this whole middle section of the Torah — what is it *really* all about? It is about…man attempting to create a version of what God created: *an apartment in His "everything" for the one that He loves.* Mankind is quite literally reenacting the steps through which his own world was brought into being.

Let's remember: How did creation unfold? First the sum total of existence was quite simply God's "everything" — Himself, in His own, glorious, utterly mysterious, divine realm. And the Almighty could well have left it at that. But God didn't do that. Instead, He chose to withdraw a bit, to create a little apartment — a universe with space, time, and all those good things in it — for the being that He would love.

So now, we humans, the beneficiaries of all that — we do the same. We look around at *our* version of "everything" — which, of course, is much smaller than God's "everything" — and what do we see? We see our apartment, this universe of space and time, with stars and planets and grass, trees and birds. We look around at that little "everything" and we say, in effect: *"What a marvelous thing my Creator did for me! I too am going to carve out a little section of this. I too am going to make an apartment in my everything for the one that I love."*

<table>
<tr><td>Exodus 25:8</td><td>וְעָשׂוּ לִי מִקְדָּשׁ וְשָׁכַנְתִּי
בְּתוֹכָם:</td><td>Make for Me a Holy Place, and I will dwell within them.</td></tr>
</table>

To carry through on that intention will not be particularly easy. To really make an apartment that will "work" for my Beloved will require a contraction of my sense of self in more ways than one. It is not just physical space I must give up. In order to really make a place I can invite Him into, I will need to go out of my comfort zone. I will need to observe special laws. In order to set up an apartment that worked for me, God needed to observe laws — laws that were not for His benefit but for mine. So the least I can do is reciprocate the kindness: I will observe laws designed to set up an apartment for Him, to set aside a space in my everything that is calibrated to His liking.

And so, there are special laws associated with the Tabernacle: laws of *tumah* and *taharah* (purity and impurity), laws of *kodesh* and *chol* (what is holy and what is mundane). We are instructed how to properly separate between these and ensure the integrity of each. These laws, at the end of the day, make little sense to the human mind, and there is a good reason for that: they're not about what it takes for us to live in our world; they are about what it takes for us to invite God into our world, what it takes to ask Him to reside among us.

Betzalel

We call this apartment we make for our beloved the *Mishkan*. The word doesn't really mean "Tabernacle," at least not literally. It more closely translates as a cozy dwelling place, the apartment we affectionately invite our

Creator into. After all, the term "*Mishkan*" is nothing less than the noun form of a verb that is suffused with love and tenderness:

וְעָשׂוּ לִי מִקְדָּשׁ וְשָׁכַנְתִּי
בְּתוֹכָם:

Make for Me a Holy Place, and **I will dwell** within them.

Exodus 25:8

The *Mishkan* is the apartment made by Little Creator to reciprocate and mirror the one made for him by Big Creator.

It is in this act of reciprocation, I want to suggest, that our destiny as humans, as creators, becomes fully realized. Remember what we suggested before: the possibility that the destiny of mankind, the beings created in the image of God, is to use *melachah* to create… *what it is that God created*. In line with this, consider who it is that builds the *Mishkan*. What, according to the Torah, is his name? His name is a curious one: *Betzalel*. What, if anything, does it mean?

On the one hand, Betzalel could be a contraction — a melding of two words:

בצלאל
Betzalel

בצל - אל
Betzel El
In the shadow of God.[9]

On the other hand, Betzalel could be an acronym, shorthand for two longer words:

בצלם אלקים
Betzelem Elokim

Either way, the meaning is the same. Betzalel is shorthand for *a being who is in the image of God*.

It is a fitting name, indeed. Betzalel is the one who represents us all, on a daring quest to realize our very humanity. He is the builder of the apartment in our everything, for the One that we love.

---

9 Consider: What would it mean to be a "shadow" of God? A shadow is a kind of reflection, a derivative image of a powerful, much more animated original being.

Two Apartments, Two Kinds of Rest

I asked before about the rationale for deriving Sabbath labor from the *Mishkan*. Why, of all things, does the work Betzalel and his craftsmen engaged in when building the Tabernacle — why does *that* end up becoming the template for *melachah* prohibited on the Sabbath? The two things seemed to have so little to do with each other. But it is now clear how related they really are. They are, indeed, two sides of the same coin.

After all, why do we rest on the Sabbath? Because God rested on the original seventh day. He rested from all the *melachah* He engaged in to make that apartment for the one He loved (that snug little domain we call our universe). So, when *we* rest, what are *we* going to rest from? We are going to rest from all the *melachah* that *we* engaged in to create an apartment for *our* Beloved. We are going to rest from the *melachah* we performed when building the *Mishkan*.

Little Creator is just like Big Creator.

A Spiritual Mission Statement

If Betzalel helps humanity writ large to actualize its destiny as *tzelem elohim*, a being created in the image of God, I wonder if a version of his quest is something we *all* embark on — not just as members of a community, but as individuals, too. We asked before whether Judaism suggests a spiritual mission statement of sorts for its adherents. Beyond overarching platitudes such as "choose right, not wrong" or "be more Godly" or "be more holy," does the Torah offer a more defined spiritual goal for us to aim for? I suspect it does. Perhaps each of us, as individuals, is meant to undertake a personal version of Betzalel's quest.

What would that mean?

Well, if the *Mishkan* is a communal home for God that we, as a nation, seek to build within our midst, perhaps we, as *individuals*, are also meant to construct a version of this home…within our own lives. Intriguingly, the very passage that instructs us to build a *Mishkan* appears to suggest as much:

Exodus 25:8	וְעָשׂוּ לִי מִקְדָּשׁ וְשָׁכַנְתִּי בְּתוֹכָם:	Make for Me a Holy Place, and I will dwell within them.

Ohr HaChaim points out that one might have expected the text to say: Make Me a Holy Place and I will dwell within "it." But the Torah doesn't say that.[10] Rather, it says: "I will dwell within *them*," which is to say, within the people. In some sense, it is not just the Tabernacle that we invite God into, but our very selves. In the immortal words of *Sefer HaCharedim*:[11]

בְּלִבָּבִי מִשְׁכַּן אֶבְנֶה לַהֲדַר כְּבוֹדוֹ, וּבַמִּשְׁכָּן מִזְבֵּחַ אָשִׂים לְקַרְנֵי הוֹדוֹ, וּלְנֵר תָּמִיד אֶקַּח לִי אֶת אֵשׁ הָעֲקֵדָה, וּלְקָרְבָּן אַקְרִיב לוֹ אֶת נַפְשִׁי הַיְּחִידָה.

In my heart a sanctuary I shall build, to the splendor of His honor…
and for an offering, I shall bring my one unique soul.

One might perhaps dismiss such a notion as mere poetry. But I think it is more than that. Building a place for God within our lives is, I believe, a serious goal to be strived for. It is a kind of anchoring quest for everything else that we do, religiously. At the end of the day, we are challenged to do something both audacious and tender with the totality of our lives: invite God in. In concert with this, perhaps we keep mitzvot not so much because they give us brownie points in Heaven, but because they elevate us, refine us, and in so doing, make us more fitting vessels to host the Divine.

Becoming Whole

A version of this mission statement, perhaps, was once articulated to the father of our nation, Abraham. It happened just before the Almighty made an eternal covenant with him. God prefaces that covenant with just four Hebrew words:

הִתְהַלֵּךְ לְפָנַי וֶהְיֵה תָמִים: Walk before Me, and be whole.   Genesis 17:1

---

10 See Alshich, Exodus 31; see also *Nefesh HaChaim* 1:4.

11 By R. Elazar Azkari. The poem has been given modern expression as the lyrics of a beautiful, popular song, *"Bilvavi Mishkan Evneh."*

The Master of the Universe asks Abraham to walk in close quarters with Him, but in conjunction with that, He asks Abraham to be "whole." Apparently, if we can just do that — achieve this elusive "wholeness" — we can have the temerity to invite God into our lives and be close to Him. But what, exactly, does it mean to be "whole"?

I can't say for sure, but I'm willing to hazard a guess. I think it might have something to do with other spaces we share. For there are others, besides God, whom we invite in to share close quarters with us.

The truth is, we build spaces and share them with others all the time. We do it with our wives, our husbands, and our children, and we call that our home; with employees and colleagues, and we call that our workplace; with neighbors, and we call that our town; with fellow countrymen, and we call that our nation. All require various doses of the ingredients we spoke of above: a willingness to contract ourselves, just a bit, to make room for others who matter; a willingness to abide by some rules of the road; and a commitment to make sure the shared space is comfortable and welcoming, not just for us, but for those we share it with, too.

When we successfully build these shared spaces and invite others in, perhaps we become more whole. In doing this, we create what Robert Nozick wryly called various kinds of "we" — composite wholes that are each larger, and more complete than our own lonesome selves.[12] When we lovingly and respectfully make room in our lives for these others, when we build successful homes, families, and societies — it is then, perhaps, that we make room for the Divine as well to take up residence in our lives, making it possible for the Master of the Universe to dwell in the apartment we've so carefully set up for Him.

---

12 Robert Nozick, *The Examined Life*, 6th ed. (New York: Simon & Schuster, 1990); see chapter 8, "Love's Bond."

A Tale of Two Clouds

וּכְבוֹד יְקֹוָה מָלֵא אֶת־
הַמִּשְׁכָּן:

And the glory of God filled the *Mishkan*.

EXODUS 40:34

A Tale of Two Clouds

PARSHAT PEKUDEI PLAYS HOST to the culmination of an astonishing pattern, one that spans almost the entire second half of the book of Exodus and which lurks just beneath the surface of the text. In these pages, I want to explore with you this pattern and what it might mean.

Making Sense of a Chiasm

The pattern takes the form of a chiasm, or what we might call an ATBASH structure. The last time I mentioned chiasms to you was in **Parshat Terumah**, so feel free to flip back to that essay for a brief refresher on how these patterns work. For the time being, suffice it to say that a chiasm, or an ATBASH pattern, is a way of structuring a section of text in an arrow-like fashion. The first element of the structure mirrors the last, the second element mirrors the second to last, the third to first pairs off with the third to last, etc., until one reaches the center.

Where does one look for meaning in a chiasm? The answer is, quite simply, everywhere. Each of the pairs in the structure are worthy of attention, for the two elements that comprise the pair often shed light on one another in fascinating ways. But although all pairs in a chiastic structure are of interest, the center of the chiasm is usually the focal point of the structure in some basic manner. The center will often offer a turning point of sorts around which the entire section of text, chiastically arranged, revolves. Moreover, the two outermost points of the chiasm — the pair formed by the first and last elements — will sometimes, like bookends on a shelf of treasured books, set the tone or context for everything that comes in the middle.

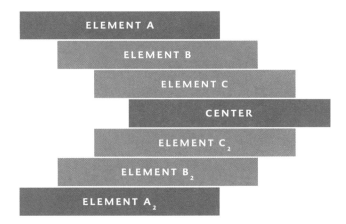

A Chiasm Spanning the Second Half of Exodus

Some chiasms are small;[1] others are much larger. The particular chiasm I'd like to show you here is probably the most extensive one I've seen, both in terms of the number of pairs it contains and the sheer amount of biblical text it encompasses. From end to end it spans no fewer than fifteen chapters of the book of Exodus, and it contains dozens of pairs. To explore the entire chiasm would require an entire book in itself, but I'll give an abridged account of it here, and hopefully we will see enough to be able to ponder together what we might learn from it.[2]

Let's begin by reviewing, for a moment, some of the grand themes the Torah speaks of in the second half of Exodus. One of the most prominent of these themes, of course, is the construction of the Tabernacle (or, in Hebrew, the *Mishkan*). This takes us from the start of **Parshat Terumah** (Exodus 25), through, more or less, the midway point of **Parshat Ki Tisa** (Exodus 31). At that point, the Torah abruptly shifts its focus. The reader

---

1   One of the smallest I know of comes early on in the Torah, in the laws that were given to Noah after the Flood:

שֹׁפֵךְ דַּם הָאָדָם בָּאָדָם דָּמוֹ יִשָּׁפֵךְ

Genesis 9:6

The one who sheds **the blood** of man, by man **shall his blood** be shed.

2   For those of you interested in diving in and seeing the whole chiasm — or at least as much of it as I've been able to discover — I invite you to listen to a thirteen-part audio series of lectures I've recorded that goes through the many, intricate pairs of the chiasm at length. That series is entitled *Shattered Tablets and a Calf of Gold*, and it is available online at alephbeta.org. The chiasm is elaborated in the last four or five of those lectures.

encounters a short series of texts commanding the people to observe the Sabbath (Exodus 31:13–17), followed immediately by the disastrous story of the Golden Calf (Exodus 32).

So, to summarize, we now see three major topics covered in the second half of the book of Exodus: the construction of the *Mishkan*, the Sabbath, and the Golden Calf.

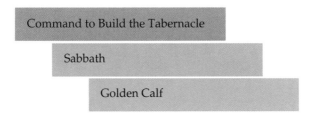

Pairs Begin to Emerge

Let's continue our outlining exercise, and you'll see how these themes begin to pair off with later elements in the book of Exodus.

Consider, for example, what happens just as the story of the Golden Calf ends. That would take us to the beginning of chapter 35, where, as if on cue, we encounter … a command to keep the Sabbath again (Exodus 35:1). Then, just a few verses later, the Torah returns to the theme of — wouldn't you know it — the actual construction of the *Mishkan* (Exodus 35:4–40:34 — earlier, we had the commands to build the *Mishkan*; now, we get the fulfillment of those commands, as the Torah details the actual construction of the building).

So you can begin to see it. The broad outlines of a chiasm are starting to emerge …

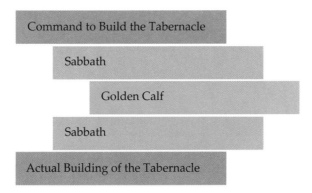

How the Structure Sheds Light on Meaning

Now, all we've seen to this point is a very broad, very rough outline of this chiasm. But even with the little we've seen, we can begin to sense some of the meaning of this structure. Think of these three themes that are being mirrored here: the *Mishkan*, the Sabbath, and the Golden Calf. At face value, the three elements seem to have absolutely nothing to do with one another. But if you meditate on them just a bit, a tantalizing common denominator begins to emerge.

Let's talk about the Golden Calf and the people's desire to build it. What catalyzed the building of the calf? According to the text, Moses was late coming down the mountain, and the people feared he had died and was never returning to them. Ramban, for one, argues on this basis that the people, in building this calf, were seeking a replacement of sorts for Moses. They needed a way to accomplish what Moses was supposed to do for them: establish a connection with the Divine on behalf of the people.[3] In other words, Moses was supposed to be their vehicle to connect to the Divine. Now there would be another vehicle…this calf.

It was a failed experiment, an illegitimate and ineffective way of bringing God into the material world. But there were other legitimate and wonderful ways to achieve this. How can one *actually* bring God into the

---

3   Ramban develops further the theory whose outlines I mentioned briefly here. He notes that what Moses was meant to do for the people — connect with the Divine — is something the people wanted but feared. Recall that before Moses left to ascend Mt. Sinai, he had encouraged the people to come closer, to hear the voice of God emanating from the mountain, but the people held back. They were afraid of directly encountering the Divine; they thought they would die. So Moses approached the mountain himself and ascended it.

   Later, when Moses was late coming down, the people figured their fears had proved to be well founded. A human can't encounter God this closely and live through the experience. So, as Ramban states, the people set about trying to create an artificial Moses for themselves. They sought a way to connect with God and to bring His Presence into the human world somehow. Because they feared the task was impossibly dangerous, they crafted a crude machine, as it were, something they hoped could be a vehicle for connecting with the Divine. They built the Golden Calf.

   Thus, the initial impetus for the calf, Ramban argues, was actually to connect with God. It was an illegitimate way of doing so, and it devolved quickly, for many, into outright worship of a false god.

material world? Through the twin elements that bracket the Golden Calf episode — through the Sabbath, and through the *Mishkan*.

Bringing God into Space. Bringing God into Time.

As I suggested above, the Sabbath and the *Mishkan* seem very different from one another. The *Mishkan*, the Tabernacle, is a tangible object, an actual building. It is something you can touch and feel. By contrast, the Sabbath isn't really even a "thing" at all. It is a period of time, a single day. In reality, though, this great difference between the two is actually that which conceptually connects them. The *Mishkan* and the Sabbath are really mirror images of one another. In a deep kind of way, what the Tabernacle is in space, the Sabbath is in time: *a place we make for God in our world.*

What, after all, is the basic environment in which everyone lives? The answer to that is: space and time. The three dimensions of space offer us the wherewithal to jump, skip, or just plain walk around, and time offers us a past, present, and future — all good things, to be sure. But living in a world of space and time can get downright lonely. For God, our Maker, lives in neither space nor time, since He is the Creator of both these elements.[4] We can therefore feel a bit marooned living within these three dimensions of ours. As much as they allow us a "place" to be, they also constrict us; they deny us immediate access to the Divine. So, to counter that, we make "homes" for God in our world. We make a *Mishkan*, a place in space that we set aside for Him to come stay with us. And we make another kind of sanctuary, too. We call it the Sabbath. The Sabbath is a place in time that we set aside for us and God to "spend time" together.

How do we make the place in space for God? By constructing a building. How do we make the place in time for Him? Ironically, by *not* constructing anything, by simply being still:

וְשָׁמְרוּ בְנֵי־יִשְׂרָאֵל אֶת־הַשַּׁבָּת לַעֲשׂוֹת אֶת־הַשַּׁבָּת	And the Children of Israel shall observe the Sabbath, [thereby] making the Sabbath.	Exodus 31:16

---

4   A creator naturally lives outside the environment he or she creates.

Look carefully at the language of that verse: When we observe the Sabbath, we thereby *make* the Sabbath. *That* is how we build it: when we are still, when we don't work on the day, and we invite God in. Indeed, if the Tabernacle is a structure we build through a creative process known as *melachah*, the Sabbath is a structure in time that we build by *refraining from melachah*.[5]

All told, the Sabbath and *Mishkan* are ways to succeed precisely where the Golden Calf failed.

Back to the Chiasm

Let's return now to our unfolding chiasm. We've now seen three macro elements: a central theme and two paired themes that branch out from the center. I call these macro elements because they each span multiple verses, or even multiple chapters, in the text. Interestingly, though, the chiasm operates on a micro level as well — sometimes at the level of a single word or phrase.

Here is an example. Go to the point in the Torah where the command to observe the Sabbath ends and the story of the Golden Calf begins. There, we find these words:

Exodus 32:1

וַיַּרְא הָעָם כִּי־בֹשֵׁשׁ מֹשֶׁה
לָרֶדֶת מִן־הָהָר
וַיִּקָּהֵל הָעָם עַל־
אַהֲרֹן

And the people saw that Moses was taking a long time coming down from the mountain, and the people **gathered** against Aaron.

Now, consider that phrase וַיִּקָּהֵל הָעָם עַל־אַהֲרֹן, "and the people gathered against Aaron." It seems fairly innocuous. But let me ask you: How many times in the Torah, before this moment, do you suppose a word spelled like *vayikahel* has appeared?

The word is comprised of a *vav*, followed by a *yod, kuf, heh*, and *lamed*. How many other times in the Torah, before this, do we encounter those exact letters, in that exact order? As it happens, this *vayikahel* ("and they gathered") is actually the first appearance of a word written like that in

---

5   See our essay on **Parshat Vayakhel** for more on this topic.

the Torah. But when is the *next* time, after this, that this particular combination of letters appears in the Torah?

It turns out that it is right where you might expect it — if you were thinking chiastically, at least. A version of the word reappears at the precise, corresponding spot on the *other* side of our chiasm. To see it, just page over to the Torah's transition *away* from the Golden Calf story, as the Torah begins to introduce the Sabbath, one more time:

וַיַּקְהֵל מֹשֶׁה אֶת־כָּל־עֲדַת	Moses then **convened** the whole	Exodus 35:1
בְּנֵי יִשְׂרָאֵל וַיֹּאמֶר	community of Israel and said to them:	
אֲלֵהֶם אֵלֶּה הַדְּבָרִים	These are the things that the Lord has	
אֲשֶׁר־צִוָּה יְקֹוָק לַעֲשֹׂת	commanded you to do: [Observe the	
אֹתָם:	Sabbath].	

The word for "**convened**" in Hebrew is composed of those very same letters: *vav, yod, kuf, heh, and lamed* (pronounced slightly differently this time, due to vowelization). The word is *vayakhel*, and it mirrors the *vayikahel* of the Golden Calf story.

Just You and the Divine, No Calves Necessary

What is particularly noteworthy about this is that the two gatherings or convenings don't just mirror each other in terms of their placement in the text; they also mirror each other conceptually. For consider what was going on the first time the word appeared: Moses was atop the mountain, the people thought he was lost forever, and the people gathered together as a group against Aaron and demanded he fix the problem somehow. The people ended up convening to do something (make a Golden Calf) that was ill-advised and destructive. But the second time you have these letters, we have a mirror image of this outcome...

The *vayakhel* that appears after the Golden Calf episode signals a moment in time when Moses has successfully returned from a (second) trip up Mt. Sinai. Back safely at the bottom of the mountain, Moses instructs the people how to do something wonderful and constructive: he tells them how they should observe the Sabbath. At the top of the mountain, Moses had communed with God, experiencing the greatest possible closeness to the Divine. And now, in giving the people the Sabbath, Moses is suggesting that he is not the exclusive holder of this privilege. The entire people can commune with the Divine, too. In *convening* them as a community, and instructing them to observe the Sabbath, he is sharing with them a way they can *all* recreate what he experienced atop the mountain. *Here is the way to engineer a true rendezvous with God. Just you and Him, spending time together; no calves necessary.*

So, filling out our chiasm a little, we now have this:

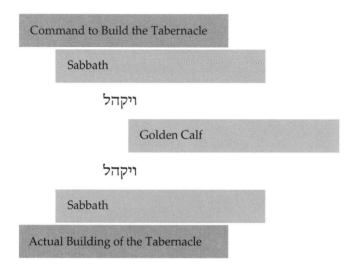

The Edges

Whenever one discovers a chiasm in biblical text, a natural question to ask is: "How far does this pattern go? What are its outer edges?" Let's wrestle with that question now. What appear to be the outer two edges of the particular chiasm we've stumbled upon here?

If we start with just the themes we've seen until now, I think it is fair to say that the two outer edges, so far, are the *command* to construct the *Mishkan* on the one hand, and the *actual* construction of the *Mishkan* on the other. I want to suggest, though, that the chiasm actually extends a little more than this. To see how, let's look at the events just a bit farther out on each edge. That is, let's examine the text that *precedes* the command to construct the *Mishkan*, and the text that *follows* its actual construction, and we can try to discern whether they perhaps mirror one another.

A Tale of Two Clouds

What comes right before the first commands to construct the *Mishkan*? As it turns out, at that point in the text, we hear of a directive God gives to Moses to ascend Mt. Sinai (Exodus 24:12). Moses complies with that directive, ascends the mountain — and there, a divine cloud is waiting for him, a cloud that, according to the text, covers the mountain:

| Moses ascends Mt. Sinai; a divine cloud covers the mountain | When Moses had ascended the mountain, the cloud covered the mountain. The glory of God rested on Mt. Sinai, and the cloud hid it for six days. On the seventh day He called to Moses from the midst of the cloud. Now the Presence of God appeared in the sight of the Israelites as a consuming fire on the top of the mountain. Moses went inside the cloud and ascended the mountain; and Moses remained on the mountain forty days and forty nights. (Ex. 24:15–18) | וַיַּעַל מֹשֶׁה אֶל־הָהָר וַיְכַס הֶעָנָן אֶת־הָהָר: וַיִּשְׁכֹּן כְּבוֹד־יְקֹוָק עַל־הַר סִינַי וַיְכַסֵּהוּ הֶעָנָן שֵׁשֶׁת יָמִים וַיִּקְרָא אֶל־מֹשֶׁה בַּיּוֹם הַשְּׁבִיעִי מִתּוֹךְ הֶעָנָן: וּמַרְאֵה כְּבוֹד יְקֹוָק כְּאֵשׁ אֹכֶלֶת בְּרֹאשׁ הָהָר לְעֵינֵי בְּנֵי יִשְׂרָאֵל: וַיָּבֹא מֹשֶׁה בְּתוֹךְ הֶעָנָן וַיַּעַל אֶל־הָהָר וַיְהִי מֹשֶׁה בָּהָר אַרְבָּעִים יוֹם וְאַרְבָּעִים לָיְלָה: |
| The very next verses give us the initial plans to build the *Mishkan* | God spoke to Moses, saying: Tell the Israelite people to bring Me gifts; you shall accept gifts for Me from every person whose heart so moves him. And these are the gifts that you shall accept from them: gold, silver, and copper. (Ex. 25:1–3) | וַיְדַבֵּר יְקֹוָק אֶל־מֹשֶׁה לֵּאמֹר: דַּבֵּר אֶל־בְּנֵי יִשְׂרָאֵל וְיִקְחוּ־לִי תְּרוּמָה מֵאֵת כָּל־אִישׁ אֲשֶׁר יִדְּבֶנּוּ לִבּוֹ תִּקְחוּ אֶת־תְּרוּמָתִי: וְזֹאת הַתְּרוּמָה אֲשֶׁר תִּקְחוּ מֵאִתָּם זָהָב וָכֶסֶף וּנְחֹשֶׁת: |

Now let's skip to the end of our emerging chiasm and take a peek at the text that *follows* the *Mishkan*'s actual completion (i.e., the analogous point on the chiasm's other end). This brings us to the very end of **Parshat Pekudei**, where we find that...the divine cloud is back. This time, it covers the newly built Tabernacle:

The construction of the *Mishkan* is complete	And he set up the enclosure around the Tabernacle and the altar, and put up the screen for the gate of the enclosure. When Moses had finished the work... (Ex. 40:33)	וַיָּ֣קֶם אֶת־הֶ֣חָצֵ֗ר סָבִ֤יב לַמִּשְׁכָּן֙ וְלַמִּזְבֵּ֔חַ וַיִּתֵּ֕ן אֶת־מָסַ֖ךְ שַׁ֣עַר הֶחָצֵ֑ר וַיְכַ֥ל מֹשֶׁ֖ה אֶת־הַמְּלָאכָֽה׃
The very next verses tell us: **A divine cloud fills the Mishkan**	The cloud covered the Tent of Meeting, and the glory of God filled the Tabernacle. Moses could not enter the Tent of Meeting, because the cloud had settled upon it and the Presence of God filled the Tabernacle. (Ex. 40:34–35)	וַיְכַ֥ס הֶעָנָ֖ן אֶת־אֹ֣הֶל מוֹעֵ֑ד וּכְב֣וֹד יְהוָ֔ה מָלֵ֖א אֶת־הַמִּשְׁכָּֽן׃ וְלֹא־יָכֹ֣ל מֹשֶׁ֗ה לָבוֹא֙ אֶל־אֹ֣הֶל מוֹעֵ֔ד כִּֽי־שָׁכַ֥ן עָלָ֖יו הֶעָנָ֑ן וּכְב֣וֹד יְהוָ֔ה מָלֵ֖א אֶת־הַמִּשְׁכָּֽן׃

The texts in the two sections are strikingly similar. In each case, there is a cloud that seems to represent the Divine Presence; in each case, the Torah uses identical language to state that the cloud is covering something special (וַיְכַס הֶעָנָן אֶת) — the mountain in one case, the *Mishkan* in the other, and in each case, the glory of God becomes present in the place the cloud covers. It therefore indeed seems fair to say that there is at least one more element in our chiasm, a new outer edge, as it were, on each side: what we might call two "cloud narratives":

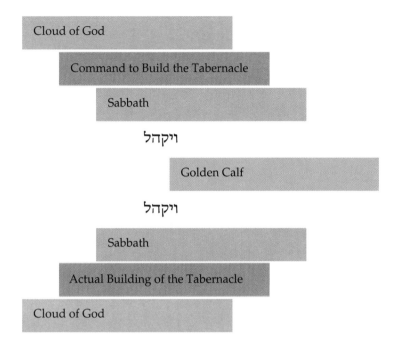

A Study in Contrasts

I want to suggest that right here, at the two edges of this vast ATBASH structure, in these two divine cloud narratives, a story is unfolding. The story is told to us, I believe, through the sum total of the similarities and contrasts between the two narratives. Because while yes, as we've seen, there are intense similarities between the two episodes, there are important contrasts between them, too. Here are a few that come to mind:

When, at the beginning of the chiasm, the cloud comes down, it covers something God made: a natural feature of the world, namely, a mountain. The second time around, at the end of the chiasm, the descending cloud covers a building that *people* made: a *mishkan*. And that brings us to the second contrast in the narratives, which concerns how, exactly, the cloud comes to rest in this world. In the first case, the cloud *covers* the mountain; in the second, it doesn't merely cover the *Mishkan* so much as it thoroughly *permeates* it:

וּכְבוֹד יְקֹוָה מָלֵא אֶת־הַמִּשְׁכָּן׃   And the glory of God filled the *Mishkan*.   Exodus 40:34

Another contrast concerns Moses' ability to enter the cloud. When it comes to the cloud atop the mountain, we read this:

Exodus
24:17–18

וּמַרְאֵה כְּבוֹד יְקֹוָה כְּאֵשׁ
אֹכֶלֶת בְּרֹאשׁ הָהָר לְעֵינֵי
בְּנֵי יִשְׂרָאֵל: וַיָּבֹא מֹשֶׁה
בְּתוֹךְ הֶעָנָן

The glory of God was like consuming fire on the top of the mountain to the eyes of all the people of Israel. And Moses went into this cloud.

Despite the fearsome and otherworldly qualities of the cloud that descended atop Mt. Sinai, Moses was able to enter it. And yet, at the other end of the chiasm, we find a cloud that Moses cannot enter. He would like to enter the *Mishkan*, which is enveloped in the divine cloud, but evidently finds himself unable to:

Exodus 40:35

וְלֹא־יָכֹל מֹשֶׁה לָבוֹא אֶל־
אֹהֶל מוֹעֵד כִּי־שָׁכַן עָלָיו
הֶעָנָן וּכְבוֹד יְקֹוָה מָלֵא אֶת־
הַמִּשְׁכָּן:

And Moses was not able to go into the *Mishkan*, because the cloud had settled upon it and the Presence of the Lord filled the Tabernacle.

So take note of the story being told here. The holiness of God's cloud in the Tabernacle is so intense that Moses can't even enter the space. God is so very "present" in the *Mishkan* in this climactic moment that although man has *made* the space, man can no longer enter it. The conclusion seems clear: However much God was present at the moment of Revelation itself, at Mt. Sinai, that is a veritable drop in the bucket compared to the intensity of the Divine Presence that comes into our world once the Tabernacle is completed. Not even Moses, the one human being privy to an otherworldly epiphany at Sinai, can enter. It's a stunning victory for the Children of Israel, a true validation of what they have made with their own hands, with the gifts that came from their own hearts.[6]

---

6 See in this regard our essay on Parshat Terumah and on the nuances the Torah seems to attach to the idea of heartfelt *terumah*, "that which lifts up."

Not Just a Cloud, but a Fire Cloud

And yet, there is still more to this story. For indeed, we are not quite through with the contrasts between the two cloud narratives. One more contrasting element remains, and we need to take a look at it. It has to do with a mysterious fire in each narrative.

At the first edge of our chiasm, when God's Presence revealed itself at Sinai in a cloud, the Torah went on to tell us something about that cloud. It was like fire, glorious and intimidating:[7]

וּמַרְאֵה כְּבוֹד יְקוָה כְּאֵשׁ אֹכֶלֶת בְּרֹאשׁ הָהָר לְעֵינֵי בְּנֵי יִשְׂרָאֵל:	And the glory of God was like consuming fire on the top of the mountain to the eyes of all the people of Israel.	Exodus 24:17

And intriguingly, at the latter edge of our chiasm, a version of that same fire seems to be back. But this time, the flames seem to have a very different quality. Look what the Torah tells us at the very end of **Parshat Pekudei** about what the fire cloud actually did:

וּבְהֵעָלוֹת הֶעָנָן מֵעַל הַמִּשְׁכָּן יִסְעוּ בְּנֵי יִשְׂרָאֵל בְּכֹל מַסְעֵיהֶם: וְאִם־לֹא יֵעָלֶה הֶעָנָן וְלֹא יִסְעוּ עַד־יוֹם הֵעָלֹתוֹ: כִּי עֲנַן יְקוָה עַל־הַמִּשְׁכָּן יוֹמָם וְאֵשׁ תִּהְיֶה לַיְלָה בּוֹ לְעֵינֵי כָל־ בֵּית־יִשְׂרָאֵל	When the cloud would lift from the top of the Tabernacle the Jews would travel, but if the cloud would not lift they would stay where they are, because the cloud was there for the Jews by day and at night it turned into fire in the eyes of all the Jewish people.	Exodus 40:36–38

---

7 The intimidating nature of the fire is suggested here by the Torah's description of the fire as "consuming," thus emphasizing the danger inherent in it. In line with this, note that the people who beheld this fiery manifestation of God's Presence were so frightened by it that after hearing the Ten Commandments, they refused to approach the mountain, even when beckoned to by Moses (Ex. 20:18).

At the end of the book of Exodus, one more time, the cloud appears as fire. One more time, the fire cloud is beheld by "the eyes of all Israel." But while the first time around, the fire was intimidating, now it is gentle and benevolent. The cloud leads us, tells us where to go, when it is time to encamp, and when it's time to leave. And when the cloud turns fiery at night, the flame illuminates the dark for us, and provides guidance, comfort, and light.

The first time the fire made us afraid. The second time it reassures us that in the dark, we needn't be so afraid.

The Two Clouds and the Turning Point between Them

As a whole, then, the chiasm beckons us to embrace a wonderful paradox. As intense as the holiness of God was in the Tabernacle, still in all, that Presence had a gentle quality to it. It served Israel; it showed them where to go; it gave them light and security. God, the Being from beyond, was there for us in our world, in the place that we made for Him with our very own hands. He had come to take care of us.

What happened in the middle, between the advent of these two clouds? Well, between the Revelation at Sinai (at the beginning of our chiasm) and the cloud's return in the *Mishkan* (at the end of our chiasm) … the Golden Calf happened. That, of course, is the centerpiece of this chiasm. *Why* is it the center? Seemingly, because the calf — while it was of course a terrible crisis; in its aftermath, we were almost destroyed — was nevertheless a kind of turning point. It was the moment everything began to change.

To explain: At the beginning of the chiasm, the people had stood at Sinai while Moses approached the cloud. And yet that first encounter with God was marred by bitter disappointment. Moses would come down the mountain and, witnessing the calf below, would smash the precious tablets he had been given. The reader wonders: If at that moment all is irretrievably lost and Israel has reached rock bottom, is it also a point of no return in their relationship with God?

As the story of the Golden Calf unfolds, Moses wins a reprieve for the people and gains God's consent not to destroy them (Exodus 32:14). But even then, the possibility that God would ever actually restore His relationship with them, that He would ever actually dwell among them, seems to be gone for good. For example, God tells Moses that although the people will enter Israel, God Himself will not be the one to escort them. An angel will need to bring the people into the land, for God can't be in the people's midst after the Golden Calf:

לֹא אֶעֱלֶה בְּקִרְבְּךָ כִּי עַם־ קְשֵׁה־עֹרֶף אַתָּה פֶּן־אֲכֶלְךָ בַּדָּרֶךְ:	I will not go up inside you, for you are a stiff-necked people, lest I consume you on the way.	Exodus 33:3

And yet, bit by bit, the Children of Israel claw back. They don't take no for an answer. They actually mourn when they hear that only an angel will lead them (33:4). Although they seemingly have everything — they won't be destroyed, and they will be able to go into the land — still, they mourn the loss of closeness with their Maker. Their desire to have God's Presence rest among them is palpable. Moses, representing the people, even goes so far as to tell the Almighty that if He won't lead the people, "don't [even bother] to take us out of here at all" (33:15).

Slowly, the people rebuild their relationship with God. And finally, at the end of the book of Exodus, and at the outer edge of our chiasm, a crowning moment arrives. God *does* come to dwell within the people after all. It is not some watered-down, dim shadow of the Divine Presence that comes now among the people. The Divine comes among them with such intensity that it dwarfs the actual Sinai experience itself. Flawed and humbled post-sin man has made a place for God in his all-too-human world — and God fills that place with more intensity, vigor, and holiness than Israel could ever have thought possible.

מָקוֹם שֶׁבַּעֲלֵי תְשׁוּבָה עוֹמְדִין אֵין צַדִּיקִים גְמוּרִין יְכוֹלִין לַעֲמֹד בּוֹ.	[In the] place that *baalei teshuvah*, those who return, stand, even those [who have always been] completely righteous cannot stand.	Berachot 34b

THE FULL CHIASM

CLOUD OF GOD

The Cloud Covered

A Consuming Fire;
Moses Could Enter

Command to Build the Tabernacle

Sabbath

ויקהל

Golden Calf

ויקהל

Sabbath

Actual Building of the Tabernacle

CLOUD OF GOD

The Cloud Covered

Moses Could Not Enter;
A Consuming Fire